P9-CLE-573

CONTEMPORARY CANADA:
ISSUES AND INSIGHTS
Editor: John Saywell

CANADA:
A MODERN STUDY

Ramsay Cook *with*

John Ricker and

John Saywell

1981

CLARKE, IRWIN & COMPANY LIMITED
TORONTO / VANCOUVER

© 1963 by Clarke, Irwin & Company Limited

Revised and enlarged edition © 1977 by
Clarke, Irwin & Company Limited

ISBN 0-7720-1133-8

First published in paperback format 1964
Revised editions published 1971, 1977

ACKNOWLEDGMENTS

The authors and publisher wish to thank Historical Services and
Consultants Limited, Toronto, Ontario, for their help in research-
ing the cartoons for this book.

The authors and publisher also wish to thank the following
organizations which made available the cartoons appearing on
the pages listed.

Canadian Liberal Monthly/189, 220; Robert Chambers in *The
Halifax Chronicle-Herald*/295, 304; Metropolitan Toronto Public
Libraries/60; *The Montreal Star*/273 (Doug Wright), 298 (Mc-
Nally); National Liberal Foundation/167; Ontario Archives/51;
Public Archives of Canada/55, 62, 88, 94, 98 (Bengough), 114,
117 (Bengough), 122 (Bengough), 125 (Weston), 135 (Ben-
gough), 138, 139, 144, 148 (Rostap), 150 (Bengough), 154
(Julien), 156 (Julien), 160, 174-5 (Julien), 195, 202, 205, 210
(Dale), 224, 225, 227, 256, 261, 290; Provincial Archives of
Manitoba/181; *Toronto Daily Star*/227 (Callan), 250 (Callan),
309 (Macpherson); *The Toronto Telegram*/172, 301 (Beaton);
Winnipeg Free Press/216 (Arch Dale), 231 (Arch Dale), 239
(Arch Dale), 281 (Arch Dale), 284 (Kuch), 288 (Kuch).

2 3 4 5 WC 81 80 79
Printed in Canada

CONTENTS

LIST OF MAPS

PREFACE

Any understanding of the present is based on a knowledge of the past. This is particularly true in the case of Canada, a country where history has created a nation to a large extent in defiance of geography but where history also has failed to accommodate easily French and English within the structure of one state.

In writing *Canada: A Modern Study* and in revising and updating the book in 1977 Ramsay Cook has brought a deep and sure knowledge of Canadian history. Born and brought up in Manitoba, he has a clear insight into Canadian regionalism. In recent years he has emerged as the foremost English-Canadian historian of French Canada, and this volume provides a clear and balanced interpretation of the evolution of Quebec and the relations between English and French in the last two centuries.

John Saywell

INTRODUCTION

It is now a number of years since the first edition of this book was written. That period has been one of the most critical in the history of Canada. The country's internal unity has been radically challenged both by the development of an aggressive nationalism among some French-speaking Quebeckers and by discontent in nearly every other region and province of the country. So, too, the perennial Canadian problem of preserving external independence has once again been acutely felt by many Canadians concerned about the high level of American direct investment in Canada.

While historical writing is by no means merely a reflection of contemporary concerns, no history of Canada today would be satisfactory if it did not provide a perspective on French-Canadian nationalism and Canadian independence. These two concerns were, among others, central themes in *Canada: A Modern Study* when it was first written and remain so in this revised and enlarged edition. These themes are fundamental to any understanding of our history; even if they were not pressing contemporary issues they would play a large part in any general interpretation of our past.

In a sense our history has centred on two events: the British Conquest in 1763 and the American Revolution in 1776. The first event severed the connection between New France and the motherland and brought *les Canadiens* into contact with the British. Ever since then French Canadians have struggled to preserve their distinct identity and to erase the state of inequality that conquest implies. Today the struggle is in a new and critical phase. The French Canadians who support Prime Minister Pierre Elliott Trudeau believe that equality can and must be guaranteed for French Canadians throughout Canada. On the other hand there are those who are convinced that equality is impossible within Canada and can only be achieved if Quebec becomes an independent nation. The roots of this debate reach far back into history and many of the issues so heatedly discussed today would have a familiar ring to the generation of Louis-Joseph Papineau and Louis Hippolyte LaFontaine.

The second result of the Conquest of 1763 was, of course, that Canada became a British colony. A gradual emergence from that status, symbolized by such events as responsible government and the Statute of Westminster, is another important theme of this book. Once in Canadian historical writing it was a theme of great urgency—perhaps even the dominant theme. Today it is more muted, for no one can seriously argue that Britain represents any constraint on Canadian independence. It is true that the Queen of England is still the Queen of Canada, but that is our choice; and our constitution is still an act of the British parliament, but this is because Canadians cannot agree on a better arrangement. Even the Commonwealth, once a focal point of Canadian foreign policy, has lost some of its significance. And as Britain turns more and more toward Europe in economic and political relations, the Commonwealth association, for all its historical significance, becomes increasingly tenuous and, to many, irrelevant.

This helps to explain, in part, the increasing significance of that second fundamental event. The American Revolution divided the continent between the United States and British North America. It also was the cause of the first large-scale English-speaking settlement in Canada. The Loyalists came to Canada for a variety of motives, both idealistic and materialistic. But they were fairly united in a desire to build new lives in a new country separate from the turbulent nation to the south. That tradition was a powerful one in our history, symbolized by the War of 1812, Confederation and the rejection of reciprocity in 1911. In the 1970's, it again became an issue of great importance for Canadians. To what degree can Canada, or should Canada, develop differently from the United States and how can this be achieved without an unsustainable loss in material standards of life?

Most Canadians would probably agree that Canadian independence is an important goal for Canadians to pursue. But there are profound differences over both what independence should mean, and how it should be achieved. In the highly developed areas of the country, Ontario in particular, it is easier to be opposed to the direct investment of American money than it is in less developed areas like Quebec, the Atlantic provinces, or Manitoba. The debate over Sir John A. Macdonald's "National Policy" is being heard again.

While French-English dualism and the impact of the United States on Canada have dominated recent history, they have not been the only controversial matters. Sectional or regional discontents, based largely on economic inequalities, have become as critical for the 1970's as they were for the 1880's or the 1930's. One result has been a series of programmes designed to stimulate the economic growth of the eastern section of the country and a gradual movement in the direction of closer cooperation among the Atlantic provinces. While Maritime union remains a distant goal, that unfinished business of the mid-nineteenth century is again on the agenda.

Western discontent has also re-emerged. Here the old sense that the prairies have been either neglected by Ottawa or subordinate to central Canadian interests has been encouraged by international marketing problems for Canadian grains, oil, natural gas and potash and difficulties in restructuring the western economy. While western separatism may not yet be a political reality, there is undoubtedly a sense of dissatisfaction on the prairies which has historical roots. In a 1971 book entitled *The Unfinished Revolt*, which seriously considers the possibility of a separate Canadian west, one writer remarks that "twice before—in the northwest and during the depression—the West rebelled against the status quo and seriously challenged its role in Canada. Both times, this rebellion produced short-term gains but failed to realize its ultimate objective—a radically reordered Confederation. Today, the basic resentments that in earlier times burst into flame are growing again." The complex character of current Canadian problems have long historical roots.

Pessimism about the future has become a fashionable feature of much recent writing about Canada. Some of the pessimism stems from the fear that the erosion of our sovereignty by the influence of the United States has passed beyond the point of return. Others see the country losing its central focus through the gradual decline of the power of Ottawa. Finally, there are those who are convinced that the destiny of Quebec lies in full or partial independence. Such pessimism is not difficult to understand, for the past decade has clearly indicated that Canada is passing through a period of profound difficulties. But these difficulties are by no means uniquely Canadian nor are they entirely national in origin. Nationalism has seen a rebirth in many parts of the world, old and new. The multi-national cooperation has infringed seriously upon the sovereignty of many countries besides Canada. The superficial affluence of the 1950's has been un-masked, and poverty, poor housing and inadequate medical treatment are apparent once more throughout the developed world. Pollution and ecological destruction have finally been recognized as the unhappy consequences of the technological revolution of the past quarter century. These problems Cana-dians share with people throughout most of the world.

The purpose of historical writing is neither to peddle optimism nor to spread doubt. Its primary goal is to provide a perspective into which contemporary concerns may be placed. That, at least, is the intention of this revised edition of *Canada: A Modern Study*.

Toronto, March 1977   RAMSAY COOK

1 THE QUESTION OF SURVIVAL

Britain's conquest of Canada created serious problems for both victors and vanquished. For the French Canadians the conquest was a tragedy and the central event in their history. British governors replaced French, while English-speaking merchants from Britain and the Thirteen Colonies quickly assumed control of the colony's economic affairs. A small number of wealthy French Canadians returned to France, but most of the habitants and small businessmen had no alternative but to remain in Canada under the conqueror and hope for the best.

The Roman Catholic Church also remained and continued to play a central role in the life of the colony. Indeed, since the Church was the only important institution in the colony that was not taken over by the Protestant conquerors, its importance actually increased after the British conquest. It not only ministered to the religious needs of its flock but it inspired in French Canada a continuing sense of mission. Cut off from their mother country and deprived of much of their secular leadership, the French Canadians turned for leadership to the Church and particularly to the parish priest. Ever since the conquest until the 1960's, the Roman Catholic Church remained one of the main sources of strength in the defence of the French-Canadian way of life.

Britain's new colony was primarily agricultural although there was a small merchant class engaged in the fur trade and in importing manufactured goods. A Swedish traveller has left the following description of New France at the time of the conquest:

All the farms in Canada stand separate from one another, so that each farmer has his possessions entirely separate from those of his neighbour. Each church, it is true, has a little village near it; but that consists chiefly of the parsonage, a school for boys and girls of the place, and the houses of tradesmen, but rarely of farmhouses. . . . The farmhouses hereabouts are generally all built along the rising banks of the river. . . . The country on both sides was very delightful. . . . The fine state of its cultivation added greatly to the beauty of the scene. It could really be called a village, beginning at Montreal and ending at Quebec, which is a distance of more than one hundred and eighty miles.

The people in general were a gay and hardy lot, faithful to their Church but enjoying boisterous good times. Years of adversity in the colony had made them strong and tough. One French observer, describing their mixed characteristics, wrote: "The Canadians are tall, well made, and well set on their legs, robust, vigorous, and accustomed in time of need to live on little. They have intelligence, and vivacity, but are wayward, light-minded and inclined to debauchery." This was the land and the people that came under British rule in 1763.

The British government's first problem was to frame a policy for the government of the new subjects. Its solution was the Proclamation of 1763, designed to transform Quebec into an English-speaking colony. The Proclamation prohibited settlement west of the Appalachians pending some solution of the Indian problem, and so determined that the American colonists would not be able to expand westward. The British hoped that this situation would produce a movement of English-speaking settlers from the thirteen colonies into Quebec in sufficient numbers to submerge the existing French-speaking population. To strengthen the attraction of Quebec for immigrants from the thirteen colonies and England, the Proclamation of 1763 promised the early establishment of English law and representative institutions in the colony.

But the policy of assimilating the French Canadians was

doomed to failure. The expected stream of immigrants never became more than a trickle. With its cold climate and foreign culture, Quebec had few attractions for American colonists when the rich lands of the Ohio valley lay beckoning. When immigration from the British colonies failed to materialize, successive governors concluded that the policy of anglicizing Quebec was not realistic. Moreover, many British officials developed a sympathy and respect for the French Canadians. General James Murray, the first British Governor, described them as "perhaps the bravest and best race upon the Globe." Murray refused to establish the assembly that had been promised by the Proclamation of 1763. He felt that such an assembly would become the tool of an English-speaking minority since the French Canadians would be excluded from the assembly, because British law still denied Roman Catholics the rights of full citizenship. One government official wrote: "An assembly so constituted might pretend to be a representative of the people there, but it would be a representative of only the 600 new English settlers, and an instrument in their hands of dominating over the 90,000 French."

Murray's refusal to introduce an assembly aroused the anger of the English-speaking minority in the colony, and in 1765 the British government appointed Sir Guy Carleton to replace him. Carleton at first disliked the French Canadians and intended to grant the wishes of the English-speaking minority. But the aristocratic British Governor soon discovered that he had little in common with the pushing and troublesome group of British merchants. The French Canadians, on the other hand, he found increasingly attractive. In 1772, Carleton informed the British government of his firm conclusion that "barring a catastrophe shocking to think of this country must, to the end of time, be peopled by the Canadian race." Since Canada would remain a colony with a French-speaking majority, Carleton believed that Britain should establish a new set of governing principles to replace the Proclamation of 1763.

The Governor had other reasons for recommending a new

policy. In view of the growing discontent in the thirteen colonies to the south, Carleton felt that the British government should take steps to ensure the loyalty of Quebec. I. the colony could be made firmly loyal to Britain, it could be used as a strategic base in the event of trouble in the American colonies. As a military man and an aristocrat Carleton felt that the real power in Quebec lay with the seigniors and the higher clergy. If Britain could win the loyalty of these two groups, all would be well for, he felt the habitants, the largest group in the colony, would natu rally follow the lead of their superiors. Carleton believed that the British merchants, while difficult and troublesome were not numerous enough to cause any serious problem For these reasons he advised the British government to work out a new system of government that would appeal mainly to the seigniors and the clergy. The result was the Quebec Act passed in 1774.

The Quebec Act recognized and guaranteed the po sition of the Roman Catholic Church in the colony and legalized its right to collect tithes from its mem bers. The Act also recognized French law insofar a it applied to such civil matters as landholding, seignioria dues and marriage rites. By these guarantees the British government hoped to weld the leaders of the French-Ca nadian community to the British Crown and to ensure thei loyalty in any future crisis.

The Quebec Act, however, denied the new colony a elective assembly, one of the traditional features of British colonial government. In spite of the repeated demands o the English-speaking merchants, Carleton and the British authorities felt that there were good reasons for refusin an assembly. Since the French Canadians had never ha elective institutions, they would not want them now. More over, since any assembly would inevitably be dominated b the British minority, its establishment would only unde mine the confidence in Britain that Carleton was so anxio to establish. In addition, assemblies in the thirteen coloni had been a chronic source of friction between Britain an

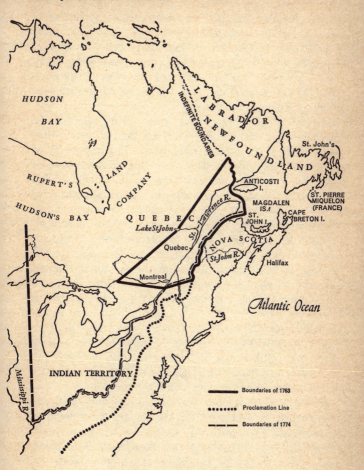

THE BOUNDARIES OF QUEBEC, 1763-1774

her American subjects, for they were constantly demanding more powers than the British government was prepared to grant. Thus, in Quebec, Britain established a system of non-representative government. Power rested with an appointed governor and an appointed advisory council composed of both English- and French-speaking members, including Roman Catholics.

The denial of representative government infuriated the merchant class who protested that the mother country had deprived them of a basic right of all Englishmen. However, two important provisions of the Quebec Act took some of the edge off their discontent. The more humane English criminal law replaced the relatively savage French penal code. The old French civil law was kept, however, and its retention remained a grievance because the merchants believed that it was not suited to the needs of a developing commerce. But, to the merchants, by far the most attractive features of the Quebec Act were the territorial changes. The Act extended the boundaries of the colony to include the rich fur-trading territory between the Ohio and upper Mississippi rivers which had formerly been part of the French empire. The new boundaries meant that the merchants in Canada would now be able to exploit the fur trade in this area without fear of competition from the merchants of Albany and New York. The developing system of the St. Lawrence region needed a rich hinterland.

As a whole, the Quebec Act satisfied fully only the upper-class French Canadians. Neither the merchants nor the lower classes found in it much to cheer about. Its most serious effect, perhaps, was the anger it aroused among the people in the thirteen colonies. One observer wrote of the Quebec Act: "It not only offended the inhabitants of the province itself, in a degree that could hardly be conceived, but alarmed all the English provinces in America, and contributed more perhaps, than any other measure whatsoever, to drive them into rebellion against their sovereign." By 1774, rebellion in the thirteen colonies was developing rapidly.

2. CANADA AND THE AMERICAN REVOLUTION

Sir Guy Carleton had been right in anticipating trouble in the American colonies. One of his main reasons for suggesting the extension of Quebec's boundaries to include the Ohio valley region had been to ensure the safety of this area if the colonists revolted. As it happened, this territorial transfer was one of several features of the Quebec Act which actually accelerated the movement towards rebellion. With the Ohio valley within the jurisdiction of Quebec the route to western settlement was closed, and the thirteen colonies were hemmed in on the seaboard. New England merchants and would-be land speculators and settlers would have to abandon their plans for exploiting the fertile western lands. In other ways, too, the Act of 1774 seemed to threaten colonial liberties, for it established on their very doorstep, and in defiance of established British tradition, a form of government that denied the people representation. Just as offensive to zealous New England Protestants was the legal recognition that the Act extended to the Roman Catholic Church. For these reasons the American colonists included the Quebec Act among the "Intolerable Acts" which helped move them farther along the road to revolution.

When the American Revolution did break out, the people of the thirteen colonies looked north hoping that Nova Scotia and Quebec would join them in the fight against the mother country. In a letter to the inhabitants of Quebec, the Continental Congress condemned the system of government in the northern colony. "We defy you, casting your view upon every side, to discover a single circumstance, promising from any quarter the faintest hope of liberty to you or your posterity, but from an entire adoption into the union of these colonies." But neither Nova Scotia nor Quebec believed that its best interests would be served by joining the rebels to the south.

Many Nova Scotians had originally come from New England and they had a deep sympathy with the revolutionaries.

There was a minor attempt to start a revolution in Cumberland county in 1776, but the ease with which it was squelched indicated the hopelessness of the revolutionary cause. Faced with large numbers of British troops and the ever-present British navy, most Maritime colonists adopted a neutral outlook. "The neutral Yankees of Nova Scotia," as they have been called, would fight neither for the British against their kinsmen, nor against the British for the cause of independence. The basic reason for this attitude was simply that most Nova Scotians did not share the grievances of their southern cousins. They had no serious complaints about the operation of the mercantilist economic regulations by which Britain bound her Empire together. In fact, Nova Scotia benefited greatly through her access to the protected British market that the system guaranteed. More immediate economic considerations also suggested the wisdom of neutrality. The American War of Independence brought prosperity to Nova Scotia as Halifax became the centre for naval and military supplies for the British forces fighting the revolutionaries. But perhaps the most important reason that Nova Scotia did not join the revolution was that it simply could not have done so if it had wanted to. Its population was very small, and scattered about the coast in isolated communities. Under these circumstances, decisive and united action by the colonists was so difficult as to be impossible.

In Quebec, too, there was an attitude of near-neutrality which surprised and dismayed Carleton, who had expected that his benevolent rule would produce widespread popular support. The Church leaders and seigniors did remain loyal, as the Governor had anticipated, but the Quebec Act had not satisfied either of the most important groups in the colony. The British merchants were still irritated because they had not been granted a voice in government through an elected assembly. The habitants, the largest group in the colony, were unhappy because the Quebec Act provided for the legal enforcement of the tithes of the Church and the feudal rents of the seigniors. To these two groups the American Revolution might well have had some appeal. Although the Roman Catholic Bishop, Briand, told his flock, "Your oaths, your religion, lay upon you the unavoidable duty of defending your country and your king with all the strength you possess," the habitants remained unenthusiastic. They were neither anxious to fight for their British conquerors nor were they willing to fight against them on the side of the traditional enemy from New England, the *Bostonais,* as they were called.

The leaders of the rebellion in the British colonies tried to win support for their cause in Canada. In October 1774, they called upon the French Canadians to "seize the opportunity presented by Providence itself." On behalf of the Continental Congress, John Brown travelled to Quebec where he aroused modest support among French Canadians and British merchants, but generally speaking the American appeal fell on deaf ears. In May 1775, some rebellious spirits covered a bust of George III with black paint and hung a garland of potatoes around his neck. An inscription left beneath the mutilated statue read: "Behold the People of Canada, or the English idiot." But more than pranks were needed to overthrow British authority. When the American armies under Richard Montgomery and Benedict Arnold invaded Canada in 1775, the habitant did little either to defend his country or to assist the invaders.

Quebec's failure to join the thirteen colonies was, then, due mainly to the attitude of the mass of the population. The sympathy which the habitant might have felt for his self-styled liberators soon dissolved when he received worthless currency for the goods which he sold to the army of the Continental Congress. Furthermore, despite their lukewarm attitude towards the British, the French Canadians could see no real advantage in joining the Americans. After all, the British were only a minority in Quebec; united with the more populous thirteen colonies, the French Canadians would be in a minority. And few French Canadians could forget that for more than a century they had fought and competed with the same Americans to the south who were now claiming to be their friends. Thus, throughout the period of hostilities, the habitants preserved an attitude of neutrality and carefully assessed their own interests. Carleton realized this truth when he wrote: "I think there is nothing to fear from them while we are in a state of prosperity, and nothing to hope for while in distress." In all probability no more than five hundred French Canadians joined the invading armies.

The English-speaking merchants in Quebec generally remained passively loyal to the Empire which was the source of their economic strength and prosperity. A few, like Thomas Walker of Montreal, joined the Americans. But most of them realized that the British Empire gave them a protected market and provided the capital they needed to extend their business activities. Moreover, the British merchants, like the French merchants before them, had come to realize that their trading system based on the St. Lawrence was in competition with the economy of the thirteen colonies, especially New York. If they were to join the rebellious colonies, they would have to share their profitable western hinterland with their southern competitors. Thus, whatever political attractions the American Revolution may have had for the inhabitants of Canada, French-speaking or British, other interests of an economic and cultural kind held them to their British allegiance.

A final and decisive factor which kept Quebec from joining the rebellion was the failure of the American invasion. For although the American army captured a poorly defended Montreal in 1775, their winter-long siege of Quebec, punctuated by a futile New Year's Eve assault on the city, was a dismal failure. When spring opened the St. Lawrence to navigation, the arrival of a British naval force compelled the Americans to give up the battle and retreat to New York. With their retreat went all hope of support for the revolutionary cause.

Yet, while neither Quebec nor Nova Scotia joined the thirteen colonies in their fight for freedom from the control of the British government, the American Revolution had an enormous effect on the history of Canada. Indeed, it helped to create Canada. After a brief two decades of North American unity under British authority, the continent was again divided in 1783, with the independent Americans masters of the southern half and the British colonies, with their French and English populations, in possession in the north.

The Treaty of Versailles, 1783, defined the new division of North America. On the seaboard, the St. Croix River became the dividing line, while in the West the British gave up all the lands south of the Great Lakes. This latter decision brought cries of dismay from the merchants in Quebec for this territory seemed to them to be essential to their fur-trading empire. Since their loyalty to Britain had stemmed in large measure from their unwillingness to share this rich hinterland with New England and New York traders, they were enraged that British diplomats, by a stroke of the pen, should now give their patrimony to the rebels. One result, however, was to force the British merchants in Canada to seek future opportunities in the British territories north of the Great Lakes.

But it was not just in the drawing of boundaries that the American Revolution helped to create Canada. Equally important were the rapid changes in the composition of the population that occurred during the last years of the war and the first years of peace. The American Revolution produced the first large-scale British immigration to Canada, and thereby helped to determine its bicultural nature, one of Canada's fundamental characteristics.

3. THE LOYALIST MIGRATIONS

The people of the thirteen colonies had not been unanimous in their opposition to British rule. One-third of the population opposed the revolution. Life in the thirteen colonies became increasingly difficult for those who refused to support the rebellion, and by the end of the war about 100,000 Americans demonstrated their loyalty to the motherland by leaving their homes to start a new life elsewhere. They came from all classes of colonial society, and included farmers and lawyers, clergymen and government employees, teachers and soldiers. Often they paid a very high price for their loyalty to Britain. Many had to abandon all their material possessions and endure long periods of intense suffering before finding new and secure homes. As late as 1786, a Loyalist petition for assistance from the British government painted this vivid picture of their hardships:

> It is impossible to describe the poignant distress under which many of these persons now labour, and which must daily increase should the justice of Parliament be delayed until all the claims are liquidated and reported . . . ten years have elapsed since many of them have been deprived of their fortunes, and with their helpless families reduced from independent affluence to poverty and want; some of them now languishing in British jails; others indebted to their creditors, who have lent them money enough barely to support their existence, and who unless speedily relieved, must sink more than the value of their claims when received, and be in worse condition than if they had never made them; others have sunk under the pressure and severity of their misfortunes; and others must, in all probability, soon meet the same melancholy fate, should the justice due them be longer postponed.

Obviously, the British authorities faced a serious human problem.

At the peace negotiations in 1783, Britain tried to gain some protection and compensation for the Loyalists, but the weak government of the newly independent thirteen colonies was neither willing nor able to ease their plight. As a result, thousands of Loyalists sought new homes in other British colonies. Because of its proximity, Canada was an obvious place to settle and eventually about 40,000 found new homes in Nova Scotia and Quebec.

The largest group of Loyalists, about 30,000, went by sea from New York to Nova Scotia. Many of these, particularly those with upper class backgrounds, found life in the struggling little colony of Nova Scotia too difficult. Despite such governmental assistance as food, land, and tools, some

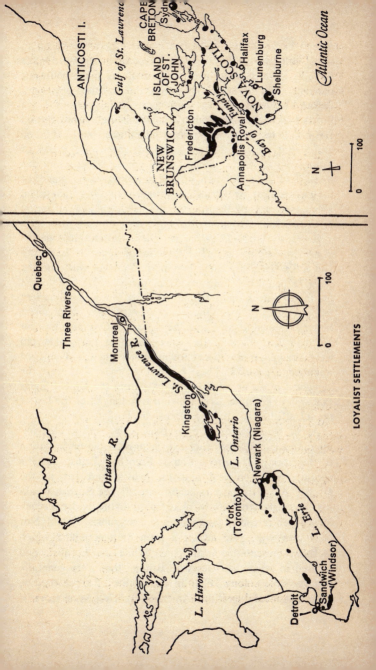

LOYALIST SETTLEMENTS

drifted back to the United States and others moved on to Great Britain. But the majority, forced by necessity to make the best of their grim situation, gradually won the battle for survival, and laid the foundations of the Maritime provinces. Before the American Revolution, the population of Nova Scotia had been only about 17,000, mainly clustered around Halifax. Some of the newcomers joined this well established group, but most settled on the north shore of the Bay of Fundy. To solve the administrative problem created by this division of the population, as well as to meet the demands of the new settlers, the British government in 1784 established a new colony, New Brunswick, with its capital at Fredericton on the St. John River.

Another 10,000 Loyalists travelled overland to Quebec. Some came up the Richelieu route to the upper St. Lawrence and Lake Ontario while others pushed farther west into the Niagara peninsula. Since many of these people had fought for the British in the revolutionary war, or were land-hungry frontier farmers from the back country, they were much better equipped to cope with the rigours of Canadian pioneer life than their counterparts in the Maritimes, many of whom were drawn from seaport towns where they had enjoyed wealth and position. These hardy Loyalist settlers were the vanguard of an army of immigrants from the United States that was to continue its northward trek long after the last of the Loyalists had trickled across the border.

As in Nova Scotia, the large-scale English-speaking immigration into Quebec dictated changes in the organization of the colony. The proportion of French to British and the accompanying political situation which had led to the Quebec Act were now radically altered. The English-speaking Loyalists strenuously objected to living under French laws which restricted land tenure to a seigniorial system. Nor were they willing to accept a form of government which lacked representative institutions. While the Loyalists had refused to sever their ties with Britain, they were generally just as firm in their belief in the virtues of representative government as were the American rebels. As a Loyalist petition in 1785 stated: "They were born British subjects, and have ever been accustomed to the government and laws of England."

In demanding a new form of government for the British colony on the St. Lawrence and the Great Lakes the Loyalists had the support of the British merchants in Montreal, who had never been satisfied with the settlement of 1774. In 1791, the British government acceded to their demands and passed the Constitutional Act which replaced the old province of Quebec with the province of Upper Canada in the west and Lower Canada in the east. In the western, English-speaking province, the new Act established British laws and institutions. Lower Canada, with its French-speaking and Roman Catholic majority, retained French civil law, seigniorial tenure and the rights granted to the Roman Catholic Church in 1774. The major innovation of the Constitutional Act was the introduction of elective assemblies in both Upper and Lower Canada.

In the western colony, the Loyalists had long demanded an assembly. In Lower Canada, however, the demand had come mainly from the British merchants and settlers; the French-speaking inhabitants were initially uninterested in the idea and some British officials were openly opposed. One British official in Lower Canada wrote: "The Canadian Habitants are I really believe an industrious, peaceable, and well-disposed people; but they are, from their want of education and extreme simplicity, liable to be misled by designing and artful men, and were they once made fully sensible of their own independence, the worst consequences might ensue." However, the British government ignored these objections and granted each colony an elective assembly. The assembly was the weakest part of the colonial government as its decisions were subject to the veto of an appointed upper house, the legislative council, and an appointed governor and executive council. Nevertheless, the assemblies soon became the centres of political activity and controversy in the colonies.

Carleton's "catastrophe shocking to think of," the American Revolution, drastically altered the character of Quebec. In the thirteen colonies, an independent republic had replaced the first British Empire in North America. North America was permanently divided. All that remained to Britain were the four provinces that had been formed out of the territory of the old French Empire, the Hudson Bay Company lands and Newfoundland. But the coming of the Loyalists had immensely strengthened the loyalty of these territories to Britain. In fact, the Loyalists placed their attachment to the Empire above everything else, and often expected others to do the same. This loyalism with its emotional attachment to the Empire and its strong anti-American flavour became one of the chief characteristics of English-speaking Canada in its formative years. But this characteristic was complicated by the bicultural nature of Canada which became increasingly evident after the American Revolution. It remained to be seen whether these two elements could be combined successfully in what was left of Britain's Empire in North America.

2 THE GROWTH AND DEFENCE OF BRITISH NORTH AMERICA

THE political settlement and geographical division of 1791 marked a fresh beginning for British North America and the British Empire. But the success of the venture depended heavily upon the growth of population, especially in Upper Canada, and the development of a sound economy. Without a growing population the colonies would remain weak, economically stagnant and in danger of absorption into the thriving American republic. The unfriendly relations between Great Britain and the United States which bred the War of 1812 were a threatening reminder that the struggle for the survival of British North America was by no means over.

1. PEOPLING THE NEW BRITISH AMERICAN COLONIES

Each colony developed in its own way in the generation after 1791. Land-hungry settlers moved into the fertile lands of the Canadas but largely by-passed the Maritimes where much of the terrain and soil was not well suited to agriculture. Nevertheless, a few hundred settlers from Scotland arrived in the Maritimes during these years. Under the direction of the Scottish philanthropist, Lord Selkirk, a group of eight hundred was settled in Prince Edward Island in 1803. By 1812, the population of the Atlantic colonies was still less than 100,000; but the population of these colonies formed a tightly-knit little society. Except in Prince Edward Island, the major industries were fishing and lumbering, neither of which supports large populations. While Nova Scotians had long been engaged in fishing, their craftsmen soon became excellent builders not only of fishing-boats, but of large sailing-ships for the oceanic trade. The great Bluenose schooners that sailed out of Halifax for

Atlantic and Pacific ports were among the finest ships in the world during the age of sail. The people of forest-covered New Brunswick depended chiefly on the lumbering trade for their livelihood. Every year great rafts of white pine logs floated down the St. John and Miramachi rivers to the coast. New Brunswick lumber fed the shipbuilding industry and was sold to Great Britain and the West Indies. During the Napoleonic Wars, when Britain was cut off from her European sources of supply, the Royal Navy relied on New Brunswick for the masts and spars of its warships.

The Maritime colonies traded extensively with the West Indian islands. Lumber and dried codfish were carried to the Caribbean where they were exchanged for sugar, molasses and rum. The Maritimes hoped to take the place of New England in the old triangular trade, among North America, the West Indies and Britain, which had existed before the American Revolution. Unhappily, New Brunswick and Nova Scotia were unable to produce enough foodstuffs to feed the sugar plantations, and despite the Navigation Acts which protected Empire markets for goods produced within the Empire, the Maritimes were unable to overcome American competition. Yet the system of imperial preferences, or mercantilism, was a fundamental source of strength for all the North American colonies. It gave the colonies a protected market for their products, and the Napoleonic Wars gave the colonial economies another push forward by forcing Britain to turn to North America for food, shipbuilding materials and ships.

In the Canadas, rapid economic progress was accompanied by a spectacular increase in population. A steady stream of pioneers poured across the Canadian-American frontier in search of fertile new lands. Some of the first settlers came from Vermont to farm in the Eastern Townships. But 9,000 English-speaking immigrants did little to alter the essentially French character of Lower Canada, for the French-Canadian population was quickly multiplying as a result of one of the highest birth rates in recorded history and a considerably reduced death rate. By 1812, there were about 330,000 people in Lower Canada, nearly three times the number in the same area at the close of the American Revolution.

While most French Canadians lived on small farms and produced food for the home market, the dynamic centre of British North America was Montreal, which, by 1812, had a population of 30,000. Here was the focal point of the fur trade, lumbering and finance in Canada. The men who controlled the economy were almost all English-speaking, for the French Canadians had been displaced by the English-speaking merchants during and immediately following the conquest and were destined thereafter to hold only secondary positions in the economic life of the colony.

Even more striking changes took place in Upper Canada. In 1791 its population was only 14,000, but twenty years later 90,000 settlers were clearing land and sowing crops. Most of these new Canadians came from the United States, restlessly following the frontier of free land regardless of political boundaries. Much of the credit for the foundation of Upper Canada belongs to John Graves Simcoe, the first Governor of the colony. Simcoe was a soldier, and a man of intense loyalty to the British connection. His main aim as Governor of Upper Canada was to develop a society that would be the "image and transcript" of Great Britain. He had grandiose but impractical plans for the development of the colony, plans which included the manufacture of hats, mining schemes, meat curing and shipbuilding. "A thousand details crowd upon my mind," he once wrote enthusiastically, "that would be productive of the most salutary consequences." While many of his projects failed, he never lost sight of the prime necessity of the colony: population. If Upper Canada were to become the "Bulwark of the British Empire in North America" as he hoped, it needed a vast increase in settlement. Since settlers from Great Britain were slow in coming, he turned his attention to attracting farmers from the United States. He was fearful that the Americans might bring republican sentiments with them, but he hoped that generous land grants would convert "the repentant sinners of the revolted colonies." These "late loyalists" represented a new element in the Upper Canadian colony, and one which the original Loyalists did not readily accept. As relations between Britain and the United States worsened in the years before the War of 1812, the American immigrants were often, and usually unjustly, suspected of disloyalty.

Nevertheless, it was these settlers who carved a rough, pioneering society out of the forests of Upper Canada. Soon dwellings and prosperous farms stretched from Kingston to the Bay of Quinte, up to the Ottawa valley and along the fertile Niagara peninsula. In the 1790's German- and French-speaking settlers began moving from the United States into Markham and Waterloo townships and Scottish settlers, sponsored by Lord Selkirk, established themselves around Lake St. Clair.

It was in the area around York on Lake Ontario that the most important developments were evident. When Governor Simcoe arrived in Upper Canada in 1792, the seat of government of the colony was at Newark, the modern Niagara-on-the-Lake. But since this settlement was too exposed to American attack, the capital was moved to York in 1793, although Simcoe himself preferred the inland site of London. While Kingston remained the largest urban centre until the 1820's, the choice of York as capital encouraged a gradual shift of population to the south central section of the colony. For the first few years the military garrison of two hundred men was the largest single element in the population of York. Not until 1797 were facilities ready for the first meeting of the government at the new capital.

Once York became the capital, roads and settlement began to branch out from it. Simcoe formed a military corps, the Queen's Rangers, whose main purpose was to clear land and construct roads such as Yonge Street, which linked York and Lake Simcoe, and Dundas Street, which ran across the Niagara peninsula from Burlington to the Thames river. By 1800 a road from York to Kingston joined an already completed road to Montreal. These roads had a dual purpose: to permit mobility of troops and to open up new lands for settlement.

A generous system of land grants was practised in Upper Canada. Loyalists and those later arrivals, who were often called "late loyalists," could obtain lands ranging in size from one hundred to a thousand or more acres in return for an oath of allegiance to the Crown. The system of course was open to abuses. Speculators frequently acquired large tracts of the most fertile lands, thus forcing settlers to move out to the frontier. But occasionally, men who acquired large holdings worked energetically to fill them with settlers. One of the most remarkable of the early settlements was organized by the eccentric Colonel Thomas Talbot. After serving as Simcoe's secretary and then in the Napoleonic Wars, Talbot retired from the army and returned to Upper Canada. In 1803 he obtained a land grant of 5,000 acres on the shore of Lake Erie. For each settler he placed on a farm, Talbot received another two hundred acres of land. Before 1850 Talbot's holdings had increased to 65,000 acres. Here, near the present-day St. Thomas, Colonel Talbot ruled his domain like a feudal baron, spurring his tenants on, entertaining in a gay fashion, and loudly denouncing Methodists because, he claimed, no total abstainer could be loyal to the Crown.

Socially, Upper Canada remained backward and underdeveloped. The provincial capital at York was slow to emerge from the position of a muddy little village to an important centre. One inhabitant wrote in 1801: "York contains about 100 houses and upwards and where about 7 years ago there was an entire wilderness there are several very handsome buildings two in particular the Chief Justice's house and Mr Jarvis secy of the province. . . ." Social and intellectual life in the province was also slow to develop. In 1799 one foreign observer wrote: "Throughout all of Canada, there is no public library, except in Quebec and this is small and consists mostly of French books." Yet at social affairs such as dinners, receptions and balls, the local population could turn itself out colourfully, though the fashion, at least according to one commentator on Kingston society in 1804, seemed somewhat out of date. He wrote:

> Among the ladies, that is, the young ones, the present exaggerated Grecian costume was further exaggerated, with the addition of cropped heads, the waists between the shoulders. Some of their elders . . . rejoicing in imitating court dresses of a half century before; long waisted, stiff silk gowns, with lace . . . aprons; high-heeled shoes and their powdered hair rolled over huge toupées stuffed with wool. . . . Some of the younger men were cropped, and wore no powder; some of the leaders wore bob-wigs, most of them had their hair tied in long queues.

But styles and fashions were less important to Upper Canadians at the beginning of the nineteenth century than roads and schools and churches.

While some of the towns gradually acquired schools, the farming communities usually depended on the travelling schoolmaster whose arrival was frequently as uncertain as his qualifications. Nor was life easy for the schoolmaster. One traveller noted that she had passed "some school houses built by the wayside; of these, several were shut up for want of schoolmasters: and who that could earn a subsistence in any other way would be a schoolmaster in the wilds of Upper Canada? Ill fed, ill clothed, ill paid—or not paid at all—boarded at the houses of the different farmers in turn."

The religious life of the colony was, perhaps, better developed. While Presbyterians and Baptists were strong on the frontier, it was the travelling Methodist ministers who attracted the widest following. Many of these preachers followed the settlers north from the United States and were prepared to carry their message into the roughest parts of the colony. Typical of these men was Nathan Bangs, who was born in Connecticut, and by 1801 had become a Methodist circuit rider in Canada. He recalled later:

> I believe that I was the first Methodist preacher that ever attempted to preach in Little York . . . and I preached in a miserable half-finished house, on a week-evening, to a few people . . . and slept on the floor under a blanket. This was in 1801. I was then attempting to form a circuit on Yonge Street . . . and I was induced to make a trial in this new little village, the settlers of which were as thoughtless and wicked as the Cana-anites of old.

Jealous of the success of the Methodists, other religious groups often condemned the circuit riders as American sympathizers, a dangerous charge during the early years of the nineteenth century when relations with the United States were very unsettled.

2. FRICTION ON THE BORDER AND THE WAR OF 1812

The peace settlement of 1783, which gave the thirteen colonies their independence, did not completely satisfy either the Americans or the British. British merchants in Canada refused to leave the fur-trading posts that lay south of the Great Lakes, on the pretext that the Americans had failed to compensate the Loyalists for property losses. After much friction the Americans sent John Jay to London in 1794 to negotiate a settlement. The British finally agreed to surrender the disputed posts, especially as the Americans had driven the Indians farther west and the eastern posts were no longer very important as centres for the fur trade.

Despite this agreement, border problems remained an unsettling influence in Anglo-American relations. British traders continued to work closely with the Indians in the American West. American settlers who suffered from Indian raids believed that the British traders encouraged the Indians and knew that the Indians got guns and ammunition from British traders in return for furs. Moreover, they suspected that the British were encouraging the Indian leader, Tecumseh, to resist American authority and to attack unguarded American settlements in the Ohio valley. Despite Tecumseh's defeat at the battle of Tippecanoe in 1811, the Americans remained convinced that only the defeat of the British in North America could satisfactorily end the Indian menace. This conviction, combined with widespread anger over the question of maritime rights, led President Madison to declare war on Britain in June 1812.

Obviously the war was a most serious threat to Canada, since it was only in North America that the United States could hope to defeat Britain. The population of the United States in 1812 was about ten times that of Canada, while Britain's European military engagements greatly restricted her ability to defend her North American colony. Since there were fewer than 5,000 British regular troops in Canada when the war broke out, it was fortunate for Canada that President Madison was never able to get his country united behind him in the war. Moreover, American conduct of the war was hopelessly ineffective.

The major battles in the War of 1812 were fought on a wide front in Upper Canada, the area most open to attack and most coveted by the "war hawks" in the western United States. As they had in 1775, the invading American armies expected that the local population in Canada would welcome this opportunity to free themselves from British rule. General Hull, who crossed the river from Detroit into Canada, issued a long manifesto to the Canadians, outlining the American view on the causes of the war and promising respect for Canadians and their property. "The United States offers you peace, liberty and security," the manifesto concluded. "Your choice lies between these and war, slavery and destruction."

Because of the large number of American settlers in the colony, there was good reason to fear that Hull's manifesto might receive a sympathetic response in Upper Canada. In July, 1812, General Brock, the commander of the British army, wrote from Fort George: "There can be no doubt that a large portion of the population of this neighbourhood are sincere in their professions to defend the country, but it appears likewise evident to me that the greater part are either indifferent to what is passing, or so completely American as to rejoice in the prospects of a change in Governments." The defection of two members of the Upper Canadian legislature to the Americans and the real or suspected disloyalty of many American settlers caused the government serious concern. To illustrate vividly the price of treason, the authorities ordered the "Bloody Assize" at Ancaster in 1814. Fifteen men were found guilty of treason and eight of these plunged to their death from the gallows on Burlington Heights.

More apparent than open treason was the apparent lack of popular enthusiasm for the war. In July 1812 Brock wrote: "My situation is most critical, not from anything the enemy can do, but from the disposition of the people — the population, believe me, is essentially bad. A full belief possesses them that all this Province must inevitably succumb." Brock realized that a defensive war would not save Upper Canada. An immediate victory was necessary to shake the people from their apathy. Attack was the obvious tactic for Brock to follow, and he sent his armies into the American territory. The British forces took Michilimackinac and their Indian allies captured Fort Dearborn, while a small army under Brock boldly crossed the St. Clair River and captured Detroit. Brock then hastily returned to defend the Niagara peninsula where American troops were massed for an attack on Queenston Heights. The attack was repulsed in October, but the gallant Brock gave his life in the Battle of Queenston Heights. Yet his brief period of command had done much to determine the final outcome of the war, for he had prevented the American from gaining the quick victory which they had anticipated, and his decisive leadership had restored confidence among the people.

In 1813 the Americans advanced as far as Stoney Creek on the Niagara peninsula and Moraviantown in the west, where Tecumseh was killed, before they were stopped or defeated. They gained control of Lake Ontario and captured and burned the muddy capital of York. In 1814 they

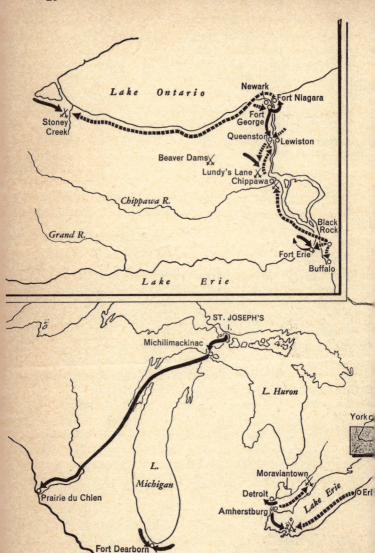

Lake Ontario

Newark

Fort Niagara

Stoney Creek

Fort George

Queenston

Lewiston

Beaver Dams

Lundy's Lane

Chippawa

Chippawa R.

Grand R.

Black Rock

Fort Erie

Buffalo

Lake Erie

ST. JOSEPH'S I.

Michilimackinac

L. Huron

York

L. Michigan

Moraviantown

Detroit

Lake Erie

Eri

Prairie du Chien

Amherstburg

Fort Dearborn

British

American

Montreal

Crysler's
Farm

Chateauguay

scott

on

Plattsburg

Sackets
Harbor

rio

Oswego

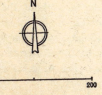

N

THE WAR OF 1812

200

once again marched across the peninsula, before being routed at Lundy's Lane.

While the major campaigns in the war were in Upper Canada, Lower Canada was not entirely spared. Here, too, the political situation was dangerous and the loyalty of the French Canadians doubted. For four years before the war the colony had been administered by a governor who was bitterly antagonistic to the French Canadians. Sir James Craig was a hot-tempered military man who believed that the French Canadians were disloyal and should be assimilated. He tried to rule with an iron hand, fighting bitterly with the leaders of the French party in the assembly, and jailing the editors of the popular French-Canadian newspaper, *Le Canadien*.

It was fortunate, therefore, that just before the war with the United States Craig was replaced by Sir George Prevost, who adopted a conciliatory attitude towards the French Canadians. Soon after his arrival Prevost reported that "several circumstances have occurred since I have assumed the administration of the Government to induce me to believe that there are persons disaffected towards His Majesty's Government amongst the Canadians as Agents of France and America." Prevost set about removing the causes of discontent by co-operating with the French Canadians, establishing better relations with the Roman Catholic Church than had existed during Craig's régime, and appointing French Canadians to the army and civil service. Thus, when the war began, Prevost was able to rely upon the services of the local militia. Under a French-Canadian commander, Lieutenant-Colonel Charles de Salaberry, a French-Canadian regiment fought bravely throughout the war. In 1812 an attempted American attack on Montreal was easily repulsed. The next year de Salaberry's troops played an important part in the defeat of the American army at Chateauguay, and two weeks later the Americans suffered a second defeat at Crysler's Farm.

In the spring of 1814 Napoleon's defeat released some battle-tested British veterans for service in North America.

The British burned Washington in retaliation for the burning of York. In the far West fur-traders, Indians and a few British troops captured Prairie du Chien, while the British successfully defended Michilimackinac, and Prevost led a powerful army along Lake Champlain as far as Plattsburg before he was forced to withdraw.

The Maritime colonies suffered none of the disadvantages of the war that were felt in the Canadas. No American invasion took place there. The British navy easily guaranteed the security of the colonies on the eastern seaboard. Here the war was limited to privateering, an activity in which many Nova Scotian captains proved themselves masters. Moreover, shipbuilders and merchants in the Maritimes seized the opportunity presented by the British blockade against American shipping to move into former American markets and capture some of the carrying trade. A period of prosperity thus marked the years of the War of 1812 in Nova Scotia and New Brunswick.

By the end of 1814 the war had dragged to a conclusion. Clearly, neither side had won. But even a draw was an impressive achievement for Canada, for despite the odds against her, Canadian independence from the United States had been preserved.

The peace settlement of 1814, the Treaty of Ghent, ended the fighting, reaffirmed the pre-war boundaries, and laid the basis for the settlement of the western boundary between the two countries. Three years later, in 1817, the Rush-Bagot Treaty between Britain and the United States prohibited large-scale naval armaments on the Great Lakes, and a Convention in the following year accepted the forty-ninth parallel of latitude as the boundary between Canada and the United States in the territory between the Lake of the Woods and the Rocky Mountains. The Convention of 1818 temporarily settled the troublesome problem of American fishing rights on the east coast of British North America, by permitting American fishermen to enter harbours for supplies, though denying them the right to fish within three miles of shore.

The peace settlement did not dispose of all the disputes between Britain's North American colonies and the United States, but it removed some of the major sources of friction. For the colonies, the war gave proof of their will to exist apart from the Republic. Both English- and French-speaking Canadians had fought to resist the invaders, and the two groups were drawn together in a common bond of anti-Americanism. This was the sentiment which underlay the remark of Egerton Ryerson, the great Upper Canadian Methodist leader, who wrote: "British and Canadian loyalty, patriotism and courage defeated their [the Americans'] dark designs against the liberty of mankind." Once more, the loyalism that characterized early Canada was strengthened by the events of the years 1812-15. The men who had proven their loyalty were among the men who were going to rise to positions of power and influence in the colonies in the post-war years. They were often men who were prepared to use their reputation for loyalty as a political weapon, branding their critics as sympathetic to the Americans and promoters of treason.

3 POST-WAR EXPANSION

THE successful defence of British North America in the War of 1812 brightened the future prospects of the British North American colonies. Moreover, the war once more confirmed the direction that the economic and commercial development of the area would follow. The Treaty of Versailles in 1783 had cut Canada off from the rich lands of the Ohio valley. While fur-trading posts had been retained in the area south of the Great Lakes for more than ten years after that, the merchants of Montreal were beginning to look more carefully at the lands north of the Lakes. Then Jay's Treaty in 1794 and, more emphatically still, the hostilities of 1812-14 made it clear that the United States had no intention of allowing British and Canadian traders to ply their trade south of the Lakes. It was to the west and north that the merchants of Canada, who were mostly based in Montreal, now had to look.

1. THE STRUGGLE FOR THE NORTHWEST

As early as 1778 a semi-illiterate American trader, Peter Pond, had crossed the prairies as French explorers had done before him and pushed north of Lake Athabaska towards Great Slave Lake. Soon his path was being pursued, and new trails blazed, by a number of trader-explorers. In 1789 Alexander Mackenzie, following Pond's lead, discovered the great river, later called the Mackenzie, which he followed to the shores of the Arctic Ocean. In 1793 Mackenzie and a small party fought turbulent waters and hazardous cliffs to become the first Europeans to reach the Pacific by the overland route. He wrote in his diary: "I now mixed up some vermilion in melted grease, and inscribed in large characters, on the south-east face of the rock on which we had slept last night, this brief memorial—'Alexander Mackenzie, from Canada, by land, the twenty-second of July, one thousand seven hundred and ninety-three.' " After Mackenzie's important journey, a host of adventurous explorers followed his path, with men like David Thompson and Simon Fraser attaching their names to two of the great rivers of the Rockies.

As the fur trade moved west, the Montreal merchants began to worry seriously about the pressure of competition from the Hudson's Bay Company. The advantages of the Hudson's Bay Company in this competition resulted from unified organization, large financial resources, and, most important, access to cheap transportation by water through the Hudson Bay. Since the Montreal merchants could do little to reduce the growing cost of transporting furs overland from points farther and farther west of Montreal, they concluded that competition among themselves must be removed. In this way they would be able to pool their resources for a combined struggle against the powerful merchants stationed on Hudson Bay. In 1788 the major Montreal groups banded together to form the North West Company. In 1804 a further step towards a completely unified organization was taken when the last substantial group of independent Montreal traders, the XY Company, was brought into the North West partnership. But in the long run, this union of forces and the enterprising spirit of the Nor'Westers was not enough to overcome the superior financial resources and cheaper transportation route of the Hudson's Bay Company.

The rivalry between the two corporations often broke into what was little less than open warfare. A major crisis arose in 1812 when Lord Selkirk, who owned much of the Hudson's Bay Company, decided to plant a colony of Scottish settlers in the Red River valley near the present site of Winnipeg. The colony was to provide food and serve as a base for the operation of the Bay men throughout the West. To the Nor'Westers the Red River settlement was a threat to their survival, for it lay across their chain of trading-posts which stretched from the Great Lakes to the Rockies. The Montrealers stirred up their half-breed allies against the colonists and, after a series of provocations which included the destruction of the crops at Red River, the colonists decided to take measures to defend themselves. But the colony was poorly armed and, when open warfare broke out at Seven Oaks in 1816, twenty-one colonists were killed and the colony fell into the hands of the North West Company.

Lord Selkirk was not prepared to give up without a fight. Bent on revenge, he hired a group of Swiss mercenaries who seized the main North West post at Fort William. This action was quite illegal, but it made Selkirk's determination to open up the Canadian West to settlement very clear to the fur-traders. Once more settlers were brought back to Red River to begin the arduous task of carving out a livelihood that would be more permanent and secure than the nomadic existence of the fur-traders or trappers.

The massacre at Seven Oaks with its aftermath was only one sign that the Nor'Westers were fighting a losing battle against the powerful Hudson's Bay Company. The older company was too strong, too experienced, too firmly entrenched and too well financed to be defeated by the Montreal men. As the arrival of traders and settlers pushed the fur-bearing animals farther north and west, the costs of the North West Company increased and profits fell. By 1821 the battle was over. In that year the two companies arranged a merger which, while certainly giving the Montreal merchants a fair settlement, marked the victory of the Bay over the River. For many years to follow, the connection between the St. Lawrence and the West, which had begun in the days of La Vérendrye, was broken.

2. THE NEW ECONOMY

With the fur trade dying, Canada had to find something to serve as the basis for a new and profitable commercial empire. The economy that developed from this search was in many ways the result of a sagging economy and heavy unemployment in Great Britain following the Napoleonic Wars, which forced hundreds of thousands of Britons to emigrate. Many of these came to Canada. To some the long sea voyage to their new homes was a nightmare:

> Before the emigrant has been a week at sea he is an altered man. How can it be otherwise? Hundreds of poor people, men, women, and children of all ages, from the drivelling idiot of ninety to the babe just born, huddled together without light, without air . . . sick in body, dispirited in heart . . . without food or medicine . . . dying without the voice of spiritual consolation, and buried in the deep without the rites of the Church.

But once ashore, the immigrants settled down to the work of clearing new farms and planting crops. In the 1820's the population grew and the area of land under cultivation expanded rapidly. One successful method of promoting settlement was the granting of large areas of land to individuals or companies. Talbot's tract was an early successful example of this practice. Another such venture was the Canada Land Company, established in 1826, which was largely responsible for settling the areas around Goderich and Guelph. A similar company in the Eastern Townships of Lower Canada, the British American Land Company, held more than 800,000 acres of land. Organizations like the Canada Land Company and the British American Land Company not only brought out settlers, they also provided such local necessities as saw mills, grist mills, brick kilns, school-houses and roads. Such developments eased the lot of the settlers and bettered their chances of success in their new occupations.

Despite the large inflow of immigrants from Britain, and the work of the land companies, there remained several serious obstacles to settlement in Canada. Some settlers expected to make a quick, easy fortune in the new land. When they found that this dream could not be realized, many moved on to the apparently greener pastures of the

United States. One reason for disillusionment was the land-grant system. In Lower Canada, where the seigniorial system was still in use, most of the large seigniories had passed into the hands of land speculators, and it was difficult for immigrants without capital to acquire good lands. Sometimes settlers found that the lands they were offered were nearly useless. The experience of one unfortunate settler was described by a traveller who met "a Scotch family returning from Canada to Columbus, Ohio, who had been decoyed away . . . with the offer of a lot of *land* for nothing—but which was found to be a complete *swamp*. When they got there the wife and children were nearly tormented to death with mosquitoes—no roads to their shanty—no friends within a considerable distance—nothing to be bought, and many other miseries we have not repeated."

In Upper Canada the orderly progress of settlement was complicated by a confusion of land policies which gave free lands to Loyalists and militia veterans of the War of 1812, and thus excluded later immigrants from some of the best lands. Moreover, large tracts, both of Crown lands and clergy reserves (lands set aside for the use of the Protestant Church), lay uncultivated, while other tracts were held by businessmen, and even public officials, for speculative purposes. As late as 1838 a British investigator reported that, although nearly all the available land had been granted, "a very small proportion, perhaps less than a tenth, of the lands thus granted, had been occupied by settlers, and much less reclaimed and cultivated."

By 1838 Upper Canada had a population of nearly 400,000. But population growth alone was not enough to produce a contented, flourishing society. The land system, inadequate provision of roads and schools, trade slumps such as the one which hit the colony in the mid-thirties, and, not least of all, the bleak contrast between Canadian backwardness and the progress of the neighbouring United States multiplied the discontent in the colony. In 1829 a petition sent from Upper Canada to the British parliament declared: "The people of Upper Canada are in the view of the United States, in daily intercourse with its citizens; they are of the same race of men, speaking one language; they see the people on their adjoining frontier thriving and contented under domestic governments instituted for the common benefit and protection. . . ." The burden of this petition was that something was seriously wrong with the governmental system of the British colonies. Others thought that the people themselves showed a lack of industry and therefore lagged behind their energetic American neighbours. One of the most vocal and witty exponents of this view was Thomas Chandler Haliburton of Nova Scotia. Haliburton's criticisms were expressed through his brilliant literary creation, Sam Slick, the "gen-u-ine Yankee" clockmaker and pedlar, who was constantly drawing an unfavourable contrast between American progress and Canadian backwardness.

Yet, despite difficulties and criticism, conditions were not as bad as they were often painted. The basis at least of a sound economy was being laid. The centre of that economy was Montreal, the traditional capital of Canadian commercial life. After the Hudson's Bay Company had defeated the Montreal merchants in the struggle for the fur trade in the northwest, Montreal businessmen turned their minds and their financial resources to new plans for commercial development. These plans were based on the rivers and lakes of the Canadian Shield, for this natural transportation system still provided the cheapest means of carrying the products of the North American hinterland to Europe. By the 1830's new staples, such as timber and grain, were replacing furs as the main exports to European markets. As the pioneers of the Canadas cleared their new lands, they had lumber and potash to sell abroad. Later the grain from their new farmlands was available for export. In return the settlers imported such European manufactured products as farm implements and clothing. Here, then, was the opportunity to create a new and prosperous trade to take the place of the fur trade.

It was not only the hinterland of Canada that the Montreal merchants were anxious to serve. The Ohio valley and the growing American West represented even more lucrative fields of activity. The Montreal merchants dreamed of nothing less than making their city the economic capital of a North American commercial empire, the focal point in the trade between inland North America and Europe.

Two conditions had to be met if the Montreal merchants were to succeed in this new venture. First, the natural waterways they used would have to be made more efficient at critical points by the building of roads and canals, for once more, as in the early days of the fur trade, Montreal and New York became keen rivals for control of the North American products that could be sold profitably on the international market. Already, in 1825, New York merchants had completed the Erie Canal linking Buffalo on Lake Erie with the port of New York. If Canadian merchants were to meet the threat of this cheap transportation system, they too needed an efficient canal system. The first improvement in the Canadian water-ways system was the short canal at the Lachine rapids upstream from the Island of Montreal. The Lachine Canal was built largely with public funds provided by the government of Lower Canada, and it was opened to traffic in the autumn of 1824. But this small canal barely touched the essential problem of tying the St. Lawrence system to the rich grain lands in the interior. This latter task was to be fulfilled by the Welland Canal. Plans for such a canal had already begun in 1818 under the direction of an energetic St. Catharine's businessman, William Hamilton Merritt; but Merritt's plan was as expensive as it was ambitious, and it was not until 1824 that he had collected sufficient funds to make it practical to have his company chartered. Before the canal was completed in 1829, heavy government assistance was required, and in the end the canal became the property of the government. Once it was opened, traffic could move from Lake Erie to the Welland River, then through the Niagara River to Lake Ontario. The first condition for the new empire had been fulfilled, but it had not solved all of the merchants' problems.

The second condition essential for success was that the Montrealers should enjoy a protected market in Great Britain and free access to the farming communities in the United States. The protected British market gave the Montreal merchants an important advantage over their American competitors. Since Britain classified United States wheat that was shipped through or milled in Canada as Imperial produce, Canadian merchants could ship both American and Canadian grain to Britain without paying the heavy duties faced by United States merchants. Moreover, if Canadian merchants could retain free access to the United States, they could sell the manufactured products imported from Britain in the American West.

It was a grand scheme. It was also a great gamble, for the objectives of the Canadian merchants actually ran counter to the trend of events in both the United States and Great Britain. In Britain the triumph of the industrial revolution was gradually pressing the country towards a policy of free trade, which would end the colonial preferences so important to the Canadian merchants. The United States, on the other hand, was just beginning to feel the first effects of industrialization, and American manufacturers were pressing for a tariff that would protect their home market from overseas competition, especially British. Thus, the Canadian merchants' hopes of selling British manufactured products in the United States were threatened, while at the same time the preferential tariff treatment that Canadian merchants enjoyed in Britain was gradually being whittled away. Nor were these the only obstacles in the way of the commercial community's ambitions.

A major problem for the Canadian merchants was the political division of Canada. While the St. Lawrence system was a geographic and economic unit, it was divided politically into Upper and Lower Canada by the Constitutional Act of 1791. This division made it extremely difficult to co-ordinate plans for economic development. English-speaking Montreal merchants found themselves stranded in an ocean of French Canadians who were not sympathetic to costly economic development programmes. After all, the French Canadians argued, canals and roads would have to be paid for with funds collected from the farmers of Lower Canada, who would not share the profits the businessmen hoped to make. As *Le Canadien* observed in 1806: "Some people wish to create a mercantile aristocracy, the most abominable, the most pernicious of governments, equally detrimental to the authority of the Crown, to the interests of the land-owners and to the liberties of the people." This quarrel between the English-speaking merchants and the spokesmen for the French-Canadian farmers was one of the root causes of the political difficulties of Lower Canada.

Even in Upper Canada, where there was no cultural division, there were deep suspicions among the pioneer farmers that the business community was little concerned about the needs of rural areas. Upper Canada was financially weak and to most struggling farmers local improvements such as roads, land surveys and schools were far more important than canals and other facilities which seemed designed only for the benefit of the commercial class. Thus, in Upper Canada, too, political discontent was closely connected with the struggle over economic policy. These disputes and struggles were made far more bitter by the form of government that had been established in the colonies in 1791.

4 REACTION, REFORM AND REBELLION IN THE CANADAS

SURVEYING the events of the American Revolution after 1783, the British government concluded that Britain had lost the thirteen colonies not because she had exercised too firm an authority over them, but because she had given them too much popular control over local governments, and allowed them too much independence from Imperial control. If the same mistake were not to be made in the remaining colonies in North America, a system of government would have to be devised that would keep any assembly firmly in check. This was the intention behind the form of government that was established under the Constitutional Act of 1791.

1. THE CONSTITUTIONAL ACT, 1791

The Constitutional Act provided for an executive consisting of the governor appointed by the British government and an executive council appointed by the governor to act as his advisers. The legislature was made up of an appointed legislative council and an elected legislative assembly. The legislative council and assembly were to be the colonial counterparts of the House of Lords and the House of Commons in the British parliamentary system. However, the elected assembly was similar to the British House of Commons in appearance only, for its legislative power was subject to a double check. Either the governor or the legislative council could refuse to approve the acts passed by the assembly. Executive control over the representative assembly was further strengthened by the fact that the members of the executive council and the members of the legislative council came to be either the same people, as in the Maritimes, or to overlap, as in the Canadas.

The executive branch of government was important not merely because of the power it was granted, but because of the men who were appointed to positions of influence. In all the colonies, the governor gathered around him men who held, and wished to protect, positions of power and influence in the community. In Upper Canada, for example, John Strachan, a leader of the Anglican Church, was a member of both the Executive Council (1818 - 1836), and of the Legislative Council (1820 - 1841). He used his position to defend the privileges of his Church against the growing criticism of other Protestant groups such as the Methodists. Another powerful member of the group was John Beverley Robinson. A former pupil of Strachan, Robinson served under Brock in 1812 and was the prosecutor at the Bloody Assize at Ancaster. After the war, he rose rapidly in the public service of Upper Canada, winning for himself the position of Attorney-General, Solicitor-General, and finally Chief Justice of the colony. Associated with these powerful men of the church and the judiciary were businessmen like William Hamilton Merritt who planned and built the Welland Canal. These men and their supporters composed a tight oligarchy, which controlled the patronage and favours that the government could dispose of as part of its offices.

In 1839, a British government report noted: "The bench, the magistracy, the high offices of the Episcopal Church, and a great part of the legal profession, are filled by the adherents of this party; by grant or purchase, they have acquired nearly the whole of the waste lands of the Province; they are all-powerful in the chartered banks." It was these men who, with the governor, ran the affairs of the colony, without regard to the wishes of the people's elected representatives. Only the governor or the British government could remove them from office.

In Upper Canada this oligarchy was known as the "Family Compact"; its counterpart in Lower Canada was the "Chateau Clique." While the governmental system under the Constitutional Act superficially resembled the parliamentary system in Britain, it was in practice very different, and it was intended to be so. As one British minister wrote: "We pretend to give Canada the same constitution as we ourselves live under. All we can do is lay the foundation for the same constitution when increased population and time shall have made the Canadians ripe to receive it."

2. THE REFORMERS AND DISCONTENT IN THE CANADAS

The differences of interests between the appointed executive, which exercised the real power, and the assembly, which represented the people, made political quarrels in the colonies almost inevitable. In each of the colonies there gradually developed two parties that we may describe loosely as conservative and reforming. The conservative or Tory element was led by the people who held positions on the executive and legislative councils and were anxious to preserve the status quo. Their opponents were the Reformers, radicals whose objective was to gain control of the government and make it more democratic and responsive to the popular will. The Tories were quick to charge the Reformers with attempting to introduce the American form of government into Canada, and therefore with disloyalty. The Reformers answered that it was the Tories whose attitude represented a real danger to the continuance of the British connection. By their selfish refusal to yield any of their authority to the elected representatives of the people, and by their mis-management of the colony's affairs, the Tories were following a course that would eventually lead to violence as it had done in the thirteen colonies. As the rebellions of 1837 were to show, the Reformers were not entirely mistaken.

The Reformers' criticisms were directed against the colonial authorities, rather than against Great Britain. One Reformer in Upper Canada wrote in 1824: "We like American liberty well, but greatly prefer British liberty. British subjects, born in Britain, we have sworn allegiance to a constitutional monarchy, and we will die before we violate that oath." Certainly, most Reformers saw clearly enough that membership in the British Empire was an advantage to colonies still much in need of British investment, and of the trade preferences Britain gave to colonial products. But the Reformers wanted the government of the colonies to conform more closely to the British parliamentary system. In the British system, the elected House of Commons had far more control over the actions of their executive than did the colonial assemblies.

There were also widespread grievances among the Reformers because of the privileged position of the Church of England. The Presbyterians, Methodists and Baptists deeply resented the privileges granted to the Anglicans. In Upper Canada, under the Constitutional Act, one-seventh of the land was specifically set aside for the support of a "Protestant clergy." The Anglicans claimed the right to all the land thus reserved, and, under the vigorous leadership of Bishop Strachan, their claim was upheld. The other Protestant groups wanted to see the clergy reserves either divided among the various denominations, or sold to support education. In Egerton Ryerson, the fiery Methodist leader, these groups found a leader who was just as determined as Strachan. But despite the strong opposition of the Reformers, the struggle over what should be done with the clergy reserves was not finally resolved until the 1850's.

Yet another grievance was the fixed belief of the pioneer farmers that the members of the Family Compact were more interested in promoting their own welfare than in providing the local improvements that would make pioneer life easier. A government which allowed the clergy reserves to lie uncultivated, and which could not find money to build roads and schools for the frontier settlements, could nevertheless find public funds to support such enterprises as the Welland Canal and the Bank of Upper Canada. To the farmer and workingman it seemed clear that the political monopoly of the minority was being used to build up an economic monopoly.

In Lower Canada, similar social and economic grievances were aggravated by cultural conflict, for the ruling oligarchy was largely English-speaking while the great majority of the people and their representatives in the assembly were French Canadians. In 1814, Sir George Prevost, the Governor-General, sent to the British government the following description of the situation in Lower Canada: "The divisions in the House of Assembly have become national in character; on one side the English minority, with whom the official class is allied, on the other side the Canadian majority backed by the mass of the people. The heat engendered by this party strife passes from the House of Assembly to its constituents. The whole country is by now divided into two parties, one the party of the administration, the other that of the people."

This racial division between French and English in Lower Canada had not been expected by the framers of the Constitutional Act. Indeed, it had been hoped that the grant of representative institutions to the French Canadians would help transform them into English Canadians. Instead the leaders of the French-Canadian majority rapidly learned to use the assembly to protect their nationality and block the plans of the English-speaking businessmen to change Quebec into a commercial society. In the first assembly of 1792, the French-Canadian members won recognition of French as an official language on a footing equal with English. Soon their rallying cry and the motto of the first French-Canadian newspaper, *Le Canadien,* established in 1806, became "Our Language, Our Institutions, Our Laws."

The opposition of the French-Canadian leaders to the English-speaking commercial class showed itself in an insistence that taxes be levied on trade rather than on land. Moreover, they fought for the preservation of the traditional system of seigniorial land tenure in the face of the desire of the British to introduce freehold tenure, a form of landholding which would make land sales and speculation easier. When the Canada Tenures Act, passed by the British parliament in 1825, permitted proprietors to change from seigniorial to freehold tenure, the French Canadians set up every possible obstacle to its application.

Gradually the leaders of the reform movements in both the colonies began to demand that the executive branch of the government be brought under popular control. They disagreed on whether this could better be achieved by adopting the United States republican system, under which the President is directly responsible to the electorate, or the British cabinet system, which makes the executive responsible to the elected legislature. This debate divided the Reformers into two groups: the moderates, who favoured the British solution, and the radicals, who looked with increasing sympathy to the United States example.

By 1815 the French Canadians had found a leader in the brilliant, eloquent, and emotional young lawyer and seignior, Louis-Joseph Papineau. As Speaker of the Assembly, Papineau became the outspoken defender of his people. Although he was liberal in his desire to increase popular control over the government of Lower Canada, he was also greatly motivated by the knowledge that popular control over government in Lower Canada meant French-Canadian control. In 1834 he declared: "One nation should never govern another." But in Lower Canada, Papineau saw that under the Constitutional Act one nation, the English, did govern another, the French-Canadian. Nevertheless, the struggle in Lower Canada was not simply one of French against English, for John Neilson, the Scottish editor of the Quebec *Gazette,* and other English-speaking Canadians, strongly supported Papineau, at least until he began to move from demands for reform to acts of rebellion. Similarly the Chateau Clique had supporters among the French-Canadian seigniors and the higher clergy who distrusted Papineau because of his "free thinking" religious views and his advanced democratic ideas.

The conflict in Lower Canada centred mainly on the question of the control of the revenue. Because it received the revenues from land sales and fees as well as the customs duties collected under the Quebec Revenue Act of 1774, the executive branch had its own source of income and was, as a result, largely independent of the elected assembly in matters of ordinary finance. Papineau and his followers soon realized that until they gained control of all revenue they could not hope to control the actions of the Chateau Clique. The executive was willing to allow the assembly control of revenues, but only on the condition that the assembly in turn would grant a permanent civil list, that is, a permanent guarantee of the salaries of government officials. Papineau refused, for obviously such an agreement would curtail the control which the assembly could exercise over these officials once their salaries were guaranteed.

One of the major reasons that the Chateau Clique in Lower Canada wanted to prevent the French Canadians from winning complete control of government was their fear that the English-speaking minority would then be at the mercy of the French. This fear was strongest among the members of the English-speaking merchant class, who realized that once the French Canadians were in control there would be little hope of levying taxes for the kind of improvements necessary to promote commerce.

In one attempt to overcome these difficulties, the British government in 1822 proposed that Upper and Lower Canada be reunited. If this were done, the English-speaking population in the Canadas would be able to work together without fear of French-Canadian domination. But the proposal so threatened the existence of the French Canadians as a cultural group, and they opposed it with such great vigour, that the British dropped the idea.

This concession to the French Canadians did nothing to weaken their desire for control over the executive. Indeed, the victory spurred them on to fight harder for recognition of the assembly's right to control the entire revenue of the colony. In 1831 the British authorities tried to conciliate Papineau and his party by granting the assembly control of the revenue, even without the guarantee of a permanent civil list. Although the assembly, led by Papineau, had won this notable victory, the Reformers were still not satisfied. Their appetite for power whetted, the French-Canadian leaders pressed for popular election of the legislative council. However, as Papineau's demands became more radical, some of his followers, notably John Neilson, drifted away from him.

In 1834, a climax came when Papineau rose in the assembly to outline a long list of real and alleged grievances. The famous Ninety-Two Resolutions contained flamboyant admiration for United States institutions and struck a new note: the threat of open rebellion. Resolution Fourteen stated what was now the heart of Papineau's demands:

> Resolved, that this House is nowise disposed to admit the excellence of the present Constitution of Canada, although His Majesty's Secretary of State for the Colonies has unseasonably and erroneously asserted that it has conferred on the two Canadas the institutions of Great Britain; nor to reject the principle of extending of frequent elections much further than it is at present carried; and that this system ought especially to be extended to the Legislative Council, although it may be considered by the Colonial Secretary incompatible with the British government, which he calls a monarchical government, and too analogous to the institutions which the several States, composing the industrious, moral and prosperous confederation of the United States of America, have adopted for themselves.

Until these demands were met, Papineau defiantly declared that his party would refuse to grant funds to carry on the government. Clearly, Papineau and his more radical followers were now moving down the road to rebellion.

In Upper Canada, despite the absence of bitter cultural conflict, similar events were taking place. Shortly after the War of 1812, an intemperate young Scotsman, Robert Gourlay, raised a furore in the colony with his criticism of the land-tenure system and the lack of internal improvements. The government quickly threw him into jail and later expelled him from the colony. Soon two American settlers, Barnabas Bidwell and his son Marshall Spring Bidwell, were in trouble with the ruling authorities for criticizing government policy and the Family Compact. When Barnabas was ejected from the assembly because of his American birth, the voters returned his son. Ejection of the younger Bidwell raised the question of the rights of thousands of American settlers, many of whom were suspected by the Compact of holding radical views. Not until 1828 did the government finally agree to allow naturalized Americans the same privileges of citizenship as others in the colony.

Meanwhile, by the 1820's, the Reformers in Upper Canada had found a fighting leader in the firebrand journalist-politician, William Lyon Mackenzie. In 1824, this red-headed Scotsman, whose passion for justice knew no discretion, began attacking the established authorities in his paper, *The Colonial Advocate*. In 1826, Tory roughnecks threw his printing-press into Toronto harbour. Mackenzie's supporters replied by triumphantly electing him to the assembly where he immediately seized on the revenue issue, just as Papineau had done in Lower Canada. Unfortunately for the Reform cause, Mackenzie was less successful than Papineau in solving it. In 1831, the Tories won a majority in the assembly and agreed to provide a permanent civil list in return for control of the revenue. Mackenzie was furious for he realized that this concession left the executive independent of the assembly. "Our representative body," he wrote, "has degenerated into a sycophantic office for registering the decrees for as mean and mercenary an executive as was ever given as a punishment for the sins of any part of North America in the nineteenth century."

Such invective was too much for the Family Compact and the Governor. An obedient assembly expelled Mackenzie for libel, and although he was re-elected four times, he was expelled on each occasion. In 1835 he was elected as the first mayor of Toronto, and, following a Reform victory in 1834, later took his seat in the assembly as well. By this time, however, Mackenzie's growing radicalism had disturbed his more moderate followers. Egerton Ryerson, the Methodist leader, had deserted the Reform cause in 1833, describing its leaders as atheists and republicans. Led by the quietly effective Toronto lawyer, Robert Baldwin, moderate

People of the County of Leeds!

Your Representatives have requested you to assemble at Farmers-ville on SATURDAY the 9th instant, at 12 o'Clock, (noon) to consider matters of public interest—Will you respond to the call? I know you will. Freemen are ever prompt to discharge their duty ; to exercise their privileges—to assert their rights.

INDEPENDENT MEN OF LEEDS!

Do you desire equal civil and religious rights ?—do you wish the Clergy Reserves appropriated to *Internal Improvement* and *General Education*, that your children and the children of your fellow-subjects throughout the Province may freely derive the benefit without distinction of sect or party ? Then turn out to a man—None will be backward—none will be absent at the time and place of meeting.

Patriots! Loyalists! Reformers! Englishmen! Irishmen! Scotchmen! Canadians!—all Subjects good and true, who abhor public abuses and desire Reform!—you regard your King—you respect his Ministers—you love your country ; then display your spirit—show your devotion—rally and come forward. Let there be a glorious assemblage of Freemen to evince their attachment to our patriotic King and testify their gratitude for the late Despatch of his liberal and enlightened Colonial Minister.

FREEMEN OF LEEDS!

You consider yourselves good subjects---None are more worthy the name---Let nothing be done on the day of meeting to tarnish your reputation---Come in peace---conduct yourselves in peace and again depart in peace---Show yourselves the friends of good order and respect the laws. No friend of the King and Government will encourage violence or disorder ; but, controlled by the dictates of reason, he will firmly and resolutely exercise his rights, and do honor to his country and King.

Freemen! be united---let your cry be "onward," and the 9th of March will be signalized in the county as a day of glorious triumph to the principles of Reform which actuate our beloved King and his faithful Ministers.
A TRUE LOYALIST.
County of Leeds, 4th March, 1833.

A Reform poster for the election of 1833 in Leeds county, Upper Canada

Reformers were unwilling to accept what appeared to be the radical American programme that Mackenzie was beginning to advocate. In 1835, Mackenzie's radicalism became plain for all to see in his Seventh Report on Grievances, which was a scathing attack on land policy, patronage and corruption, the power of the Family Compact, and the iniquities of oligarchical government and appointed councils.

Into this troubled situation stepped Sir Francis Bond Head. Bond Head's knighthood had been granted by William IV for his adeptness with a lasso, an art he had learned in South America, but of colonial government he knew nothing, and his Tory temperament made conflict with the Reformers inevitable. At first, however, he acted moderately, appointing Baldwin and two other moderate Reformers to the Executive Council. But Baldwin soon realized that his new position gave him no real power since Bond Head felt free to ignore the advice of his Council. When the Governor's position became clear, the entire Council, Tory and Reformer alike, resigned and the assembly passed a resolution supporting their action. At this point, the assembly of Upper Canada for the first time refused to vote funds for the use of the Executive. The elected members also demanded that the Executive Council be formed of men who had the confidence and support of the assembly. What was necessary, a resolution of the assembly declared, was "a responsible executive council to advise the lieutenant-governor on the affairs of the province."

Like the old soldier he was, Governor Bond Head took the initiative. Dissolving the assembly, he made a personal appeal to the electorate. It was a furious and bitter election campaign in which Bond Head branded his critics as traitors scheming to destroy the British connection. He called upon "every noble-minded Englishman, Irishman, and United Empire Loyalist" to support him. To a friend in England he wrote: "I am playing a game here in which I am king, and all the rest of the cards knaves; and yet I believe I have at last managed to trump them, but it is hard work. . . . This is a fine country, if we could but get it quiet, in which I have nearly succeeded by upsetting the radicals." Where emotional appeals were inadequate, Bond Head successfully used bribery and intimidation to ensure the return of government supporters. The result was an assembly which could be relied upon to support him. With this successful election behind him, Bond Head threw moderation to the winds and refused to make any concession even to the moderate Reformers. As for Mackenzie's radical followers, they now lost all hope of change by constitutional means.

In Lower Canada, Papineau had reached almost the same conclusion. Following the assembly's refusal to grant funds in 1834, the British had sent Lord Gosford, as Governor-General, to Quebec with orders to investigate the deadlock and adopt some conciliatory measures. Gosford offered to appoint some of Papineau's followers to the Legislative Council, but refused to recommend that it be elected. Papineau rejected the compromise. The deadlock continued and the assembly refused to grant funds for the salaries of government officials. In March 1837, Lord John Russell, the British Colonial Secretary, intervened. In his famous Ten Resolutions he bluntly rejected the appeal for an elected legislative council and an executive in any way responsible to the assembly. Russell felt that to grant responsible government would be nothing less than to make the colonies independent. If the Empire were to be maintained, the governor and his council had to be responsible to the British government, not to the local assembly. Moreover, one of Russell's Resolutions declared that if the assembly refused to grant funds for the carrying on of government, the governor could legally spend money without the approval of the assembly. In short, taxation without representation, the situation which had helped to bring on the American Revolution, could be practised in Canada.

The radicals in Canada concluded that nothing was to be gained by further appeals to the British government. William Lyon Mackenzie wrote angrily in his newspaper:

> The secret is told at last—The screeds and councils and constitutions, the pledges and kingly declarations, the proclamations and acts of parliament and ministerial statements, to which the judge on the bench, the representative in the legislature, and the loyalist in his family circle referred as proofs that colonists were freemen are swept away in one instant by an almost unanimous resolution in the House of Commons in England, agreeing to rob, plunder, steal and defraud the people of Lower

Canada of their money, the produce of taxation, to apply that money to purposes the people by their representatives would not consent to apply it, and to refuse them all substantial redress of the grievances under which they have so long and so patiently laboured.

Mackenzie's vigorous and rousing attack found a ready audience, for by the summer of 1837 a depression had hit the Canadian colonies. A financial panic in the United States, a trade depression in England, poor crops and low prices, bankruptcies and unemployment provided fertile ground for the seeds of political revolt that Mackenzie and Papineau had been sowing.

3. THE REBELLIONS OF 1837

The rebellion came first in Lower Canada. Although Papineau and his supporters had certainly been talking the language of revolutionaries, its outbreak was accidental. E. B. O'Callaghan, a hot-headed Irish supporter of Papineau, wrote that the reply to Russell's Resolutions should be resistance. He declared: "HENCEFORTH, THERE MUST BE NO PEACE IN THE PROVINCE—*no quarter for the plunderers.* Agitate! *Agitate!!* Destroy the revenue; denounce the oppressors. Everything is lawful when the fundamental liberties are in danger." This loud talk had not been backed up by any serious preparations for a rebellion. Yet, the mass meetings organized by "les Patriotes," as the Reform party was called in Lower Canada, resulted in rioting in Montreal on November 7, 1837. Believing that his presence in the city might lead to further trouble, Papineau decided to leave Montreal. Ironically, the government interpreted this move as an attempt by the Patriote leader to gather support among the country people. Attempts to arrest the leaders of the Reform party led to a series of armed clashes at St. Eustache, St. Denis, and St. Charles. At St. Eustache, hastily gathered rebel forces took cover in a church. A British officer described the scene as British troops moved in: "The rebels were found stationed in the gallery still defending them-

4,000 Dollars
REWARD!

PROVINCE OF LOWER CANADA. | **GOSFORD.**

By His Excellency the Right Honorable Archibald Earl of Gosford, Baron Worlingham of Beccles, in the County of Suffolk, Captain General and Governor in Chief in and over the Provinces of Upper and Lower Canada, Vice Admiral of the same, and one of Her Majesty's Most Honorable Privy Council, &c. &c. &c.

A Proclamation.

WHEREAS by information upon oath it appears that,

Louis Joseph Papineau,

of the city of Montreal, Esquire, is charged with the crime of High Treason. And whereas the said Louis Joseph Papineau has withdrawn himself from his usual place of resort, and there is reason to believe he has fled from justice ; and whereas it is expedient and necessary for the due administration of justice and for the security of Her Majesty's Government in this Province, that so great an offence should not escape unpunished. Now therefore know ye, that I the said Archibald Earl of Gosford, by the advice of Her Majesty's Executive Council of this Province, have thought fit to issue this Proclamation, and I do hereby require and command all Her Majesty's loving subjects in this Province to discover, take and apprehend the said Louis Joseph Papineau, wherever he may be found therein, and carry him before a Justice assigned to keep the Peace or Chief Magistrate in either of the cities of Quebec or Montreal, aforesaid. And for the encouragement of all persons to be diligent in endeavouring to discover and apprehend the said Louis Joseph Papineau, and who shall bring him before such Justice assigned to keep the peace or Magistrate aforesaid, I do hereby offer

A REWARD OF
One Thousand Pounds,

Current money of this Province, to whomsoever shall so apprehend the said Louis Joseph Papineau, and deliver him up to justice.

Given under my Hand and Seal at Arms, at the Castle of Saint Lewis, in the City of Quebec, the first day of December, in the year of Our Lord, one thousand eight hundred and thirty-seven, and in the first year of Her Majesty's Reign.

By His Excellency's Command,

D. DALY,
Secy. of the Province.

Printed by JOHN CHARLTON FISHER, and WILLIAM KEMBLE, Printer to the Queen's most Excellent Majesty.

selves, and having cut away the staircase, every attempt to dislodge them for awhile proved utterly fruitless, but on a sudden the church was in flames and on the part of the rebels all was lost. These unfortunate and misguided people were then to be seen dispersing in every direction; few escaped. One hundred and twenty were made prisoners, but the estimated loss in killed and wounded was great." The rebels in Lower Canada were easily defeated by the better equipped and trained troops that the government had at its command. Papineau and his chief lieutenants escaped to the United States where they hoped to regroup their forces and gain American assistance.

The rebellion in Upper Canada was precipitated by events in the lower province. When Mackenzie heard the news of the battle in French Canada, he began to organize his forces. A handbill entitled "Independence," which was circulated among Mackenzie's sympathizers, illustrated the revolutionary spirit that had captured the radicals. It read: MARK MY WORDS, CANADIANS! The struggle has begun—it might end in freedom; but timidity, cowardice, or tampering on our part, will only delay its course. We cannot be reconciled to Britain. . . . We are determined never to rest until independence is ours. . . . Up then brave Canadians! Get ready your rifles, and make short work of it." But despite revolutionary enthusiasm among the leaders, the revolt was a hopeless, mis-managed affair from the beginning. Mackenzie gathered his disorganized force of ill-armed farmers and workingmen at Montgomery's Tavern, which stood near the present intersection of Yonge and Eglinton in Toronto. Sir Francis Bond Head proved almost as incapable of organizing his forces as Mackenzie was of leading the rebels. The major clash occurred on December 7, and the rebels were quickly dispersed. After the "battle," Mackenzie wrote: "And never did men fight more courageously. In the face of a heavy fire of grape and cannister, with broadside following broadside of musketry in steady and rapid succession, they stood their ground firmly, and killed and wounded a large number of the enemy, but were at length compelled to retreat."

Defeated, Mackenzie followed Papineau across the border into the United States. There the exiles from both provinces attempted to reorganize their men and win support from the Americans for a new attempt to overthrow the government in Canada. Apart from a few minor raids and border skirmishes, nothing came of their efforts. While some Americans along the border gave private aid to the exiled rebels, the American government had no desire to provoke war with Great Britain. The chief result of the border raids was to encourage repressive measures by the ruling authorities in the Canadas, who took the opportunity to make arrests on very slight suspicion of disloyalty. Only two men were executed but many others were exiled to such penal colonies as Van Diemen's Land and Australia.

Despite the widespread discontent in both Upper and Lower Canada, the majority of the population refused to believe that rebellion was the only solution. The radical views of Mackenzie and Papineau, which implied both republicanism and independence, alienated many of those who shared their dissatisfaction with the existing order. In Upper Canada both Loyalists and more recent British immigrants were unwilling to jeopardize the British connection, while in Lower Canada the Roman Catholic Church and many of the habitants distrusted the democratic, anti-clerical and, to some, revolutionary views of Papineau and his followers. Yet, while the rebellions had failed, they had also succeeded; for the British government, abruptly reminded of the disastrous consequences of 1776, decided that a thorough-going investigation of the British North American problem was necessary.

5 DURHAM'S REPORT AND THE TRIUMPH OF RESPONSIBLE GOVERNMENT

NO better man than John Lambton, first Earl of Durham, could have been selected to investigate the crisis in the Canadas. Durham was an extremely wealthy man, fully in sympathy with the nineteenth-century industrial and commercial revolution. Yet he was also a convinced reformer, who had won the title "Radical Jack" for his prominent role in the struggle for the Reform Bill of 1832. Well-read and highly intelligent, he had learned the finer arts of diplomacy as British ambassador to Russia. Although he was charming and tactful when the occasion demanded, he had a haughty and arrogant temperament, often accentuated by the severe headaches which were a symptom of the disease that was to kill him at forty-nine. Durham was reluctant to accept the assignment to British North America. "The undertaking is a fearfully arduous one," he wrote, "and nothing but the extreme emergency of the case could induce me to make such a sacrifice."

1. DURHAM'S REPORT

The "extreme emergency" was not just the problem of the Canadian uprisings. At stake, too, was the continued existence of the British Empire. By 1837 many people in Britain believed that the time had come to emancipate the colonies, particularly those like the British North American colonies, which were a problem to govern and an expense to defend. The sentiment was strengthened by the growing belief that Imperial trade preferences were a liability and that Britain should adopt free trade. Of what use was an empire if it were not profitable?

Durham did not share these sentiments and staunchly

maintained his belief in the value of the Empire. He belonged to the group of colonial reformers who argued that a liberal grant of self-government, an enlightened administration, free trade and large-scale British emigration to the colonies would promote the welfare of both Britain and the colonies and strengthen the bonds between them.

To assist him in British North America, Durham enlisted the support of two prominent and able colonial reformers, Edward Gibbon Wakefield and Charles Buller. A powerful advocate of a freer system of colonial government, the charming and witty Buller was a valuable addition to Durham's staff. The imaginative Wakefield was well known for his ideas and achievements in the field of large-scale emigration to the colonies. More widely publicized was his ill-fated attempt to abduct an heiress, for which escapade he had spent two years in jail.

As Durham descended the gangplank at Quebec late in May 1838, the guns roared in salute and the guard of honour in their scarlet tunics stood rigidly at attention. In a magnificent uniform, heavily embroidered with silver and decorated with the Order of the Bath, Durham rode up the rocky streets of Quebec on a prancing white horse. The crowds cheered, sensing that perhaps upon the shoulders of the new Governor-General rested not only their future but that of the Empire as well.

Yet even as the crowds cheered, there were sporadic outbursts of violence and threats of new uprisings in Lower Canada. To pacify the colonies and restore order would require determination and humanity. Durham revealed both qualities when he pardoned most of the rebels and exiled eight to Bermuda. Complete pacification of the Canadas, however, was impossible while there remained the danger of an attack from the United States. In Buffalo, William Lyon Mackenzie had received an enthusiastic welcome, and soon a thousand men, armed with guns removed from the United States arsenal, were waiting for the signal to march. All along the border—at Troy, Burlington, Rochester, Ogdensburg and Montpelier—Americans voted money and supplies

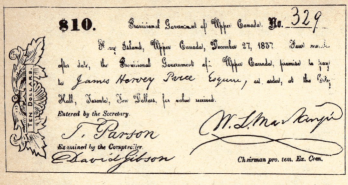

Only an optimist would have accepted this promise to pay by Mackenzie's provisional government.

for the "patriots" and formed Hunters' Lodges whose members swore "never to rest until all tyrants of Great Britain cease to have any Dominion or footing whatever in North America."

Shortly after his arrival Durham travelled to Niagara Falls where he ostentatiously reviewed British and Canadian troops. Crossing the border he attended lavish dinner parties and held sociable conversations in which he convinced the Americans that whatever British policy in the Canadas had been in the past, under him it would be liberal, democratic, and just. Durham's charm was irresistible and, while the border remained unsettled, the immediate threat of invasion disappeared. As Charles Buller wrote:

> A million of money would have been a cheap price for the single glass of wine which Lord Durham drank to the health of the American President. . . . It is only the man of statesmanlike mind who can produce a great result out of things so small as an invitation to dinner, or the drinking of a glass of wine.

Durham and his staff had also been carefully studying the causes of the 1837 rebellions. As Durham's Report later revealed, they saw at once that the economic and social problems of the colonies centred on the conflicts between the

Family Compact or Chateau Clique and the elected assembly. They also accepted the argument of Robert Baldwin, the Upper Canadian Reformer, that the solution of these problems was a system of government under which the governor would choose his advisers in the executive council from men who had the confidence of the legislative assembly. As Durham wrote in the majestic prose that graced his entire Report:

> We are not now to consider the policy of establishing representative government in the North American Colonies. That has been irrevocably done. . . . To conduct their Government, harmoniously, in accordance with its established principles, is now the business of its rulers; and I know not how it is possible to secure that harmony in any other way, than by administering the Government on those principles which have been found perfectly efficacious in Great Britain. . . . [The Crown must] submit to the necessary consequences of representative institutions; and if it has to carry on the Government in unison with a representative body, it must consent to carry it on by means of those in whom that representative body has confidence. Every purpose of popular control might be combined with every advantage of vesting the immediate choice of advisers in the Crown, were the Colonial Governor to be instructed to secure the co-operation of the Assembly in his policy, by entrusting the administration to such men as could command a majority.

The governor would still have an important role to play, but it would be in working with the assembly rather than supporting the executive and legislative councils in opposition to it. Government would thus spring from the popular will, and, said Durham, "If the colonists make bad laws and select improper persons to conduct their affairs, they will generally be the only, always the greatest sufferers; and, like the People of other countries, they must bear the ills which they bring on themselves, until they choose to apply the remedy." The alternative to responsible government, he warned, was an army strong enough to prevent further rebel-

In November 1838 the Patriotes once again took up arms. For a few days the region southwest of Montreal was controlled by the Patriotes, and at Napierville three thousand rebels issued a declaration of independence. But Sir John Colborne, commander of the Canadian troops, moved quickly and the rebellion was soon put down. This time little mercy was shown the rebels. Over seven hundred were captured. Of the 108 brought to trial, 99 were condemned to death. Only 12 were executed, however, and 58 were banished to Australian penal colonies.

lions against the oligarchic rule of the Compact and Clique.

Durham attempted to reassure his readers that responsible government did not mean complete self-government and separation from Britain. On the contrary, Britain would retain control of these matters of Imperial interest: the management of public lands, in deference to Wakefield's hope for large scale emigration to the colonies; the regulation of external trade and foreign affairs; the form of the constitution itself; and relations with the Indians. But in all ordinary questions of domestic policy the colony would govern itself.

Although he fervently believed in responsible government, Lord Durham refused to recommend its introduction in

Lower Canada, for it would mean placing the English-speaking minority under the French-Canadian majority. He had seen that the constitutional conflict in Upper Canada had economic and social roots, but he attributed the Lower-Canadian crisis almost exclusively to a conflict of races. As he wrote in one celebrated passage: "I expected to find a contest between a government and a people; I found two nations warring in the bosom of a single state: I found a struggle not of principles but of races." There was no doubt in his mind that, however gracious and hospitable the French Canadians were, the future lay with the British. It could hardly be otherwise. Like the English-speaking merchants in Montreal, he believed in industry and commerce, in the development of transportation facilities and the encouragement of a business-like and progressive spirit. He shared their views of the commercial possibilities of the St. Lawrence system, and deplored the unprogressive and stubborn nature of the French Canadians who blocked its development.

Union of the two colonies appeared to be the ideal solution to both the economic and the political problem. Union would end the fatal division of the St. Lawrence water-way system. It would also solve the constitutional dilemma. With Upper Canada's rapid increase in population, the English-speaking Canadians would soon be the majority. They would then not only dominate political life in the united colony, but by sheer superiority of numbers, Durham thought, they would assimilate the French Canadians.

Durham had come to these conclusions, which he later embodied in his Report, within six months of his arrival in Canada. His investigations were cut short in September when the British government refused to support his banishment of the exiles. Outraged by this lack of confidence, Durham returned home to write his Report at breakneck speed and face his enemies in the last few months of life remaining to him. The publication of the Report in 1839 aroused a storm of protest. Upper Canadian Tories charged that his analysis of Compact rule was inaccurate and biased, and denounced responsible government as a reward for disloyalty and rebellion. The English-speaking minority in Lower Canada applauded the idea of union, but suspected that responsible government would give power to the French. The French Canadians, understandably, were enraged. Only the Upper Canadian Reformers greeted the Report with enthusiastic approval. On the evils of oligarchy and the need for responsible government Durham had completely vindicated the position they had held for ten years. But more important than the mixed cries of joy and anger in the Canadas was the official reaction of the British government.

2. RUSSELL'S COMPROMISE

The Imperial government readily accepted the arguments for union of the two Canadas, and in 1840 passed the Act of Union to come into effect a year later. Like Durham, the British ministers maintained that the French Canadians should not be placed in a position to dominate the legislature of the Canadas. Since English-speaking Canadians were then in a slight minority in the two colonies the British ministers gave equal representation to Upper and Lower Canada, or Canada West and Canada East as they now became known, failing to realize that the rapid immigration to Upper Canada would soon place English-speaking Canadians in a commanding majority.

Despite the power and logic of Durham's arguments for responsible government, the British ministers remained unconvinced. As long as the colony remained a colony, the governor must be responsible to the British government and not to an executive council chosen from the legislative assembly. As Lord John Russell, the Colonial Secretary, wrote:

> It may happen . . . that the Governor receives at one and the same time instructions from the Queen and advice from his Executive Council, totally at variance with each other. If he is to obey his instructions from England, the parallel of constitutional responsibility en-

tirely fails: if, on the other hand, he is to follow the advice of his Council, he is no longer a subordinate officer, but an independent sovereign.

Responsible government, then, was synonymous with independence. Durham's argument that this conflict would not arise because matters of Imperial concern would remain in Britain's hands was considered to be unrealistic and impossible. Russell wrote:

> There are some cases of internal government, in which the honour of the Crown or the faith of Parliament, or the safety of the State, are so seriously involved that it would not be possible for Her Majesty to delegate her authority to a Ministry in a colony.

Nevertheless, the Liberal government* in Great Britain, of which Russell was a member, had no desire to return to the system of oligarchic government that had caused the rebellions of 1837. In the future the people of Canada were to have a greater voice in their own government, and the governor was to select his advisers from "men whose principles and feelings were in accordance with the majority" and administer the colony in co-operation with the legislative assembly. However, the governor was not to be bound to follow the advice of his council, which was still responsible to him and not to the assembly. What remained to be seen was whether this compromise, so easily stated on paper, could be worked out in practice.

3. THE CRITICAL YEARS 1840-1846

The man selected for the difficult task of initiating the Russell compromise was Charles Poulett Thomson, who was elevated to the peerage as Lord Sydenham. Sydenham was a man of considerable experience in business and politics. He realized that to succeed he had to persuade a majority in the assembly to follow him instead of any other combination of political leaders. In short, the Governor

* It was also known as the Whig or Reform government.

had to be his own Prime Minister and party leader. With an Imperial loan to provide the necessary means he reduced the provincial debt and undertook an ambitious programme of public works. As Sydenham suspected, most Canadians were more concerned with obtaining material improvements than with solving their constitutional problems. Even the restless members in the assembly were seldom a match for the shrewd Governor whose parliamentary skill was highly regarded even in England. There were two men, however, who did not fall under the Sydenham spell. Louis LaFontaine held the ranks of the Lower Canadian Reformers solid in opposition to the new Governor. Sydenham shared Durham's views of the French-Canadian problem, and refused to invite the "disloyal" French to serve on the council. Robert Baldwin, who had supported Sydenham until he realized that he would not accept the full implications of responsible government and intended to govern himself, continued to press in the assembly for full responsible government. Baldwin's stubborn and insistent pressure and the increasing strength of the Baldwin-LaFontaine alliance on the principle of responsible government forced the Governor to seek the assembly's approval for a set of resolutions introduced by Harrison, one of his ministers. The resolutions stated that the governor was responsible "to the Imperial authority alone" but:

> That in order to preserve between the different branches of the Provincial Parliament that harmony which is essential to the peace, welfare and good government of the Province the chief advisers of the representative of the Sovereign, constituting a Provincial administration under him, ought to be men possessed of the confidence of the representatives of the people. . . .

The Harrison resolutions were little more than a restatement of Russell's policy, but they were sufficient to appease men less determined than Baldwin and LaFontaine. What would happen if the Governor could not find men "possessed of the confidence of the representatives of the people" remained to be seen. Sydenham had avoided such a crisis by governing himself and building up his own party in the assembly, but Sydenham fell from his horse the day after the Harrison resolutions were passed and died two weeks later.

As his successor, Sir Robert Peel's Conservative government, which had defeated the Liberals in 1841, appointed Sir Charles Bagot. Unlike Sydenham, Bagot had no parliamentary experience, but his charm, tact and impartiality had helped him to build an extremely successful diplomatic career. Peel instructed him to follow the general policies of Sydenham, but suggested that the blanket rejection of all the French Canadians might be reconsidered. This conciliatory policy towards the French had been urged upon Peel by Charles Buller:

> We have put down their rebellion, destroyed their nationality, and in doing this reduced them to a miserable state of social subjection. The Governor that would raise them up to a social equality by mere justice and kindness would make them the instruments instead of the enemies of Government. The French Canadians if rightly managed are the natural instruments, by which the Government could keep in check the democratic and American tendencies of Upper Canada.

Upon his arrival in Canada, Bagot immediately decided that he neither could nor would adopt Sydenham's techniques. As he informed his superiors in London: "It was only by dint of the greatest energy, and I must add the unscrupulous personal interference of Lord Sydenham, combined with practices which I would not use, and your Lordship would not recommend, in addition to the promise of the Loan and the bribe of Public Works, that Lord Sydenham managed to get through the Session." Moreover, Bagot soon realized that the precarious personal party that Sydenham had built up had disintegrated, and the defeat of the executive in the assembly was almost certain. To Bagot the solution was equally clear. Since Baldwin and LaFontaine jointly possessed a majority in the assembly, they should form a new executive council. Bagot knew only too well that Baldwin and LaFontaine were committed to the principle of responsible government, which he had been instructed to reject. He knew also that opinion in England, at the Colonial Office, and in influential circles in Canada was utterly opposed to giving any power to the French-Canadian Reformers, so many of whom, like LaFontaine, had supported Papineau. Yet in Bagot's opinion both political necessity and a generous humanity pointed to the same end. In September 1842 he persuaded the Reform leaders to take office.

Bagot's "Great Measure," as it was called, was really an admission that responsible government existed. As he wrote to the Colonial Secretary, Baldwin was "the actual and deservedly acknowledged leader of the strongest party in the House, and in the Country. . . . Whether the doctrine of responsible government is openly acknowledged, or is only tacitly acquiesced in, virtually it exists." While the Montreal *Gazette* charged that Bagot had handed over "the British party . . . to the vindictive disposition of a French mob," the Governor patiently explained the significance of his action to the outraged Colonial Secretary, who had advised conciliation of the French but no more.

> I have removed the main ground of discontent and distrust among the French Canadian population; I have satisfied them that the Union is capable of being administered for their happiness and advantage, and have consequently disarmed opposition to it. I have excited among them the strongest feelings of gratitude to the Provincial Government; and if my policy be approved by Her Majesty's Government, I shall have removed their chief cause of hostility to British institutions, and have added another security for their devotion to the British Crown.

Unfortunately, illness soon forced Bagot to resign and the British government seized the opportunity to send a new governor to Canada who would at least stop the clock, if not turn it back. Sir Charles Metcalfe was an experienced administrator and a man of liberal views, but his experience in India and Jamaica had not given him much faith in colonial assemblies nor had it led him to look kindly upon men whose profession of loyalty to the British connection he regarded as "utterly worthless." His own position was clear: "Whether my contest be with a malignant minority, or with a majority of the House of Assembly, or with the whole colony run mad, my duty must be the same. I cannot surrender Her Majesty's authority, or the supremacy of the Mother Country."

Inevitably, Metcalfe differed with his Canadian advisers, and, in November 1843, Baldwin and LaFontaine resigned. For a year the Governor vainly attempted to find a majority in the assembly. Finally, in November 1844 he appealed directly to the people to elect a more sympathetic assembly. Led by Metcalfe, who campaigned personally in the election, the Conservatives denounced the Reformers as petty office-seekers interested only in patronage, as traitors and republicans, who would break the British connection. This appeal to loyalty and patriotism won the support of Egerton Ryerson and the Methodists and gave Metcalfe and the Conservatives a precarious majority. As in 1837 there were murmurings of revolt, and in 1845, when Metcalfe went home to die, it remained to be seen whether Canada was to have responsible government or government by bayonet.

4. THE VICTORY GAINED, 1846

The issue was largely determined by events in England. In 1846 the British government, secure in its industrial and commercial supremacy, swept away the old policy of mercantilism and adopted free trade. With the abandonment of the old economic base of the Empire, it no longer seemed as important to retain firm political control over the colonies. An even more decisive factor was the victory of the Liberals in the 1846 election. Since their defeat in 1841 the English Liberals had been reconsidering their attitude towards responsible government for the colonies. As they observed the course of events in Canada and studied the arguments of Durham and Buller and of Baldwin in Upper Canada and Joseph Howe in Nova Scotia, the logic of responsible government appeared irresistible. When the new government took office, Lord Grey, a brother-in-law of Lord Durham, became Colonial Secretary, and among his staff was Charles Buller. Grey immediately made it clear that responsible government would be granted to the North American colonies.

The first colony to benefit was Nova Scotia. Under the leadership of the brilliant journalist, Joseph Howe, the Reformers in Nova Scotia had struggled for responsible government as vigorously as the Canadians, although they had never resorted to rebellion. Joseph Howe's *Letters to Lord John Russell* in 1839 had been as eloquent a statement of the need for constitutional change as was Durham's Report. In one sentence the fiery "tribune of Nova Scotia" had summed up his case: "We seek for nothing more than British subjects are entitled to; but we will be content with nothing less."

No sooner was he installed in office than Lord Grey informed Sir John Harvey, the Lieutenant-Governor of Nova Scotia, that a new policy had been adopted in colonial affairs. Grey's dispatch was one of the most important that had ever crossed the Atlantic to British North America.

> I have ... to instruct you to abstain from changing your Executive Council until it shall have become perfectly clear that they are unable, with such fair support from yourself as they have a right to expect, to carry on the government of the province satisfactorily, and command the confidence of the Legislature.... In giving, therefore, all fair and proper support to your Council for the time being, you will carefully avoid any acts which can possibly be supposed to imply the slightest personal objection to their opponents.... A refusal to accept advice tendered to you by your Council is a legitimate ground for its members to tender to you their resignation, a course they would doubtless adopt should they feel that the subject on which a difference had arisen between you and themselves was one upon

which public opinion would be in their favour. Should it prove to be so, concession to their views must, sooner or later, become inevitable, since it cannot be too distinctly acknowledged that it is neither possible nor desirable to carry on the government of any of the British provinces in North America in opposition to the opinion of the inhabitants.

When the Nova Scotia election of 1847 returned a majority of Reformers and the government lost a non-confidence motion early in 1848, Sir John Harvey accepted the resignation of his ministers and called upon Howe and the Reform party to form a new administration. Responsible government in Nova Scotia had become a fact.

A year earlier Lord Grey had sent Lord Elgin, Durham's son-in-law, to Canada as Governor-General. Before Elgin's departure, he too had been given a copy of the dispatch quoted above with instructions to "act in conformity with the principles there laid down ... and to withdraw from the position into which Lord Metcalfe had, by unfortunate circumstances been brought ... and to make it generally understood that, if public opinion required it, he was equally ready to accept [the Reformers] as his advisers, uninfluenced by any personal preferences or objections." When the Canadian electorate returned a Reform majority in the 1847 elections, Elgin immediately asked Baldwin and LaFontaine to form a new government.

Although this decision caused grumbling among the Conservatives, the real test did not come until 1849, when the assembly passed the Rebellion Losses Bill to compensate those people in Canada East who had suffered property damages during the 1837 rebellion. To the English-speaking community in Canada East the Bill was nothing more than a reward for treason and rebellion, and an act of revenge by LaFontaine and his friends, many of whom had been rebels. Lord Elgin and the British government had misgivings about the justice of the Bill. But Elgin realized that responsible government meant following the advice of his ministers on matters of local concern, and assented to the Bill.

The reaction was violent. The Tories who opposed responsible government hurled a stream of insult and abuse at the Reform leaders, who actually feared for their lives. Elgin's carriage was pelted with stones as it passed through the streets of Montreal. On April 7, 1849, opponents of the Bill stirred a street mob to rioting which ended only after the skies over Montreal were lit up by the flames of the burning Parliament buildings. But the flames were really the death of the old order, for responsible government had triumphed. Lord Durham had also triumphed, but only in part. For responsible government was won not by the assimilation of the French but by the co-operation of both communities in Canada. Baldwin and LaFontaine had proved Durham right while also proving him wrong.

5 THE UNEASY UNION

1. REORGANIZING THE ECONOMY

The number and magnitude of the evils that afflict our country, and the universal and increasing depression of its material interests call upon all persons animated by a sincere desire for its welfare to combine for the purposes of enquiry and preparation with a view to the adoption of such remedies as mature and dispassionate investigation may suggest. . . . THIS REMEDY CONSISTS IN A FRIENDLY AND PEACEFUL SEPARATION FROM [THE] BRITISH CONNECTION AND A UNION UPON EQUITABLE TERMS WITH THE GREAT NORTH AMERICAN CONFEDERACY OF SOVEREIGN STATES.

This manifesto appeared in the Montreal *Gazette* on October 11, 1849. It was not drafted by fanatical crackpots but represented the considered opinion of the most prominent, respectable and powerful businessmen in Canada East. The three hundred and twenty-five men who signed it were the "solid" citizens of the community, men who instinctively voted Conservative. Their proposed solution, however, was the most radical one imaginable for Canada's problems for it meant the end of Canada as a community separate from the United States. Priding themselves above all on their loyalty to the British connection, the English-speaking merchants were driven to this desperate extreme by the conviction that the mother country had abandoned them. Britain had not only supported responsible government, which seemed to put control of the colony in the hands of the "disloyal" French Canadians; even more serious, between 1846 and 1849 the British government had established free trade and abolished the Navigation Acts, thus ending the old colonial system. The tariff privileges enjoyed by the

Canadian merchants in the Imperial market disappeared and they lost their important advantage over American merchants. Their vision of a great commercial empire, based on the St. Lawrence water-way system, and stretching into the rich lands of the West, was now just a mirage. Disillusioned, fearful and angry, the Montreal businessmen concluded that if they could not defeat their competitors in The United States, they had better join them.

The Annexation Manifesto found little support among most Canadians. The economic problems were undoubtedly serious, but as in 1837 most people in 1849 were unwilling to accept the political consequences of the Manifesto. Even the Tories in Canada West turned deaf ears to the proposal. Rejecting annexation as a solution, they proposed a federation of all the British North American colonies, an adventurous suggestion that foreshadowed the later creation of the Dominion of Canada.

A more practicable solution for the present was the attempt to develop freer trade with the United States. Lord Elgin was an enthusiastic supporter of this idea of reciprocity with the United States and pressed his views on the British government: "You have a great opportunity before you—obtain reciprocity for us and I venture to predict that you will be able shortly to point to this hitherto turbulent colony with satisfaction in illustration of the tendency of self-government and freedom of trade to beget contentment and material progress."

The lever that might be used to pry open the American market for Canadian natural products was the American desire to use the rich Canadian inshore fisheries denied to them by the Convention of 1818. Despite the prohibition, New England fishermen attempted to fish in British North American waters. By 1850, squadrons of the American and British navies sailed off the coasts of Nova Scotia and Newfoundland to protect their citizens, and the danger of an armed clash was imminent. Since the British were anxious to resolve this troublesome problem, Lord Elgin was authorized to negotiate a settlement which would include trade questions with the United States. Despite the American desire to have access to the fisheries, Lord Elgin needed all his personal charm and diplomatic skill in Washington to secure acceptance of a treaty. Over cigars and champagne, Southern Senators were persuaded that reciprocity would keep Canada out of the Union, while their Northern colleagues were not discouraged from seeing reciprocity as a way of obtaining new markets and as a prelude to annexation. Elgin took Washington society by storm, but, as his secretary observed, he "never loses sight for a moment of his object, and while he is chaffing Yankees and slapping them on the back, he is systematically pursuing that object. The consequence is, he is the most popular Englishman that ever visited the United States." In the end Elgin was successful. The reciprocity treaty of 1854 provided for free exchange of natural products between the United States and the British North American colonies, free navigation of the St. Lawrence and Great Lakes waterways, and mutual access to the inshore fisheries.

The reciprocity agreement strengthened the Canadian economy. Natural products such as grain and timber from the Canadas, and fish and timber from the Maritimes, found wide markets in the United States. One-half of the trade of the Canadas and two-thirds of the trade of the Maritimes remained with Great Britain despite reciprocity, but the newly opened market in the United States provided a very necessary addition. Perhaps more important, by decreasing the dependence of the colonies on Britain, the reciprocity agreement helped to encourage a growing sense of maturity in British North America.

One practical sign of this new maturity was the decision of the Canadian government in 1859 to impose a customs tariff which protected Canadian manufacturers against British imports. When Britain protested against this measure, Canada argued that responsible government meant full Canadian control over the colony's economic life. A. T. Galt, the Canadian Minister of Finance, bluntly informed the British that "the Government of Canada acting for its Legislature and people cannot, through those feelings of deference which they owe to the Imperial authorities, in any manner waive or diminish the right of the people of Canada to decide for themselves both as to the mode and extent to which taxation shall be imposed." The British reluctantly accepted the Canadian argument, and self-government was thus recognized in another area of the colony's life.

The reciprocity agreement of 1854 was also significant in a more general way. The fact that the treaty had been negotiated for all the British North American colonies suggested that the area could be treated as a unit rather than as a group of totally separate colonies. Did this not suggest the possibility of a political union of all British North America? If the colonies could be linked together by new means of communication, and if their populations grew large enough to provide a prosperous home market, political union would become feasible.

2. RAILWAYS AND WESTWARD EXPANSION

The population of the British North American colonies grew rapidly in the 1850's. The number of people in Canada West jumped from 445,000 in 1841 to 952,000 in 1851, when for the first time it exceeded that of Canada East. While growth in the Maritime colonies was slower, by 1861 they contained 662,000 people compared with 2,500,000 in the Canadas. This population growth was the result of economic changes important enough to justify the title of a revolution. At the core of the commercial revolution was the coming of the railway and, with it, a spirit of buoyant optimism. The St. Thomas *Weekly Despatch* declared in 1853:

> It is exceedingly gratifying to witness the spirit of enterprise and progress which has of late sprung up as it were simultaneously in every section of Upper Canada. We hear nothing but Railways, Steamers and Telegraph lines. A few years since it was not so. It seems but yesterday when the projection of a costly line of Rail-

way such as the Grand Trunk or even Great Western would have been considered a mere chimera, an idle fancy of speculative imagination. This state of things has disappeared, the spirit of improvement is abroad, the march of Canada from end to end is onward, its prosperity is astounding the dormant settlers who were content to live in peaceful retirement enjoying the comforts derived from hard toil and incessant plodding.

Railways were needed or demanded everywhere in British North America. Many local lines were built by enterprising companies in all the colonies, but it was the more grandiose projects in the Canadas that caught the imagination of both politician and businessman. A. T. Galt, who was both, underlined the importance of railways to Canada when he remarked: "Unless Canada can combine with her unrivalled system of inland navigation a railroad system connected therewith and mutually sustaining each other, the whole of her large outlay must remain forever unproductive." What Galt and others realized was that the old St. Lawrence commercial system could only be revived if British North America was bound together and extended by rails of steel. A network of railways running north and west from Toronto was built to tie the western and northern hinterlands to the centres of trade and commerce. Among these was the Northern Railway, running north from Toronto to Lake Simcoe and thence to Georgian Bay, which was designed to reach into new areas of settlement north of Toronto and draw farm products to the city's markets. A second project was the Great Western, developed to link Hamilton with American railways which ran to Buffalo and Detroit. A third was the St. Lawrence and Atlantic from Montreal to Portland, Maine, which gave the Canadians a winter port when the St. Lawrence was ice-bound.

But what British North America needed most was a single line that would join British North American terminals rather than run to American ports. The greatest of such projects was the Grand Trunk, which was to run from Sarnia to Halifax. Much of the money and engineering skill needed to begin this vast enterprise came from Britain. Construction had scarcely started when it was realized that the project would require more capital than was originally anticipated, and local governments were repeatedly called upon to provide funds to save the railway from bankruptcy. By 1860 the Grand Trunk was completed in the Canadas, but its eastern outlet was provided by the line running to Portland, Maine.

There still remained the major problem of building an all-Canadian line to link the Maritimes with the Canadas. In 1858, A. T. Galt summed up the dangers which this situation created: "The position of Canada is both peculiar and exceptional. A population now numbering three millions of British-born subjects resides in the interior of America and during the winter season are absolutely proscribed from any intercourse with either Great Britain or the other colonies except through a foreign country [the United States] jealous of the power of England upon the continent. . . ." The Grand Trunk lacked the resources to build the line itself; indeed, each year it sank more deeply into debt. The British government refused to provide the capital. And as long as the colonies remained politically divided they, too, lacked the necessary concerted effort and financial resources.

The financial problems of the railways produced many headaches for Canadian politicians in the 1850's. The heavy costs of construction and operation meant that railway promoters had to appeal repeatedly for public funds, with the result that railway development and politics became closely interwoven. This situation was not always good for either the railways or the politicians since it opened the door to extravagance and corruption. One Grand Trunk representative wrote:

> My work was almost exclusively "lobbying" to get a Grand Trunk Bill through. . . . The Canadian Ministers were willing but weak—the majority a doubtful quantity. Although up to the last minute I felt that there was a chance of getting the bill through I was always doubtful, since it was clear that some twenty-five mem-

bers, contractors, etc., were simply waiting to be squared either by promise of contracts or money. As I had no authority to bribe, they simply abstained from voting and the bill was thrown out. £25,000 would have bought the lot. . . .

In an underdeveloped country like Canada, the government was the only institution rich enough to provide the railway builders with the capital they needed. And one thing was certain: if the country were to thrive it had to have railways.

By the end of the 1850's much had been achieved in the field of railway building. In 1850 only sixty-six miles of railroad existed in all of British North America. Ten years later the mileage had increased to 2,065. From the strictly financial point of view, the railways never achieved the success expected, but they did contribute a great deal to the growth of such industries as foundries, rolling mills and locomotive shops. The major industrial centres were Toronto and Hamilton, though smaller industries such as the manufacture of boots and shoes, the fabrication of cotton goods and the production of agricultural implements developed in other towns.

More important than these economic changes were the social and political changes that came with the railways. Railways broke down the isolation of pioneer communities. It was obvious that in the same way railways could tie together the whole of British North America into one vast economic unit; and economic union might bring political union with it. Thus, political and business objectives for the building of railways were tied together. As one newspaper noted in 1854: "Railway operations are calling into existence new wants and new enterprises, creating new markets and filling men with bigger thoughts."

Many of these "bigger thoughts" were directed towards the northwest, which seemed to provide the key for the further growth and prosperity of British North America. The Grand Trunk had failed to win control of the traffic from the American West, but the great expanse of the Canadian northwest above the forty-ninth parallel lay open and virtually untapped. By the 1850's, businessmen and politicians were beginning to examine the possibility of transforming this area into the kind of settlement that would fill an important role in building a prosperous economy. This was the dream of many easterners and it was summed up by the Toronto *Globe,* one of the first eastern newspapers to recognize the potential of the West.

> If Canada acquires this territory, it will rise in a few years from a position of a small and weak province to be the greatest colony any country has ever possessed, able to take its place among the empires of the earth.

If the West could be acquired and settled, it would not only provide farm products for eastern cities and for export, it would also furnish a market for the new manufactured products being developed in the Canadas.

In 1850 all of the British lands in the West were owned by the Hudson's Bay Company, which continued to carry on its lucrative fur-trading enterprise. As always the Company discouraged settlement, for settlers drove out the fur-bearing animals. But to the south the westward movement of settlers in the United States was growing so great that some of them began to look enviously at the fertile, un-populated lands of the Hudson's Bay Company. The Oregon boundary dispute in 1846 illustrated what could happen in such a situation.

The Convention of 1818 had made the forty-ninth parallel the Canadian-American boundary as far west as the Rockies. Beyond that the border was undefined. Until the 1840's the Hudson's Bay Company remained in undisputed control of the lower Columbia River valley and had its headquarters near the southern end of the river, at Fort Vancouver. In the 1840's, however, American settlers were flooding into the Oregon territory and soon demanded its formal annexation to the United States. Their appeal found a ready response in the United States and James Polk, the Democratic candidate for the Presidency in 1844, won the election on the campaign cry of "Fifty-four Forty or Fight,"

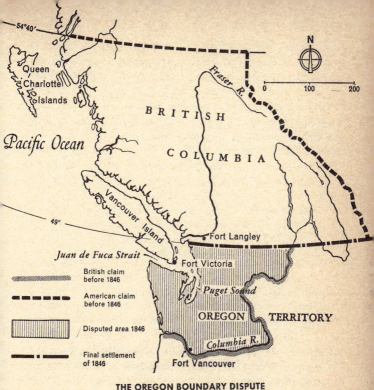

THE OREGON BOUNDARY DISPUTE

which was a claim not just to the Oregon territory, but to all of the Pacific coast south of Alaska. Britain refused this extravagant demand, but finally agreed to relinquish the territory south of the forty-ninth parallel.

The Oregon compromise set Canadians thinking more seriously about the future of the West. Fear of American expansion was heightened when the discovery of gold on the Fraser River in 1858 brought thousands of American prospectors to British Columbia from the exhausted gold fields of California. Firm action by Governor James Douglas kept the tumultuous gold seekers under control, but the danger remained that the Americans might once again demand annexation to the United States. Isolated from Brit-

ain's other North American colonies, British Columbia
and Vancouver Island were likely areas for American expansion unless, somehow, these areas could be drawn closer
to the rest of British North America.

Between British Columbia and the Canadas lay the large
open spaces of the prairies and the Rockies. Here, the only
important settlement was Fort Garry on the Red River,
where Selkirk's Scottish settlers had been joined by those
offspring of the fur trade, the half-breeds. As one Hudson's
Bay Company officer wrote, Red River became:

> The favourite retreat of the Company's servants. . . .
> Here they find themselves with the companions of their
> youth, their fellow adventurers; those with whom they
> tugged at the oar, and shared the toil of the winter
> march; and when they meet together to smoke the social
> pipe, and talk of the scenes of earlier days, "nor prince
> nor prelate" can enjoy more happiness.

Long isolated in the centre of the continent, the settlers
at Red River were first drawn into the mainstream of North
American life by pioneers passing westward across the
United States. By 1850, three hundred Red River carts
rumbled along the prairie trail from Minneapolis to Fort
Garry carrying supplies and mail, and by the end of the
decade steamboats on the Red River had cemented the
north-south bond. Minnesota had become a state in 1858
and ambitious local politicians cast envious eyes on the
unoccupied territory to the north. By 1860 it was clear that
unless Canada established communications with Red River,
the fertile western colony would fall prey to the expansion-
ist ambitions of the United States. Land-hungry farmers in
Canada West, who saw their sons emigrating to the United
States, supported the western expansion of Canada. So did
eastern manufacturers, who dreamed of a settled West as
a market for their goods. But as long as the Canadas were
unable to solve their own political problems, territorial
expansion was impossible.

3. POLITICAL TROUBLES

In the 1850's Canadian politics entered a new and unsettled
period. The source of the trouble lay in the Union Act
of 1841. The Act had never really united the two sections
of Canada, for, by granting equal representation to Canada
East and Canada West, it perpetuated a division based primarily on race. For ten years the system worked well enough
because the Reform supporters of Baldwin in Canada West
and LaFontaine in Canada East shared a common objective:
responsible government. Once responsible government was
achieved, however, in 1849, the interests of French- and
English-speaking Canadians began to diverge. And it was
the nature of the constitution itself that caused the most
serious dissension.

Until the early 1850's Canada West had the smaller population and was satisfied with equal representation. But
as soon as the population of Canada West exceeded that of
Canada East, some English-speaking Canadians began to
demand that representation in the legislature should be
based on population. Since this would mean an increase
in the number of English-speaking members, the French
Canadians firmly opposed the idea, fearing that an English-
speaking majority might interfere with the language, religion
and schools of the people in Quebec.

In Canada West the advocates of "rep-by-pop" found a
vigorous leader in George Brown, editor of the Toronto
Globe. Brown's demand for a reform of the system of representation was popular in Canada West, and after Baldwin retired in 1851 Brown soon became the real leader of
the Reform party. The French Canadians distrusted and
feared Brown, an ardent Presbyterian who opposed state
support for Roman Catholic separate schools and attacked
what he called "French domination" of the union.

Since the French Canadians were no longer willing to
co-operate with the Reformers from Canada West, they
gradually moved closer to the English-speaking Tories. Like
the French Canadians, the Tories from Canada West were
opposed to constitutional changes. Their main interest was

economic development and many of their leaders were associated with the Grand Trunk Railway and the businessmen who were developing the commerce of the St. Lawrence. By 1854 the alliance of French Canadians and English-speaking Canadian Tories had been moulded into the Conservative party by the capable hands of John A. Macdonald and Georges Etienne Cartier.

Macdonald was a young Kingston lawyer whose wit, attractive personality and ability to work with others gradually won him the leadership of his party. He was a practical man who believed that the union as it existed could work if the government promoted a favourable climate of economic development. Moreover, he realized that his party could only win a working majority if French- and English-speaking Canadians co-operated. As he told a friend: "If a Lower Canadian Britisher desires to conquer, he must stoop to conquer. He must make friends with the French. Without sacrificing the principle of his race or lineage, he must respect their nationality. Treat them as a nation and they will act as a free people generally do—generously. Treat them as a faction and they become factious."

Georges Etienne Cartier, a French Canadian, was, like Macdonald, anxious to promote a new alliance of the moderates from Canada East and Canada West. Like LaFontaine before him, Cartier believed that the cultural rights of French Canada, as well as the interests of the Montreal business community with which he was closely connected, could be protected and promoted by co-operation of English and French political leaders. Although the Macdonald-Cartier party became the strongest alliance in the union, its cohesion was precarious and it was threatened with disintegration whenever sectional issues arose.

Nevertheless, the Macdonald-Cartier government, formed in 1854, did manage to enact a number of important measures without stirring up sectional divisions. For example, in 1854, after years of heated controversy, both the clergy reserves and seigniorial system were abolished. Moreover, the government actively supported the construction of the Grand Trunk Railway. But the sectional problem persisted, and Macdonald's support in Canada West declined because he refused to accept "rep-by-pop." Macdonald and Cartier even found it impossible to select a permanent capital, for the French Canadians favoured Quebec or Montreal, while English-speaking Canadians insisted on Toronto or Kingston. When the matter was referred to Queen Victoria, the backward lumbering town of Ottawa was selected as a compromise. But the legislature refused to accept the decision, and the Macdonald-Cartier ministry was driven from office. It was soon back in power, however, for George Brown's Reformers had no success in finding a majority that would keep them in office. Their only possible supporters were members of the *parti rouge* in Canada East, whose French-Canadian nationalism made them difficult allies and whose radicalism and anti-clericalism alienated them from the conservative rural voters and the powerful leaders of the Roman Catholic Church.

Brown's failure to retain office increased the discontent of his followers in Canada West. Some of the more radical Reformers, who were known as "Clear Grits," demanded that the union should be dissolved completely. Brown was not prepared to go so far. Instead he proposed that the existing legislative union should be replaced by a federal union which would place most power in the hands of local legislatures, with the central government controlling only a few matters of common interest to both sections, such as tariff and defence.

Brown was not the only Canadian politician who, by the 1860's, was convinced that the union was no longer workable. Although Macdonald and Cartier preferred to work within the union, they were willing to consider the possibility of a federal scheme that would include not just the Canadas, but also the Maritimes. In 1858 A. T. Galt, the Montreal railway man, had joined the Macdonald-Cartier ministry as Minister of Finance on the condition that the government seriously consider the creation of a federal state. Galt believed that only under a federation of all the colonies could the railroad problem be met, and the West brought into closer association with the rest of British North America. Moreover, by the 1860's sectional disagreement within the union had become so acrimonious that the colony could not even agree on measures to strengthen the militia at a time when relations with the United States threatened to lead to war. Despite two elections and three separate governments between 1861 and 1864, it proved impossible to reach an agreement even on this question of defence.

In 1864 George Brown pronounced the failure of the union when he declared: "We have two races, two languages, two systems of religious belief, two systems of everything, so that it has become almost impossible that, without sacrificing their principles, the public men of both sections could come together in the same government. The difficulties have gone on increasing every year." A constitutional renovation was obviously necessary.

7 FOUNDING A NEW NATION

POLITICAL paralysis in the Canadas in the 1860's made the idea of a union of all the British North American colonies an attractive prospect. With all the colonies brought under a single roof, the economy of the entire area could be united and the means provided for a solution to the problem of railways and western expansion. But it was not only the internal political and economic difficulties of the colonies that emphasized the need for a new political arrangement. Developments outside British North America pointed towards the same conclusion. In the 1860's, as so often happens in Canadian history, events in Great Britain and the United States gave impetus, and even definition, to developments that were taking place within British North America itself.

1. AMERICAN THREATS AND BRITISH CONCERN

From the middle of the nineteenth century, Great Britain had been following a policy of free trade, and colonies were no longer regarded as being of economic advantage to the mother country. Sometimes they were even looked upon as "millstones around the Mother Country's neck," as Benjamin Disraeli put it in 1852. Canada's decision in 1859 to erect tariff barriers to protect Canadian manufactured goods against competition from British as well as other foreign imports increased British doubts about the colonies as markets.

If the Empire was no longer of economic benefit to Britain, some of the more extreme British anti-Imperialists (or "little Englanders" as they were called) questioned the value of having colonies at all. An English Liberal was

JOHN BULL KICKING AWAY THE LADDER.

HE THINKS HE CAN DO WITHOUT IT, BUT MAY FIND HIS MISTAKE..

A Canadian view of British colonial policy in the 1860's and 1870's.

thinking particularly about Canada when he remarked that if colonies "are to be constantly applying to us for guarantees for railways, and for grants for fortresses, and for works of defence, then I think it would be far better for them and for us—cheaper for us and less demoralizing for them—that they should become an independent state, and maintain their own fortresses, fight their own cause, and build up their own future without relying upon us." While such extreme views never won full acceptance, they did influence the development of Britain's colonial policy. Their effect was indicated in the growing desire of the British government in the 1860's to have colonies, such as those in North America, assume financial responsibility for such matters as defence in order to reduce the tax burden on British electors. The British were sympathetic therefore to plans for larger unions, like the federation plan suggested in British North America, for such unions would be better able to stand on their own feet without continued financial and military support from the mother country. The London *Times* was expressing this view when it commented on the federal scheme in 1864: "Conscious as we are of our inability to protect these colonies by land in case of war, we must naturally rejoice at any event which seems to place them in a position in which they would be better able to protect themselves." Britain's desire to cut costs was particularly important to Canada in the 1860's, and not only because the British were reluctant to provide financial support for such colonial projects as railway building. What concerned the colonial politicians much more was Britain's apparent indifference to British North America's fate when trouble with the United States began to develop during the American Civil War.

While neither Britain nor the North American colonies were directly involved in the bloody war which began in April 1861 in the United States, the four years that followed were times of serious crises in Anglo-American relations. As always in such crises, Canada found herself in the centre of the storm. The resulting fear of American aggression was a powerful factor in bringing federation to completion. In fact, in 1865, Cartier went so far as to suggest that the British colonies had either "to obtain British North American Confederation or be absorbed in an American Confederation."

The bad relations between Britain and the United States grew out of the North's conviction that Britain's sympathies were with the Confederacy. Many upper-class Englishmen undoubtedly favoured what they thought of as the aristocratic South, and some British politicians went so far as to express publicly their hope that the South would win freedom from Northern domination. In the United States there were Northerners who felt that the country's attention could be turned from the Civil War to the annexation of Canada. Although President Lincoln had no interest in this wild plan, it was enthusiastically advocated by his Secretary of State, William Seward. Seward's plan was even popularized in a little song, which was sung to the tune of "Yankee Doodle":

> *Secession first he would put down*
> *Wholly and forever,*
> *And afterwards from Britain's crown*
> *He Canada would sever.*

Clearly, if there were a threat to Canada, the colony's defences would have to be greatly strengthened. While this need was, or should have been, obvious from the beginning of the Civil War, it became urgent after a series of incidents brought Anglo-American relations close to the breaking-point. In November 1861, two envoys who had been sent to Britain by the Southern Confederacy were removed from the British steamer *Trent* by sailors from a Northern warship. Britain's vigorous protest at this interference with a British ship aroused tempers on both sides of the Atlantic. As partial preparation for a possible war with the United States, Britain dispatched nearly fifteen thousand troops to Canada. In the end the *Trent* dispute was settled peacefully, though the incident left many Canadians fearful of American aggressive intentions towards Canada. Good relations with the United States were only slowly restored. In December, 1861, the Buffalo *Express* stated: "Out of this *Trent* affair has come one permanent good. The old, natural, instinctive and wise distrust and dislike for England is revived again in the American heart, and will outlive all the soft words and snivelling cant about international brotherhood and reciprocity."

Thus Anglo-American relations remained tense. The North

had good reason to complain when the warship *Alabama*, built in a British shipyard, was sold to the Confederacy. Used as marauders, the *Alabama* and other ships plied American coastal waters bombarding Northern posts and sinking Northern shipping. Northerners felt that the sale of the *Alabama* was definite proof of the British government's hostility to their cause. Southern conspirators also used British territory as a base from which to plan attacks on the North. Confederate agents in Canada had little difficulty obtaining supplies, gathering information about Northern troop movements, and raising men for border raids. All of these incidents, threats and rumours made Canada's position precarious. As we have seen, Britain, recognizing the seriousness of the situation, sent troops to Canada late in 1861. Since winter had already set in when the troops arrived at Halifax, their trip to Quebec by sleigh was agonizingly cold and slow. Nothing could have emphasized more forcefully the need for the much discussed intercolonial railway from Halifax to the Canadas. But railway building had to wait until the colonies' political difficulties could be solved.

2. THE POLITICS OF CONFEDERATION

The idea of a federal union of all British North America had been under discussion in the Canadas, at least, since Galt had made his proposal in 1858. But it was not until 1864 that a ministry was formed which was definitely pledged to place federation before all other policies. The man chiefly responsible for this action was the Reform leader, George Brown. In June 1864, a committee to consider federation, which had been appointed at Brown's urging, reported in favour either of a local federation of the two Canadas, or a larger scheme to include all the British colonies. On the same day that this report was presented to the Legislature, the Macdonald-Cartier ministry was defeated.

George Brown decided that the time for decisive action had arrived. Swallowing his personal dislike of Macdonald, the Reform leader announced that he was prepared to enter into a coalition government with any Conservative who was willing to support the idea of federation. In a speech he delivered explaining his position, Brown expressed his strong desire to end the political troubles of Canada. He declared: "I do frankly confess, Mr. Speaker, that if I never have any other parliamentary success than that which I have achieved this day in having brought about the formation of a Government more powerful than any Canadian Government that ever existed before, pledged to settle, and to settle forever, the alarming sectional difficulties of my country, I would have desired no greater honour for my children to keep years hence in their remembrance than that I had a hand, however humble, in the accomplishment of that great work. . . ." Although Macdonald had opposed the federal proposals earlier in committee, he immediately saw that Brown's conciliatory gesture offered a real opportunity for settling the problems of the union. He accepted Brown's offer and years of bitter political feuding between the two men were temporarily put aside by a common resolve to establish a new nation.

But whether Brown and Macdonald were to succeed in achieving their common goal depended on the decision of another well-known figure, Georges Etienne Cartier. Without the agreement of the French Canadians, no alteration of the existing union would be possible. The French Canadians had always been the strongest opponents of any change in the existing political arrangements, but in 1864 Cartier realized that the time for negative opposition to such changes had passed. French-Canadian rights could be made even more secure in a federal union. Cartier also shared with Macdonald and Brown the desire to see the economic promise of a wider union fulfilled. He therefore joined the coalition of Conservatives and Reformers and brought with him a crucial bloc of French-Canadian votes. Macdonald, Brown and Cartier formed the core of the new government but they were ably supported by men like A. T. Galt, E. P. Taché, William McDougall and the stirring orator, Thomas D'Arcy McGee.

The formation of the "Great Coalition" was merely the beginning of a strenuous search for a new constitution for British North America. The coalition represented only Canada, and, before their aims could be achieved, allies would have to be found in the Maritimes. In 1864 the time was ripe to approach the politicians in the Atlantic colonies, for these men were slowly moving towards the consideration of a Maritime union. Such a union could either be the first step towards the union of all British North America, or an obstacle to that larger union. The Canadian politicians determined to take the initiative and forestall talk of Maritime union by placing the idea of a union with the Canadas before the Maritimers. The Maritime leaders had made plans for a meeting among themselves in September 1864 at Charlottetown. The Canadian government asked if it could send delegates to this conference to present a plan for federation. The Maritimers agreed that they might.

In September all the important Canadian leaders attended this first conference at Charlottetown. Brown, Macdonald, Cartier and Galt had their arguments well prepared, and the delegates from the Maritimes listened to them attentively. The Maritimers had never been very enthusiastic about a local union, but perhaps this wider federation that the Canadians presented so persuasively would be advantageous. At any rate it would be well worth discussing further. Therefore it was agreed that a second meeting should be held at Quebec in October. The most important result of the Charlottetown meeting was that the leaders of Canada and the Maritimes, in coming together to discuss common problems, had realized that common solutions might be found for those problems. The Halifax *Witness* remarked after the meeting: "There is less aversion to Canada. Indeed, there seems to be a positive desire for union . . . the distinguished men whom Canada has sent . . . have succeeded in removing some prejudices, and greatly modifying some real obstacles to union. As things look at present we must have a Colonial Union of some kind with the least possible delay." This was a substantial achievement. The paper might have added that the Charlottetown conference had also produced some very

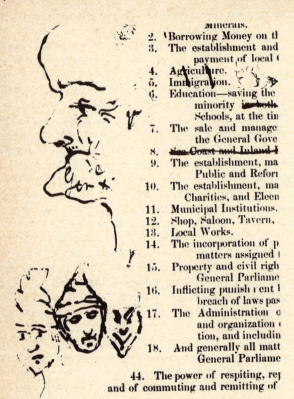

Minerals.
2. Borrowing Money on th
3. The establishment and
            payment of local (
4. Agriculture.
5. Immigration.
6. Education—saving the
            minority in both
            Schools, at the tin
7. The sale and manage
            the General Gove
8. Coast and Inland F
9. The establishment, ma
            Public and Refor
10. The establishment, ma
            Charities, and Eleen
11. Municipal Institutions.
12. Shop, Saloon, Tavern, .
13. Local Works.
14. The incorporation of p
            matters assigned t
15. Property and civil righ
            General Parliame
16. Inflicting punish r ent l
            breach of laws pas
17. The Administration o
            and organization (
            tion, and includin
18. And generally all matt
            General Parliame

44. The power of respiting, rep
and of commuting and remitting of

As the form of the new federal system was being debated at Quebec in 1864, an unknown member of the group drew caricatures of his colleagues. This set of resolutions was found in the Macdonald Papers but is not John A's work and is on the page where the provincial powers, which ultimately became Section 92, were being outlined.

effective Maritime leaders for the cause of federation. One was the hard-working and somewhat long-winded Dr. Charles Tupper, the Conservative Premier of Nova Scotia. The other was the capable Reform Premier of New Brunswick, Leonard Tilley.

On October 10, the federation discussions were resumed

at Quebec City. There was now great impatience to get on with the work. "We can't wait," George Brown wrote, "we are *not going to be tied to Lower Canada for twelve months more.*" The ever present fear of attack from the United States created an even greater sense of urgency. In the middle of the Quebec conference a new incident focused the attention of the delegates on the American danger. On October 19 a small group of Confederates slipped across the border from Canada into Vermont and attacked the village of St. Albans. When the Confederate agents who slipped across the border and attacked St. Albans in Vermont were allowed to escape unpunished by a Canadian court, talk of war was heard in the United States. "It may be said that this will lead to war with England," the New York *Times* declared, "But if it must come, let it come. Not ours, the guilt. . . . We were never in better condition for war with England." As the war scare grew, Canadian troops were made ready for defence; by January 1865 two thousand Canadian militiamen had been placed along the American border.

The threat of American action was close to the thoughts of the delegates at Quebec as they discussed the Macdonald-Tilley motion "that the best interests and present and future prosperity of British North America will be promoted by a federal union under the Crown of Great Britain, provided such union can be effected on principles just to the several provinces." The discussion centred on the division of powers between central and local governments, and the debate recalled many of the arguments that were heard at Philadelphia in 1787 when the American constitution was being drawn up. Macdonald hoped that the gathering would approve a legislative union in which there would be a single government, because he was convinced that the American Civil War had revealed the fatal weakness of a federal system. But delegates from Quebec and the Maritimes were anxious to preserve local autonomy, and it became clear, as Brown noted, "there was but one choice open to us—federal union or nothing." Nevertheless, most of the delegates agreed on the need for a union with a strong central government. One delegate described the discussions:

> For the first few days the leading delegates of the Lower [Maritime] Provinces exhibited caution and vigilance upon every question affecting the interests of these provinces. . . . As the business proceeded and the details of the federal union were from day to day laid down, parties evinced a visible elasticity of judgment, and were observed gradually to harmonize with those whose opinions they had previously met in a style more polemical in character. The current seemed to set with the Canadians. The Maritime delegates, one after the other, were observed to drop into the stream; and, with few exceptions, the members appeared to float along with it, scarcely producing a ripple on its now gentle surface.

Eventually the persuasiveness of the Canadians won over all the Maritime delegates except those from Prince Edward Island.

The conference adjourned on October 29, and the delegates returned to their provinces to begin the hard fight to win popular approval of the Quebec Resolutions. "Will the people follow the example and rise to the level of the occasion—to settle now the destiny of this northern country and the people that dwell here?" asked the Montreal *Gazette*. The question was now more pressing than ever, for relations with the United States were so unsettled that the possibility of war hung darkly over the British North American colonies. The Civil War was moving into its final stages, and the powerful Northern armies would soon be free to threaten Canada. But a more immediate danger than an organized American attack was the threat of border raids by the fanatical Irish-American Fenian Brotherhood. By late 1864 Irishmen in the United States of America were devising plans to free Ireland from British rule by embroiling the United States in a war with Britain. This they proposed to do by attacking Canada. Macdonald learned from a secret agent, shortly after the Quebec conference, that the Fenians were training in New Jersey in preparation for a drive across the border in Mid-January, 1865.

Canada could easily deal with the Fenians as long as the American government remained friendly. But by the end of 1864 another American action brought new fears to British North America. Since 1860 pressure had been mounting in the United States for the abrogation of the reciprocity treaty of 1854. In January 1865 the United States Senate passed a resolution calling for the termination of the treaty in 1866. While this action was in keeping with the provisions of the treaty, it was interpreted as a sign of American unfriendliness, and gave further point to the arguments that the economy of British North America could only survive and expand if it were directed by a single political authority.

When the Canadian Legislature met in February 1865, most members were conscious of the critical stage that had been reached in the affairs of British North America. In the lengthy debate on the resolutions drawn up at Quebec, the leading Canadian politicians and many of their followers had an opportunity to express themselves on the federation proposals. Macdonald defended the scheme against those who felt it was too weak to succeed and warned of the dangers that faced the colonies if they remained disunited. Cartier tried to quiet the misgivings of those in French Canada who feared that the federal plan would threaten French-Canadian rights. "In our Confederation there will be Catholics and Protestants, English, French, Irish and Scotch, and each by its own efforts and success will add to the prosperity, to the might and to the glory of the new federation. We are of different races, not to wage war among ourselves, but to work together for our common welfare," Cartier argued. Galt explained the economic advantages of the scheme, and assured the English minority in Canada East that its rights, too, would be protected.

As the debate continued through many days, it was George Brown, speaking for the Reformers in the coalition, who voiced the thought that was weighing heavily on the minds of many members. "There is one consideration," he

Speaking in the Confederation Debates in 1865, Macdonald appealed for immediate acceptance of the Quebec Resolutions. "If we do not take advantage of the time," he declared, "if we show ourselves unequal to the occasion, it may never return and we shall hereafter bitterly and unavailingly regret having failed to embrace the happy opportunity now offered of founding a great nation under the fostering care of Great Britain and our Sovereign lady Queen Victoria."

said, "that cannot be banished from this discussion, and that ought, I think, to be remembered in every word we utter; it is that the constitutional system of Canada cannot remain as it is now [loud cries of Hear, hear]. Something must be done. We cannot stand still. We cannot go back to chronic sectional hostility and discord—to a state of perpetual Ministerial crises." When the vote was finally taken, the Quebec Resolutions won the approval of the Canadian Legislature by a solid ninety-one to thirty-three vote, with twenty-two of the opposing votes coming from representatives of Canada East, who believed that French Canada would suffer a loss of its rights in a federation in which English-speaking Canadians would make up the great majority. This vote in the Canadian Legislature was the only occasion on which the plan of federation was submitted to even this limited form of popular approval in the Canadas.

In the Maritimes the struggle between the supporters and opponents of the Quebec Resolutions was bitter and its outcome long remained in doubt. Enthusiasm for the scheme had never been great in the Atlantic colonies and even the promised intercolonial railway failed to overcome the Maritimers' deep suspicion of the Canadians. Although Prince Edward Island and Newfoundland rejected the plan immediately, it could still succeed if the two larger colonies, Nova Scotia and New Brunswick, gave it their approval. But in Nova Scotia Joseph Howe, the popular leader of the Reform forces since the 1840's, turned his powerful influence against Confederation. Howe had not been a member of his colony's delegation at Quebec, and a combination of personal jealousy of Tupper and a genuine belief that Nova Scotia's interests were being sacrificed turned him against the federal plan. He used his effective pen to attack what he sarcastically called "the Botheration Scheme." The effect of Howe's attack was so great that Tupper decided not to place the Quebec Resolutions before the Nova Scotia assembly, lest they be defeated.

In New Brunswick, matters were even worse. In March 1865, Tilley called an election and the anti-confederation forces defeated him. But the new government had no positive policies, or any workable scheme to meet the obvious need for a railway linking New Brunswick with the Canadas. A complete stalemate seemed to have been reached in the Maritimes when outside events again intervened. The British government, anxious for the success of Confederation, instructed the Governor of New Brunswick, who had previously shown no enthusiasm for Confederation, "to further the cause of union by every means within his powers." As the anti-Confederation government was already falling apart, the Governor was able to carry out his orders by forcing a new election early in 1866. In the midst of the campaign Tilley's argument for union with the Canadas received forceful support by threatened Fenian raids on the New Brunswick border. With the support of the Governor, fear of the Fenians, and lavish financial aid from Canada to assist him, Tilley swept back into office. The Confederation scheme was on the move again. Tupper in Nova Scotia now took heart. He issued a call to arms: "If we remain disunited . . . the time may come when we shall have the British flag lowered beneath the Stars and Stripes, and the last gun fired from the Citadel as a British fort." The Legislature harkened to the appeal, and authorized delegates to attend a further conference in London to discuss Confederation.

Before the London Conference the long-expected Fenian invasion arrived. "Fenians mounted two deep upon horses; Fenians in lumber wagons, carrying boxes of ammunition; Fenians on foot, whistling bayonets about their heads, frantically leaping mud-puddles and shouting 'Come on' " was the way the New York *World* described the movement of Fenian invaders on Fort Erie on June 1, 1866. The next day local Canadian volunteers met the invaders at Ridgeway and were driven back, having suffered six dead and more than thirty wounded. War fever swept the western part of the province and the militia made ready to fight. By June 4, the Fenian raiders, some fifteen hundred strong, retreated across the Niagara River. The next week, a similar raid took place in Canada East, raising a further temporary scare. But by the end of the first week in June, the threat had passed as the American government began to take action to halt the raids.

At the Westminster conference in London in December 1866, the Quebec Resolutions remained the basis for the new constitution, though some final touches were added. In London, a British official wrote: "Macdonald was the ruling genius and spokesman and I was greatly struck with his powers of management and adroitness. The French delegates were keenly on the watch for anything which weakened their securities; on the contrary, the Nova Scotia and New Brunswick delegates were jealous of concession to the *arrière* province." The only major changes that were made provided larger financial grants to the Maritimes and a constitutional guarantee that an intercolonial railway would be built.

In March 1867, the British parliament passed the British North America Act. "We are laying the foundation of a great state," the British Colonial Secretary declared, "perhaps one which at a future day may even overshadow this country." At last the scheme was complete. The delegates, filled with elation at their success but wearied from the long discussions and the round of social activities, were anxious to get home and begin preparations for July 1, the day on which Confederation would become a fact.

3. THE NATURE OF THE NEW GOVERNMENT

The intention of the men who wrote the British North America Act was to adapt the traditional British parliamentary system to the needs of the new North American nation. The most obvious and necessary modification arose from the fact that British North America's regional and cultural diversities made a unitary system of government impossible. Therefore, like the United States, the new country was given a federal constitution. At the same time, Canadian leaders were well acquainted with the American system of government and were determined to avoid the features of the American system which they believed had helped to provoke the bloody Civil War.

They believed that the main weakness of the American system lay in a division of powers between the states and the federal government which had left the states too strong. To guard against this weakness, the framers of the Canadian constitution tried to establish a central government so powerful that it would be impossible for any local government to challenge its authority. They carefully divided authority between the federal and provincial governments, giving to the provincial authorities only certain specifically enumerated powers that were clearly local in their application. These included direct taxation within the province, authority over municipal institutions, construction of roads, the passage of laws concerning "property and civil rights" within the province, and many other powers of a purely provincial nature. In addition, the control of education was placed within the jurisdiction of the provinces, but the federal government was given the right to act in educational matters to protect the rights of minorities. This latter provision was designed to protect both Roman Catholic minorities in English-speaking Canada, and the Protestant minority in Quebec.

The federal government, under the British North America Act, was empowered to make laws for the "peace, order and good government" of Canada in *all areas not specifically granted to the provincial legislatures.* In giving this general residual power to the federal government the Fathers of Confederation hoped to avoid the problem of states' rights, which had caused such serious friction in the United States. In 1866 Macdonald explained the Canadian solution to the states' rights difficulty: "Ever since the [American union] was formed the difficulty of what is called 'State Rights' has existed, and this had much to do with bringing on the present unhappy war in the United States. They commenced, in fact, at the wrong end. . . . Here we have adopted a different system. We have strengthened the General Government. We have given the central legislature all the great subjects of legislation. . . . We have thus avoided that great source of weakness which has been the cause of the disruption of the United States." Some of the main powers of the federal government were listed in Section 91 of the British North America Act. These included the regulation of trade and commerce, defence, the power to raise money by any form of taxation, banking and currency laws, and criminal law. But the list of powers set out in the Act was not intended to be exhaustive. It was given merely to illustrate some of the powers that were included in the general authority of the central government.

The wide authority of the federal government was also made clear in a number of other ways. The central government was given the power to appoint the lieutenant-governors of the provinces. This meant that the lieutenant-governor was to act as an officer of the federal government. An even more important example of the authority of the federal government was the federal power of disallowance which gave the central government the right to veto acts of the provincial legislatures which it judged not to be in the national interest. So strong was the federal government that Macdonald, its chief architect, claimed that it had "all the advantages of a legislative union," that is, a unitary rather than a federal union.

The structure of the new Canadian government followed closely the British practices that had always guided the colonies. An executive officer, or governor-general, was placed at the head of the governmental pyramid. The governor-general was not only to play the role of monarch in the Canadian system, but was also to represent the British Colonial Office in Canada. The governor-general was not to be completely powerless. In certain limited circumstances he could refuse to grant a dissolution of parliament to a prime minister. But in most matters the governor-general was expected to follow the advice of his cabinet according to the well-established principles of responsible government.

Under the British North America Act the Canadian parliament, like its British model, was to be composed of two houses, the Senate and the House of Commons. The Commons was the more important of these two chambers because its members were elected, while those of the second chamber, the Senate, were appointed. Representation in the House of Commons was determined upon the principle of representation by population, with Quebec granted sixty-five members and the representation of the other provinces determined in proportion. It was assumed that most of the important members of the cabinet would be drawn from the House of Commons.

The upper house of parliament, or Senate, like the British House of Lords, was non-elective. But since Canada lacked an hereditary aristocracy, the appointed house of parliament could not be called a House of Lords. Therefore the American name, Senate, was adopted. In theory the powers of the Senate were equal to those of the Commons, except that money bills could originate only in the elected house. In practice, the House of Commons, as in England, exercised far more power, for it was to this house that the cabinet was responsible.

Members of the Senate were to be appointed by the federal government. They had to be at least thirty years old and own property valued at $4,000. The Senate was expected to serve two special purposes. First, it was to be a check on any hasty action taken by the House of Commons. As Macdonald noted in 1865, the Senate "must be an independent House, having a free action of its own, for it is only valuable as being a regulating body, calmly considering the legislation initiated by the popular branch, and preventing any hasty or ill-considered legislation which may come before that body, but it will never set itself in opposition against the deliberate and understood wishes of the people." The Senate's second important function was to protect provincial rights and represent sections. This feature was emphasized by the stipulation that Ontario and Quebec would each have twenty-four Senators and the Maritimes another twenty-four. But since the Senators are appointed by the federal government and not the provinces, the Senate has not in practice been a very adequate reflection of provincial interests. Indeed, apart from preventing hasty and imprudent legislation, the Senate's chief purpose today is to provide a means of rewarding political services rendered to the governing party.

These, then, were the main features of the new government established in 1867: a federal system with a strong central government, a bicameral legislature with the House of Commons exercising the primary authority, and a governor-general advised by a cabinet which acted as a body collectively responsible to parliament. It was, in short, Britain's traditional system of government modified to meet the needs of Canada.

In the new constitution, Macdonald thought he had won acceptance for a form of government that would undermine local loyalties and defeat the sectional forces that had destroyed the earlier union. It was his hope that the whole scheme would be capped by a name that would announce to the world the establishment of a new nation. The name he wanted was the Kingdom of Canada. But the British government, concerned that this title might irritate the republican United States and convinced that the colony was seeking too elevated a status, rejected Macdonald's suggestion and substituted the title of Dominion. This title did not alter Macdonald's view that Confederation marked the appearance of a new nation on the world's stage. He had defined his view in 1865 when he told the Canadian assembly that under the new scheme Canada would be "able from our union, our strength, our population, and the development of our resources, to take our position among the nations of the world. . . . Instead of looking upon us as a merely dependent colony, England will have us as a friendly nation—a subordinate but still a powerful people—to stand by her in North America in peace or in war."

On July 1, 1867, the first step was taken towards fulfilling Macdonald's vision when the federation of the four British colonies came into effect. The Toronto *Globe* exulted on that first Dominion Day: "With the first dawn of this gladsome summer morn we hail this birthday of a new nationality." But realistic politicians like the country's first Prime Minister, now Sir John A. Macdonald, realized that despite the great step that had been taken, some of the hardest work still lay ahead. It remained to be seen whether policies could be found that would transform and expand the federation into a prosperous nation.

8 THE UNCERTAIN NATION

"WE don't know each other. We have no trade with each other. We have no facilities or resources or incentives to mingle with each other. We are shut off from each other by a wilderness, geographically, commercially, politically and socially. We always cross the United States to shake hands." This description of the "New Nation" by the *Acadian Recorder* was pessimistic, but it did indicate the enormous difficulties that Canada faced. The new nation needed imaginative leaders if these divisions were ever to be overcome.

The man on whom the heaviest responsibility fell was Sir John A. Macdonald, the Dominion's first prime minister. The first quarter-century of Canada's history was to be almost completely dominated by this gay and shrewd politician. While Macdonald's first government still contained some representatives of the Liberal party, it rapidly became a purely Conservative administration. Brown had left the coalition almost as soon as Confederation had become a certainty. Indeed, it was somewhat amazing that the puritanical Scot from Toronto had been able to co-operate for so long with his debonair countryman from Kingston. In forming his first Dominion government, Macdonald had to bring in men from the Maritimes. Charles Tupper from Nova Scotia, who was later to become Macdonald's most faithful colleague, had to be left out of the first cabinet but Leonard Tilley from New Brunswick was given a portfolio. A. T. Galt and G. E. Cartier remained as the two chief pillars of strength in central Canada, which now became Ontario and Quebec. It was on these men that the greatest onus fell for making the experiment in nation-building a success.

1. ROUNDING OUT THE UNION

The first task of Macdonald's new government was to complete the physical structure of Confederation. Newfoundland and Prince Edward Island had remained aloof in 1867, while Nova Scotia had been absorbed reluctantly. To the West lay the territories of the Hudson's Bay Company, which, if not united to Canada, might fall into the hands of the United States. Beyond the Rockies lay Vancouver Island and British Columbia, united in 1866, whose population was overwhelmingly American. Each of these colonies would require different bait if they were to be attracted into the net of Canada's Manifest Destiny. In the end Macdonald caught all but Newfoundland, though none came without resistance.

In the East, Nova Scotia was the immediate problem. Out of the nineteen federal members of parliament from Nova Scotia, only one, Charles Tupper, was elected as a supporter of the new union. At the same time a provincial government with an anti-Confederation majority of thirty-six to two won power at Halifax. The leader of the forces which preached secession from Confederation was the powerful Joseph Howe. When his efforts to have the British government annul the union failed, and the United States turned a deaf ear to requests for a trading agreement, a compromise with the federal government became inevitable. In 1869 Macdonald used all his charm and persuasiveness to convince the Nova Scotians that a new financial arrangement involving "better terms" would redress their grievances. The price paid for an end to the secession movement was a cabinet post for Joseph Howe and an increase of $140,000 in the federal subsidy to Nova Scotia. Macdonald in his usual realistic way remarked: "Nova Scotia is about to take the shilling and enlist, though I am afraid it will consider itself for some time, a conscript rather than a volunteer."

It was another four years before Macdonald could overcome the sturdy independence of the little colony of Prince Edward Island. However, as the colony slipped further and further into debt in its efforts to build a railway, the prospect

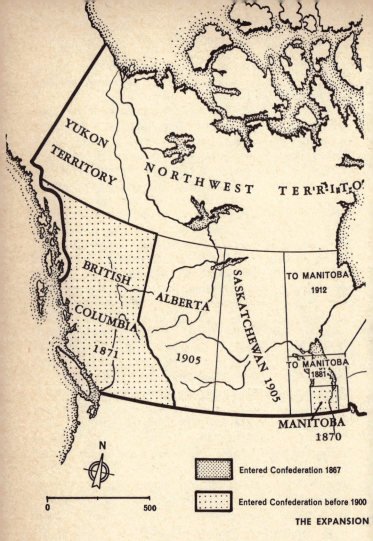

YUKON
TERRITORY

N O R T H W E S T T E R R I T O..

BRITISH

COLUMBIA

1871

ALBERTA

1905

SASKATCHEWAN 1905

TO MANITOBA
1912

TO MANITOBA
1881

MANITOBA
1870

N

0   500

Entered Confederation 1867

Entered Confederation before 1900

THE EXPANSION

of assistance from the Canadian treasury grew more and
more appealing. Moreover it became increasingly clear that
large tracts of land owned by absentee landlords could never
be purchased by Prince Edward Island without outside
financial assistance. Assumption of its railway obligations,

F CONFEDERATION

and a promise to buy out the absentee landholders were the
main features of the agreement which, in 1873, brought
Prince Edward Island into the Canadian union. In addition,
however, the federal government agreed to pay a generous
annual subsidy to the Island government and to provide a

means of communication with the mainland. The advantages to Canada of this union were both strategic and economic, for Prince Edward Island was desirable for the defence of Canada and for the control of the valuable Atlantic fisheries. For the same reasons, Canada wooed the colony of Newfoundland. Separated geographically from Canada and supported by the fisheries and commerce of the North Atlantic, the Newfoundlanders repeatedly resisted union with Canada until 1949.

The federal government faced even greater difficulties in extending its authority to the West. The western area presented four immediate difficulties: it was owned by the Hudson's Bay Company which was most reluctant to give up its valuable fur-trading territories without compensation; there was no established means of communication between Canada and the Red River colony; the settlers at Red River, most of whom were French and British half-breeds or Métis, showed no interest in becoming Canadians; and finally the United States, which had the most direct communications with Red River, was suspected of harbouring ambitions to annex the area. These factors, combined with the blunders of the federal government and the tactlessness of a small but noisy group of recent settlers from Ontario, help to explain the outbreak of the Red River Rebellion in 1869.

In November 1869, after a long series of negotiations, the Hudson's Bay Company gave up its claim to the Canadian West in return for a million and half dollars in cash, 45,000 acres of land around its posts, and large tracts of land elsewhere. The purchased territory was transferred to the British government, which was to turn it over to Canada when the Dominion was ready for it. All of these negotiations had taken place without any consultation with the people in the Red River colony, who suspected that their property and cultural rights were in jeopardy These suspicions were confirmed both by Canadian government land surveys in Red River, and by the boasts of many Canadians who had recently moved into the colony that they would soon be in command.

Under the leadership of Louis Riel, an eloquent and intelligent young Métis of unstable temperament, the half-breeds decided to defend their rights by force. Riel had no desire to make the colony an independent country, but only to make sure that the people had some voice in determining their own fate. "If we rebel against the country which wishes to buy us, we are not rebelling against the supremacy of England, which has not yet given its approval for the final transfer of this country. . . . We wish only that the people of Red River be a free people." The first step that Riel's followers took to protect their rights was to prevent the entry of William McDougall, the man appointed by Macdonald to assume authority in Red River on behalf of Canada following the transfer of that territory to the Canadian government. Riel then set up a provisional government to negotiate an agreement with Macdonald on the future of the colony. Unfortunately, the continued opposition of the Canadian minority in the colony enraged Riel, and, in March 1870, he undertook to show the Canadians that he meant business by executing a young Ontario troublemaker, Thomas Scott, on grounds of insubordination and striking his guards.

The execution of Scott brought a sudden calm to Red River but it complicated the problem of reaching an agreement with Macdonald's government. Ontario demanded the head of Riel, and warned the government not to negotiate with "men who come here with their hands red with blood." Quebec, on the other hand, sympathized with Riel and his followers in their attempt to preserve their cultural identity. Thus Macdonald faced not only a rebellion in the West, but also a racial crisis in central Canada and within his own party, which demanded all the political agility he could muster.

To appease the Red River colony and Quebec, he agreed to negotiate with delegates from Red River on terms of entry into Confederation. The result was the Manitoba Act of 1870, which created the small province of Manitoba with the same institutions and powers as the older provinces. The

Act guaranteed French language rights, Roman Catholic schools, and Métis land titles. The federal government gave the new province a generous financial subsidy but maintained control over unsettled lands in order to use them for the promotion of immigration and railway construction.

While these negotiations were under way, Macdonald's government tried to appease Ontario by sending a force of British regulars and Canadian militia to Red River to subdue the Métis, and also to show the United States that Canada meant to increase her authority in the West. But Riel had achieved his object and, not wishing to tempt fate, disappeared before the army reached Red River. Gradually relations between British and French in Canada returned to normal. But while Canada's political structure had survived a severe test, Sir John Macdonald had not heard the last of Louis Riel.

The final step in pushing the sovereignty of Canada to the Pacific was the incorporation of British Columbia. The Pacific colony was sparsely settled and heavily in debt after the gold rush had subsided in the 1860's. Before it lay the alternatives of union with Canada or annexation to the United States. The fear that the coastal colony would join the United States was enough to convince Macdonald and his colleagues that a generous offer should be made to British Columbia to attract it into the Confederation.

The Imperial authorities also believed that union with Canada offered the best solution to British Columbia's difficulties. In 1871, led by a colourful politician, who had changed his name from Smith to Amor de Cosmos (Lover of the Universe), the unionists in British Columbia triumphed and a delegation journeyed to Ottawa. The terms of union included not only a generous subsidy but, more important, the promise of a railway to the Pacific to be started in 1873 and completed in ten years. Macdonald wrote: "The terms can, I think, be fully justified on their own merits; but we may expect considerable opposition in our parliament on the ground that they are burdensome to the Dominion and too liberal to British Columbia." The Prime Minister was right. There was heavy criticism of the terms both in 1871 when they were accepted, and later when economic depression made them difficult to fulfil.

Thus by 1873, with both Prince Edward Island and British Columbia in the union, Canada stretched from sea to sea. It was a substantial achievement in five short years, but Canada remained a fragile union whose brittle skeleton had still to be clothed in the flesh of economic and social development.

2. DIPLOMACY, RAILWAYS AND SCANDAL

Macdonald's plans for the development of Canada were strongly influenced by the fear that the United States had unfriendly intentions towards the new Dominion. At the same time he was fully aware of the importance of the large United States market for Canadian goods. Indeed, he never entirely gave up the hope that a new reciprocity agreement could be negotiated between the two countries. Unsettled relations between Britain and the United States, and also the strength of the protectionist interests in the United States, made it impossible to restore reciprocity in the first years after Confederation. But in 1871, when a conference was called in Washington to consider a variety of Anglo-American problems, Macdonald thought that the opportunity had arrived to begin discussions of the trade question.

Many of the questions considered at Washington directly affected Canada. The United States claim against Britain for damages caused by the British-built Confederate raider, *Alabama*, was the most important problem from the American point of view, but several disputes touched Canada more closely. There was a disagreement over the boundary between Canada and the United States in the Straits of Juan de Fuca off Vancouver Island; there was the question of damages claimed by Canada for the Fenian raids; and above all, there was the problem of the rights of American fishermen to fish in eastern Canada coastal waters. These latter rights had been granted to the United States

MOTHER BRITANNIA: "Take care, my child!"
UNCLE SAM: "Oh! never mind, if she falls, I'll catch her!"

In 1870, as the Washington Conference approached, many Canadians feared that Britain might desert Canada, allowing the new nation to fall into the hands of the United States. And there were certainly Americans who looked forward to the destruction of British influence in North America. Senator Charles Sumner insisted in January, 1871: "The greatest trouble, if not peril, being a constant source of anxiety and disturbance, is from Fenianism, which is excited by the proximity of the British flag in Canada. Therefore, the withdrawal of the British flag cannot be abandoned as a condition or preliminary of such a settlement as is now proposed. To make the settlement complete the withdrawal should be from this hemisphere, including provinces and islands."

by the 1854 reciprocity treaty, but that treaty had now been terminated. Nevertheless, American fishermen were naturally reluctant to abandon these rich fishing-grounds.

Since all these questions related to Canada, Macdonald himself was made a member of the British delegation, an appointment which represented recognition of Canada's new status. Unfortunately for Canada, Macdonald was caught in a very awkward situation at Washington, for the British were prepared to pay a fairly high price to win the friendship of the Americans. Macdonald described his difficulties in a letter to Charles Tupper in Ottawa:

> If a majority of my colleagues should at any time conclude to accept terms that I do not approve of, I must, of course, either protest and withdraw, or remain on the Commission and trust to non-ratification of the Treaty by Canada. If I take the first course it will disclose to the Americans the fact of a difference of opinion, a conflict, in fact, between Canada and England. This the Americans are anxious to establish, in order to get up a sort of quarrel between the two, and strengthen that party in England which desires to get rid of the colonies as a burden. If I continue to act on the Commission, I will be attacked for making an unworthy sacrifice of Canada's rights. . . .

Macdonald could not stand alone against the Americans and the British, and it soon became clear that Canada was going to make several sacrifices for the cause of better Anglo-American relations. After a period of hard bargaining, during which the Canadian Prime Minister put up a stiff but futile fight for reciprocity, the Treaty of Washington was signed. Under that agreement the Juan de Fuca boundary and the *Alabama* claims were referred to an arbitration board. Moreover, United States fishermen were to be allowed access to Canadian fisheries for a price which was also to be settled by arbitration. The British privately agreed to compensate Canada for Fenian damages. Macdonald knew that the treaty would not be popular at home; for while he had failed to get reciprocity the Americans had secured access to the Canadian fisheries.

Shortly after the acceptance of the Washington Treaty, the Canadian voters were given another reason to be dissatisfied with the Macdonald government. While it had been assumed since the first discussions of Confederation that a transcontinental railway would eventually bind the whole country together, the method of carrying out this expensive project had remained unsettled. The first railway to be built was the Intercolonial, which had been promised to the Maritimes in the British North America Act. In return for a British loan the Canadian government agreed to build the line to Halifax through the uninhabited forests of northern New Brunswick so that in the event of war with the United States it could not easily be destroyed by the Americans. Militarily the route made sense, but commercially it was a poor choice and politically it alienated the inhabitants of southern New Brunswick.

Building a railway to the Pacific coast also presented difficulties. The government decided that the railway could best be constructed by a private company with substantial government assistance of thirty million dollars and fifty million acres of choice land. So attractive were the terms that two companies were anxious to obtain the contract. One company, led by Senator D. L. Macpherson, was largely a Toronto organization. The other, headed by Sir Hugh Allan of Montreal, had the financial support of a group of American capitalists. Allan used all of his great influence with Macdonald and Cartier to win the contract. Not only did he exclude some of the Americans from the company on the request of Macdonald but he also contributed heavily to the Conservative campaign fund in 1872. A telegram from Macdonald during the campaign which read, "I must have another ten thousand; will be the last time of calling; do not fail me; answer today" was only one of the pieces of evidence which later brought about the Conservatives' downfall.

Macdonald was re-elected in 1872 and shortly afterwards gave Allan the contract. But a diligent Liberal Opposition soon uncovered the unsavoury details of Allan's $300,000 donation to the Conservative election fund. While Macdonald and Allan indignantly denied that the $300,000 had anything to do with the granting of the contract, even Macdonald's followers were disillusioned by what came to be called the "Pacific Scandal" and the Prime Minister was forced to resign in November 1873.

3. THE HESITANT LIBERALS AND CONSERVATIVE REVIVAL

The Liberals, who replaced the Macdonald government, were led by Alexander Mackenzie, a Sarnia stone-mason. Mackenzie was honest and a good administrator, but he lacked imagination and a capacity for leadership at a time when his party needed both. In 1873 the Liberal party was strongest in Ontario, but even there Mackenzie's grip on the party was not secure. His staunchest supporter was the sharp tongued Richard Cartwright; but Cartwright was a free trader and was not very popular with business leaders in Canada who were anxious for tariff protection. Another Ontario Minister was the brilliant but unpredictable Edward Blake who moved in and out of the cabinet at will and refused to bow to Mackenzie's leadership.

In Quebec the party was much weaker. The chief cause of this weakness was the strong opposition to the Liberals by a wing of the Roman Catholic Church, very powerful in Europe at that time, which held that the Church was superior to the state, and that a Catholic's first loyalty should be not to the state but rather to the Papacy which was "beyond the mountains." Thus the term "ultramontane" was applied to them. In Canada, by the middle of the nineteenth century, the ultramontane party in the Quebec Church was led by the strong-willed Bishop of Montreal, Monseigneur Bourget.

Bishop Bourget watched his diocese carefully in order to detect and stamp out any signs of anti-clericalism. Since European liberals were clearly anti-clerical, and even anti-religious, Bishop Bourget suspected that Liberals in Canada were guilty of the same sins. This suspicion was based not only on similarity of names, but also because he found in the Institut Canadien signs of the views he hated most. The Institut Canadien had been established in Montreal in 1844 with the purpose of organizing discussions and providing a library for its members. Before this apparently innocent institution was very old, however, Bishop Bourget discovered some facts about it that deeply disturbed him. In the first place, speeches were being made at the Institut's meetings which contained sentiments very like the anti-clerical doctrines frequently expressed by European liberals. One speaker had gone so far as to state that "the government of Pope Pius IX is the most despotic which exists in the world." Other members, including the old revolutionary, Louis-Joseph Papineau, who had returned to Canada from his long exile in France, maintained that the Church had no right to meddle in secular affairs. These anti-clerical speeches were bad enough, but the Bishop also learned that the Institut's library contained books that Roman Catholics were forbidden to read without the approval of the Church. The Bishop therefore decided to take firm action against the offending organization.

When Bishop Bourget insisted that the interdicted books be removed from the Institut's library, the members replied that, since their organization was secular and had a civil charter, the Church had no control over it. This was an open challenge to the authority of the Bishop. The war between the Bishop and the Institut raged for several years until finally, in 1869, Monseigneur Bourget, with Papal support, issued a pastoral letter forbidding Roman Catholics to belong to the Institut. Anyone who refused to follow the Bishop's instructions was to be denied the sacraments of the Church.

The matter might have ended there, for membership in the Institut was already declining, but shortly after the issuing of the Bishop's pastoral letter an obscure member of the Institut named Joseph Guibord died. Since Guibord had refused to renounce his membership in the Institut the Church refused to allow his body to be buried in that part of the cemetery reserved for Roman Catholics. Guibord's friends took the case to the courts in an attempt to force the Church to allow the body to be buried in the Roman Catholic cemetery. The essential issue in this case was whether the matter was to be governed by civil or Church law and, in effect, whether the Church was subordinate to the state. It was not until 1874 that the legal question was finally settled when the Judicial Committee of the Privy Council, the final court of appeal, ruled that Guibord had a right to be buried in a Roman Catholic cemetery.

Thus, nearly six years after his death, Guibord was to be buried properly. The first attempt to move his body to the

Roman Catholic cemetery was a failure, for his funeral cortège was halted by a mob of irate citizens. A few days later, under the protection of a thousand armed soldiers, Guibord was finally buried and his grave covered with cement to prevent any attempt to remove the body. But Bishop Bourget was not yet defeated. The day after the funeral, he announced that the ground which contained Guibord's body was not to be considered consecrated ground!

In itself the Guibord case was not important, but it threw into relief the strength of the hostility that some leaders of the powerful Roman Catholic Church in Quebec felt towards anti-clerical organizations. The Liberal party, some of whose supporters had belonged to the Institut, was looked upon with deep suspicion by clerics like Bishop Bourget. Thus the party found itself seriously handicapped in Quebec. "Our great weakness," Wilfrid Laurier, a young Quebec Liberal, told a friend in 1874, "is the everlasting one: the hostility of the priests."

The young Laurier took it upon himself to try to bring the running battle between the clergy and the Liberal party to an end. To do this he believed that he had to convince the Roman Catholic Church that Canadian Liberals had nothing in common with the revolutionary, anti-clerical liberals of Europe. In June 1877, he put forward his views in a brilliant speech on "Political Liberalism" in which he denied the charges made by the Church against his party. He claimed that Canadian Liberals accepted the evolutionary, reformist views of British liberals rather than the radicalism of European liberalism. He added that the Roman Catholic Church had nothing to fear from his party, though he made it clear that he did not believe that priests had any right to use the spiritual power of the Church to influence the political opinions of their parishioners.

A second point in Laurier's famous speech was a warning that it was dangerous for Quebec to listen to those politicians and priests who wanted to form a Roman Catholic party:

You wish to organize all Catholics into one party, without other bond, without other basis than a common religion; but have you not reflected that by that very fact you will organize the Protestant population as a single party, and that then, instead of the peace and harmony now prevailing between the different elements of the Canadian population, you will throw open the doors to a war, a religious war, the most terrible of all wars?

Laurier's opposition to a Roman Catholic party, or a French-Canadian party was a view he continued to hold throughout his long political career.

Laurier made his speech at an opportune moment, for Bishop Conroy had been sent by Pope Leo XIII, a far more liberal prelate than Pius IX, to examine the Church-state problem in Quebec. Conroy accepted Laurier's definition of liberalism in Canada and agreed that clerical intervention in politics was unwise. In future, the Quebec bishops were forbidden "to teach from the pulpit or elsewhere that it is a sin to vote for any particular candidate or party; even more it is forbidden to announce that you will refuse the sacraments for this cause. You are never to give your personal opinions from the pulpit." It was a striking triumph for the young Laurier.

The Mackenzie administration secured a number of important reforms in the political system. Under the direction of Edward Blake, the Minister of Justice, several important steps were taken to widen Canadian powers of self-government. In 1875 a Canadian Supreme Court was established which limited the number of appeals taken to the Privy Council in England, though it did not end them. In addition, Blake succeeded in having the powers of the governor-general clarified in order to limit further his right to act without the advice of the cabinet. Other reforms included the introduction of the secret ballot, a Corrupt Practices Act to prevent bribery of public officials, and legislation to control election expenses, all of which helped to reduce corruption and raise the level of Canadian political life.

ANCIENT TROY TACTICS
OR

To the Liberals, who had often heard the Conservatives trumpet the values of reciprocity and free trade, the National Policy looked suspiciously like a ruse to secure office.

When the Liberals moved from constitutional and political reforms to plans for economic development, however, their record was much less impressive. No sooner was the Mackenzie government in office than a world-wide trade depression slowed down the growth of the Canadian economy and caused a serious decline in government revenues. While the Intercolonial railway was pushed ahead and completed in 1876, the Pacific railway problem was more difficult to solve. The Mackenzie government constructed seven hundred miles of line through northern Ontario, largely to connect existing water-ways, and surveyed much of the route. But the pace was much too slow for Manitoba and British Columbia, while Ontario complained of the heavy taxes necessary to build a railway across a sea of muskeg and mountain. To bolster the country's sagging economy, Mackenzie's government made another attempt to secure reciprocity with the United States in 1874, only to see an indifferent American Senate reject the bill without any serious discussion.

The rumblings of economic discontent mounted and as the 1878 election approached the electoral pendulum was clearly swinging back towards the Conservatives. The people were beginning to believe the Conservative posters that proclaimed: "The weevil came in with the Grits [Liberals] and prosperity with John A." Shrewd Sir John and his able colleague, Tupper, were convinced that they knew the desires of the country when they began campaigning for a "National Policy." In its most elementary form, the National Policy meant a protective tariff for Canadian industry; but it meant more than just a tariff. It also meant a return to vigorous government support for railway building, immigration, and overall economic development. In the election of 1878 the voters forgot past Tory sins and voted for the National Policy. Macdonald was to be given another chance.

9 RAILWAYS, RIEL AND SECTIONALISM

SIR JOHN A. MACDONALD had already announced his plans for the economic development of the country when he and the Conservatives returned to office in 1878. He intended to replace the hesitant Liberal programme of railway building with a vigorous new scheme. During the election campaign he had also promised to raise the tariff to protect Canadian industry and to stimulate new economic growth within a transcontinental economy. Finally, more people were needed to build up the home market for Canadian products. When the empty plains were filled, they would become the breadbasket of the nation. Western wheat would be shipped along the new railway line to be exchanged for Eastern manufactured goods. But as Macdonald was to learn, it was far easier to plan the National Policy than it was to guarantee its success.

1. IMPLEMENTING THE NATIONAL POLICY

In 1879 the first of the new policies was implemented when the tariff was increased on both agricultural and manufactured products entering Canada. The new duties on manufactured products, amounting to twenty-five per cent and higher, were the most important features of the tariff, for Canadian farmers had little to fear from foreign competition. The high protection thus given to industry later caused farmers and Maritimers to criticize the tariff as a policy designed to meet only the needs of central Canada. But Macdonald and his Finance Minister, Leonard Tilley, argued, and expected, that the tariff would benefit all sections of the country by helping to encourage a diversified

In this cartoon entitled "On the Fence" Officer Macdonald is saying, "No more jumping over the fence, Jonathan. You must go around by the gate and pay your toll."

In advocating the National Policy of tariff protection, Sir John Macdonald had said: "Not only is this country made a slaughter market by being overwhelmed by the sweepings of the United States, but it has sometimes been made a sacrifice market by ruinous proposals for the purpose of suppressing any given trade. We all remember what the salt manufacturers of the United States did when the salt manufacturers first opened work in Goderich. The salt manufacturers of Syracuse and Selena sent in their salt with instructions to undersell Canadian salt on the Canadian market, to crush this infant industry. The shoe trade was dealt with in the same way by the leather manufacturers of the United States." Canadian manufacturers, he said, could not compete; plants would close and the people move to the United States.

and prosperous economy. Perhaps the importance of Macdonald's tariff policy is best illustrated by the fact that few

governments after 1879 have seriously attempted to change
it.

Rapid completion of the Canadian Pacific Railway was
vital to the Conservative prescription for a prosperous
economy. Liberal policy had been for the government to
build the railway on a "pay-as-you-go" plan, in order to
keep taxes and government expenditure low. Once back in
office Macdonald returned to his original policy of appealing to private contractors to build the line by offering lavish
government assistance. In 1880 a new Canadian Pacific Railway syndicate was formed under George Stephen of the
Bank of Montreal, and Donald Smith of the Hudson's Bay
Company. The government offered these businessmen
twenty-five million dollars, twenty-five million acres of the
best land in the West, seven hundred miles of completed
railway, permanent tax exemptions on railway property,
duty-free importation of necessary building materials, and a
promise to prohibit the construction of competing lines to
the south or southwest of the Canadian Pacific Railway line
for twenty years. The railway was to be completed by 1891.
The generosity of these terms demonstrated Macdonald's determination to get the railway built. In February 1881, the
Prime Minister wrote to A. T. Galt: "At last the C.P.R. is
a fixed fact. Royal assent given, Royal charter under the act
issued, company organized, and it now remains for Stephen
and Company to show what mettle they are made of."

But Macdonald's troubles were just beginning, for the
generous assistance given to the builders of the C.P.R. in
the original contract was not enough to ensure completion
of the railway. By 1883 the company was at the government's door with a request for a loan almost as large as
the original cash grant. Macdonald's first impulse was to
reject the request, but he was quickly reminded by one of
his advisers that "The day the Canadian Pacific busts, the
Conservative party busts the day after." Macdonald knew
that the fate of the government and perhaps even the fate
of the country depended on finishing the railway. He granted
the loan. Two years later, another loan was requested and

granted, this time with less hesitancy, for the railway had just proven its worth by transporting troops to the Northwest during the second Riel rebellion.

Although building a transcontinental railway was a very expensive project for a young country, Macdonald insisted that it was imperative for Canada's survival. Only with a railway to provide the basis for economic development could the widely separated sections of the country be welded into a single nation. As he explained in 1878: "Until this great work is completed our Dominion is little more than a 'geographical expression.' We have as much interest in British Columbia as in Australia, and no more. The railway once finished, we become one great united country with a large interprovincial trade and a common interest."

On November 7, 1885, Macdonald received a long-awaited telegram. "The first train from Montreal is approaching Yale, within a few hours of the Pacific Coast. The last spike was driven this morning by Honourable Donald Smith at Craigellachie, in Eagle Pass, some 340 miles from Port Moody. On reaching the coast our running time from Montreal, exclusive of stoppages, will be five days, averaging twenty-four miles per hour." It was a great day for Canada, rivalling in importance July 1 itself.

The completion of the Canadian Pacific Railway was perhaps the major achievement of the Macdonald government. The results of the government's immigration policies were much less impressive. Immigration, too, was of major importance to Canada, for the railway would be of little value if it passed through a sparsely populated country. The government hoped that, once the railway made the prairies accessible, immigrants, especially from Great Britain, would flock to Canada. "The most important subject which can engage the attention of the High Commissioner in England," Macdonald told A. T. Galt, Canada's first High Commissioner, "is the development of the North-West Territory." But only a few settlers came. A world depression lowered prices and dried up trade throughout North America. Canada was particularly hard hit because as an underdeveloped country she depended heavily on outside sources for capital investment. Moreover, as a producer of grain and raw materials, Canada prospered only when there was an expanding foreign market for these products. Since there was no expanding foreign market in the late eighties and early nineties, Canada's economy stagnated and it was very difficult to attract new settlers. Many of those who came soon found life too hard and moved on south to the United States. By the 1890's even natural increase failed to enlarge the population, as many native-born Canadians gave up hope of better times and moved to the United States.

Thus, by the 1890's the hopes upon which Macdonald's National Policy were built remained largely unfulfilled. The government was not entirely to blame, for it had no control over the external economic forces which had such a profound effect on Canadian development. Even more serious than Canada's economic difficulties, however, were the cultural and sectional clashes that threatened the very existence of the new Dominion.

2. RIEL AGAIN

Macdonald had naturally designed his immigration policies to people western Canada. In the early 1880's the pace of settlement had increased and the West was experiencing its first real boom. When the Canadian Pacific Railway reached Winnipeg in 1881, a stream of settlers and fortune seekers poured into Manitoba. Between 1871 and 1883, the population of the province grew from 25,000 to 150,000. As land prices soared, new settlers moved on to the Northwest Territories where the population expanded from a few hundred in 1871 to 50,000 twenty years later.

But by 1883, this short-lived bubble of western prosperity had burst. As world grain prices fell, western farmers felt the pinch of economic depression and attacked the federal government's economic policies. The farmers resented the high rates charged by the Canadian Pacific Railway for carrying grain to market. They criticized the tariff as a device to force them to pay high prices for goods produced by eastern manufacturers. By 1884 many western farmers were convinced that the federal government was completely ignoring their needs. A few agrarian leaders talked of open rebellion. One organizer of the Manitoba "Farmers Union" wrote in 1884 that the time had come for direct action. "The fact of the matter is, we have nothing to resist us, the military here is nothing but a pack of boys, and we have easy access to the store rooms." Farther west the British and European settlers were equally unrestrained. An editorial in the Edmonton *Bulletin* asked:

> If it was not by—not threatening, but actual rebellion and appeals to the British government for justice that the people of Ontario gained the rights they enjoy today and freed themselves from a condition precisely similar to that into which the Northwest is being rapidly forced, how was it? Was it not by armed rebellion coupled with murder, that Manitoba attained the rights she enjoys today from the very men who now hold the reins of power at Ottawa? If history is to be taken as a guide, what could be plainer than that without rebellion the people of the Northwest need expect nothing, while with rebellion, successful or otherwise, they may reasonably expect to get their rights.

The Prince Albert *Times* agreed with this view: "There is a ring of true metal about it which indicates pretty plainly the temper of the Nor'Wester."

But despite dissatisfaction and even rebellious muttering among these settlers, the most serious discontent in the West was among the Indians and the Métis. Both groups felt that the pressure of the expanding European population threatened their lands and their nomadic way of life. The Dominion government's Indian policy aimed at gradually settling the wandering tribes on reservations. Though not a very generous policy, it was fairer in its treatment of the Indians and was more successfully carried out than the policy of the United States, where settlement of the West had cost a good many lives—mainly Indian. But not all the Indians in western Canada were prepared to exchange their freedom and independence for a quiet life on a reservation. A few tribes remained sullenly suspicious of the threat implicit in advancing settlement. In 1884 a government agent wrote: "I never saw the Indians mean business before, the thing has got to be looked at seriously and precautions taken before it is too late." In Ottawa the warning was largely ignored.

The claims of the Métis received no more attention than those of the Indians. Many Métis had moved to the Northwest Territories from Manitoba after 1870 to establish their own independent community free from the influences and controls of a dominant Anglo-European civilization. By the 1880's a new crisis jeopardized their dream of freedom, for once again the vanguard of a new wave of surveyors and settlers threatened their landholdings, to which they had never legally established claims. No doubt the Métis had been careless about legal technicalities but the Macdonald government casually and consistently ignored all their pleas for a settlement of their land claims. The new advance of settlement was particularly serious for the Métis because there remained no new attractive uninhabited areas into which they could move.

In Ottawa Macdonald's government seemed to have too many other problems to consider the grievances of the westerners. Although the warnings of approaching disaster became more and more urgent, Macdonald, the Minister responsible for the West, continued to ignore petitions which demanded generous treatment for the Indians and Métis, settlement of land titles, lower tariffs and local self-government. In the fall of 1884 the government agent in the West wrote to the Prime Minister: "If the half-breed question is arranged this winter it will settle the whole business; if not a good force in the North will be necessary." But Macdonald took the light-hearted and cynical view that "no amount of concession will prevent people from grumbling and agitating." By the beginning of 1885, the troubles in the Northwest were far more serious than Macdonald realized.

In March 1884, the Métis had invited Louis Riel to return from Montana, where he was teaching, to lead them once again. Their invitation mentioned some of the grievances:

> We may say that the part of the North-West in which we are living is Manitoba before the troubles with the difference that there are more people, they understand things better, and that they are more determined; you will form an idea as to the conditions upon which the people base their claims, for the reason that there are many people in the North-West whom the government has recognized less than Indians; and yet it is these poor half-breeds who have always defended the North-West at the price of their blood and their sacrifices for a country which is stirring up the whole world today.

The letter concluded: "The whole race is calling you!" Riel returned reluctantly. He was now fifteen years older and his mental instability had increased. For a time, after the 1870 uprising, he had undergone treatment in an asylum and suffered from religious delusions. The Riel who arrived in Prince Albert in the spring of 1885 was a man suffering from religious and political delusions which made him entirely unfit for the task he had assumed.

With Riel's return the Métis' discontent rose to fever pitch. The situation was even more explosive than in 1869, for this time it also involved several Indian tribes led by two powerful warriors, Poundmaker and Big Bear. Fighting broke out in March at Duck Lake when a North West Mounted Police detachment, sent to investigate a Métis gathering, was driven off by force. Immediately after this victory, Poundmaker seized Battleford, and Big Bear's Indian followers massacred settlers in the little village of Frog Lake.

These events at last roused Ottawa. Macdonald dispatched a force of 8,000 men, under General Middleton. The swift

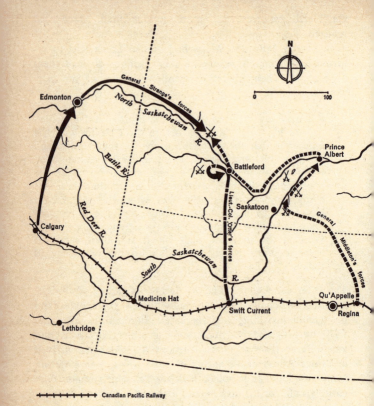

THE NORTHWEST REBELLION

arrival of this force, made possible by the newly completed Canadian Pacific Railway, ended the threat of a general Indian uprising. But complete pacification was not gained without further bloodshed. At Fish Creek the Métis forces won a last victory, before the superior number of government troops forced the rebels to surrender at Batoche. On May 15, 1885, Louis Riel surrendered and was taken to Regina to stand trial.

The fate of Louis Riel had raised a furore in central Canada in 1870. Once more in 1885 English-speaking Canadians demanded Riel's life as a revolutionary and as the murderer (in 1870) of Thomas Scott. In Quebec French Canadians, overlooking Riel's religious heresy, sang the praises of the Métis leader as the defender of French-Canadian minority rights. Even the moderate Laurier declared: "Had I been born on the banks of the Saskatchewan I would myself have shouldered a musket to fight against the neglect of governments and the shameless greed of speculators."

Riel stood trial in Regina in the summer of 1885. His defence lawyers argued that he was insane and therefore not responsible for his acts. Riel denied that he was unbalanced. An English-speaking Protestant jury found him guilty and sentenced him to hang, although his English-speaking lieutenant, William Jackson, was quickly found innocent because of insanity. Macdonald now had to face the difficult question of whether to grant the Métis leader a reprieve. Subjected to pressure from all sides, the Prime Minister finally decided to let Riel die, thinking that Quebec would stand by him anyway. "We will have lively times in Quebec," he wrote, "but I feel pretty confident that the excitement will die out."

On November 16, 1885, Louis Riel was hanged. In death he became a martyr to the cause of French-Canadian rights. "Riel, our brother, is dead, victim of his devotion to the cause of the Métis of whom he was the leader, victim of fanaticism and treason," declared Honoré Mercier, who would soon be Premier of Quebec. Riel's execution opened a Pandora's box of sectional and cultural discontents which plagued Macdonald until his death and eventually destroyed his Conservative party.

3. CONSTITUTIONAL AND SECTIONAL TROUBLES

Riel's execution caused Quebec to turn in on herself and re-examine the position of a cultural minority within Confederation. Macdonald's decision to allow Riel to die, despite

Quebec's opposition, was the first warning to French Canadians after 1867 that on issues which united English-speaking Canada the minority would have to accept defeat. Fortunately for Quebec, English-speaking Canadians were united on few public questions.

The immediate result of Riel's execution on the political level was to weaken the Conservative party's hold on Quebec, a hold which had been loosening since Cartier's death in 1873. In federal politics this weakening was not immediately apparent. Macdonald's French-Canadian colleagues stood by him because they feared their resignations would start a racial war. But on the provincial level the Conservatives were driven from office by a coalition of Liberals and French-Canadian nationalists led by the passionate orator, Honoré Mercier. Now the Liberals had a strong foothold in Quebec, which, combined with their strength in Ontario, could be used to launch an attack on the Conservatives in Ottawa. Macdonald recognized the danger at once. "The triumph of the Liberals over the corpse of Riel," he told Charles Tupper, "changes the aspect of affairs *quoad* [with respect to] the Dominion government completely. It will encourage the Grits and opposition generally; will dispirit our friends, and will, I fear, carry the country against us at the general election." Macdonald's prediction was not entirely accurate, for the Conservatives did win the election of 1887.

Mercier in Quebec was not the only thorn in Macdonald's flesh. By the late 1880's the premiers of both Ontario and Manitoba were attacking his conception of the Canadian federal system. Sir John A. Macdonald believed in the necessity of strong central government, with the provinces holding minor positions. One way in which the Conservative leader had restricted the activities of the provinces was by exercising the federal power of disallowance. Under the British North America Act the federal government could veto provincial laws which it considered were unconstitutional or which seemed to conflict with the national interest. Between 1867 and 1896, the federal government disallowed

LET THE BIG CHIEF BEWARE!

A cartoon by Bengough shows Manitoba borne down by the C.P.R.
monopoly. Macdonald's response to the complaints from the West was
revealed in a confidential letter written to a supporter: "When the North
West is filled with people, they may agitate as they please against it,
but it is not for the present population of Canada or the provinces east
of Manitoba to exclaim against a monopoly (if it be one) created for
their special benefit. Manufacturers might as well complain of a Protective Tariff especially made for their advantage."

sixty-eight provincial laws. Among them were laws passed
by the Manitoba government to charter railways to run to the
United States boundary and destroy the Canadian Pacific
Railway's monopoly, which Manitoba farmers blamed for
high freight rates and inadequate branch lines and elevators.
Since these acts were in conflict with the monopoly that the
railway had been granted in 1880, Macdonald had them disallowed, even though they had been passed by a Conser-

vative government in Manitoba. The result was serious discontent in Manitoba, and the defeat of the provincial government by one pledging itself to an anti-Macdonald crusade. Ontario, too, felt that it had suffered unjustly from Macdonald's free use of the power of disallowance, especially in the matter of control of navigation on rivers and streams.

Discontent also developed in the Maritimes during the 1880's. Confederation had not brought prosperity to the Maritimes and the depression of the 1870's and 1880's had hit them badly. While their economic problems were due largely to changes in the world economy and transportation systems (such as the widespread use of the iron ship which destroyed their shipbuilding industry) they laid the blame squarely on the doorstep of the federal government. The chief criticism was levelled at the tariff, which not only increased the cost of manufactured goods, but also, by reducing imports, made it more difficult for foreign countries to buy Canadian exports. To the Maritimer the tariff looked like an instrument of the devil, the latter only faintly disguised as an Ontario or Quebec manufacturer. By 1886 discontent in Nova Scotia had reached such a pitch that Premier W. S. Fielding's Liberal government passed a motion upholding the province's right to secede from Confederation.

These conflicts between the federal government and the provinces came to a head in 1887, when the premiers of Ontario and Quebec summoned an Interprovincial Conference to discuss the grievances of the provinces. British Columbia and Prince Edward Island, which had Conservative governments, refused to send delegates, and Macdonald, who had been invited to send representatives, chose to ignore the meeting and condemned it as a Liberal party rally. Nevertheless, the representatives of five provinces met, and passed a series of resolutions which were designed to alter the constitution and weaken the federal government. The dissident provinces called for increased subsidies, a voice for the provinces in choosing senators, and the transfer of the federal power of disallowance to the Imperial government. Far more important than the resolutions passed by the Interprovincial Conference was its illustration of the opposition that had developed to Macdonald's policies.

Although the provincial premiers failed to weaken the powers of the federal government, Macdonald faced another kind of attack that was not so easy to withstand. He could fight the provinces to a standstill at home, but when they carried their cases to the Judicial Committee of the Privy Council in England, the last court of appeal, he was less successful. As early as 1883 the Privy Council had begun to hand down decisions whose effect was to emphasize the legislative powers of the provincial governments and restrict the federal authority. Though Macdonald believed that the constitution was being misinterpreted by the Judicial Committee, he had no way of fighting the decisions. By 1896 the provinces, with the aid of the English judges, had won for themselves a breadth of power that Macdonald thought had been effectively denied to them in 1867.

4. THE OLD MAN, THE OLD FLAG, THE OLD POLICY

In the last years of Macdonald's life the country that he had led for so long suffered under strains that seemed to threaten its very existence. After the hanging of Louis Riel in 1885, relations between English-speaking and French-speaking Canadians moved slowly towards a crisis. But the "Old Chieftain's" most serious problem was the depressed economic condition of the country. By the late 1880's it was evident that the National Policy had not produced a prosperous and united Canada. The main difficulty was the world-wide economic depression, but as conditions grew worse, many people became convinced that the basic cause of Canada's economic difficulties was the high tariff. This view found strong support among farmers, and people living in the Maritimes, who believed that the high tariff benefited only the manufacturers of central Canada. What Canada needed was not protection, but free trade with the United States, which would not only allow Canadians to sell their products on the huge American market, but would reduce the cost of goods imported from the United States.

THE "TARIFF OF ABOMINATIONS."

Mr. Foster: Accept my congratulations, Mr. Farmer, on your magnificent harvest.
Nor'west Farmer: Thank ye kindly, sir, but somehow it doesn't seem to pan out much for me after all!

As conditions in the country became more serious, the Liberals, who had always fought for freer trade, intensified their attack on the Conservative tariff policy. In 1887, the Liberal party advocated complete free trade with the United States, or "unrestricted reciprocity." In the federal election campaign of 1891, the chief issue was the National Policy versus unrestricted reciprocity.

The Liberals argued that unrestricted reciprocity would mean the removal of all tariffs between Canada and the United States, but each country would maintain its own tariff against the rest of the world. Macdonald and the Conservatives claimed that unrestricted reciprocity was im-

THE GRIT TOBOGGAN SLIDE, AND WHERE IT LEADS TO!

GRIT POLICY

UNRESTRICTED RECIPROCITY

But the Canadian People will come to the Aid of their Patriotic Premier on the 5th of March, and Rescue their Country from the impending Danger.

A Conservative poster for the 1891 general election

possible unless Canada and the United States adopted a single, uniform tariff against other countries. If this were not done, products imported into the United States could move freely into Canada without being subject to Canadian tariff laws. The Conservatives believed that a common tariff would mean commercial union between Canada and the United States. The inevitable consequence of commercial union, they argued, would be the political union of the two countries and the disappearance of Canada.

Macdonald was not opposed to a limited trade agreement with the United States, provided that it did not threaten the basis of the national economy that he was attempting to establish. Indeed, in 1891 his government attempted to negotiate a new trade treaty with the Americans. But the effort failed. Therefore, in order to counter the growing popularity of the Liberal proposal, Macdonald condemned unrestricted reciprocity as disloyal and a threat to Canadian independence. In the election campaign, the Conservative slogan was "the old man, the old flag, the old policy." Macdonald set the tone of his campaign with his famous declaration:

> The question which you will shortly be called upon to determine resolves itself into this: Shall we endanger our possession of the great heritage bequeathed to us by our fathers... with the prospect of ultimately becoming a portion of the American Union? As for myself, my course is clear. A British subject I was born, a British subject I will die. With my utmost effort, with my latest breath, will I oppose the "veiled treason" which attempts by sordid means and mercenary offers to lure our people from their allegiance.

The emotions stirred up by Macdonald's plea, the support of the businessmen whose interests were protected by the high tariff, and the fear of many people that the Liberal policy would lead to political union with the United States, enabled the Conservatives to limp back into office by the narrowest possible margin. Macdonald had once more succeeded in winning his countrymen to his concept of Canada as an independent British nation in North America. Even the Liberals concluded that unrestricted reciprocity was not a policy that the electorate would support, and in 1893 it was dropped from the party's platform.

Nevertheless, the result of the election of 1891 was as much a personal victory for old Sir John as it was for his party or his policy. For more than thirty years he had been at the centre of events in British North America. The shaping of the new nation, both its successes and its failures, had taken place under Macdonald's guidance. Even his opponent, Laurier, admitted that Macdonald's "actions displayed unbounded fertility of resource, a high level of intellectual conception, and, above all, a far reaching vision beyond the event of the day, and still higher, permeating the whole, a broad patriotism, a devotion to Canada's welfare, Canada's advancement, Canada's glory."

Even as Macdonald formed his new cabinet in 1891, there were frightening signs of new cultural conflicts that would be difficult to settle. But Macdonald did not have to face these problems. Tired out from the hard winter of campaigning, the old man died on June 6, 1891. Goldwin Smith, an English historian living in Canada, wrote: "When this man is gone who will there be to take his place? Who else is there who knows the sheep or whose voice the sheep know? Who else could make Orangemen vote for Papists, or induce half the members for Ontario to help in levying on their own province the necessary blackmail for Quebec? Yet this is the work that will have to be done if a general break-up is to be averted." During the five years that followed Macdonald's death, no one was found in the Conservative ranks who had the master magician's touch.

10 RACE, RELIGION AND VICTORY FOR LAURIER

WHILE Macdonald had successfully countered the major challenge to his National Policy by defeating reciprocity, he had not conjured away other threats to the national unity. Above all, he had been unable to soothe the increasing bitterness of the relations between French- and English-speaking Canadians. After his death, the Conservative party was unable to find a leader of similar stature and ability. For five unhappy years a succession of Conservative leaders wrestled with problems of race and religion, as their party was torn apart by internal divisions and external pressures.

1. MOUNTING CONFLICT

After the hanging of Louis Riel, the relations between French- and English-speaking Canadians grew increasingly strained and acrimonious. In Quebec, the martyred Riel became a symbol of the injustice and tyranny of the English-speaking majority. As one French-Canadian leader remarked: "In killing Riel, Sir John has not only struck a blow at the heart of our race, but above all he struck at the cause of justice and humanity, which represented in all languages and sanctified by all religious beliefs, begged mercy for the prisoner of Regina, our poor brother of the North West." Conscious as never before of their minority position in Canada and their weakness in the face of a united English-speaking community, the French Canadians became increasingly nationalistic and sensitive to any assaults on their culture.

In English-speaking Canada, Riel also became a symbol, a symbol of the British nature of the new Canadian nation.

By the late 1880's, many English-speaking Canadians were loud in their assertions that Canada was an English and Protestant country and vigorous in echoing Lord Durham's contention that the nation could not survive as a country of two cultures. While most realized that the people of Quebec could never be assimilated, they were adamant in opposing the spread of French culture beyond the borders of that province. Claims of the French Canadians for recognition of their minority rights and respect for their culture outside of Quebec were treated with contempt by English-Canadian extremists. As the *Orange Sentinel,* spokesman for the anti-Catholic Orange Order and other like-minded English-speaking Canadians, declared in 1886: "Must it be said that the rights and liberties of English people, this English colony, depend upon a foreign race? The day is near when an appeal to arms will be heard in all parts of Canada. Then, certainly, our soldiers, benefiting by the lessons of the past, will have to complete the work they have begun in the North West." The basic question facing Canada, exclaimed D'Alton McCarthy, a prominent Conservative, was "whether this country is to be English or French." The Liberal John Charlton observed that "the sentiment that received the greatest applause was when I asserted that a successful French nationality in the North American Continent was a hopeless dream, for that question had been settled upon the Plains of Abraham." The *Orange Sentinel,* McCarthy and Charlton represented the extreme view, but the extremists seemed often to drown out the moderates who, like Sir John Macdonald, believed that "there is no paramount race in this country, there is no conquered race in this country; we are all British subjects and those who are not English are none the less British subjects on that account."

The racial and religious conflict became even more intense in 1888 when Honoré Mercier passed the Jesuit Estates Act. In 1773 the Society of Jesus had been abolished by the Papacy and its property in Canada had reverted to the Crown. When the Society was re-established in 1842, the Jesuits naturally requested either the restoration of their

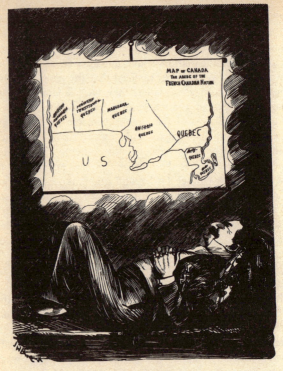

MERCIER'S DREAM
OF THE FUTURE MAP OF THE DOMINION.

To many English-speaking Canadians the emotional Honoré Mercier, who had won power in Quebec in the aftermath of the Riel crisis, represented a threat to Anglo-Saxon Protestant supremacy in Canada. The Toronto *Mail* declared, "The French priest, it is true, cannot formally import into Ontario his Church Establishment and his system of Tithes. But this matters little, if he can thrust out the British population and plant in its room a population which will be under his sway, and from which he can swing practically any payments which he thinks fit. . . . He will, to all intents and purposes, detach Eastern Ontario from the British and Protestant civilization of which it now forms a part, and annex it to the territory of the French race, which is also the dominion of the priest." The fear that the French population was spreading throughout Canada was one of the reasons which led D'Alton McCarthy to begin his campaign for the abolition of the French language in the Northwest Territories and in Manitoba.

property or compensation. After forty years of disputes and negotiations, Mercier sought to settle the long-standing and contentious problem by valuing the estates at $400,000. Of this sum, $60,000 was to go to Protestant schools in Quebec, while the remainder was to be divided among the Jesuits and other Roman Catholic bodies as the Pope saw fit. The bill passed the Quebec Legislature unanimously.

But in Ontario the Jesuit Estates Act aroused a storm of protest, although the province was in no way affected by the measure. Outraged by the appeal to the Pope, many English-speaking Canadians echoed the fears and threats of the Toronto *Mail*: "If the British and Protestant element in Quebec [which supported the Bill!] will not save itself, we must try to save it for our own sakes. That the abandonment of Quebec to the ultramontane and the Jesuit will be the death of Canadian nationality is clear enough. But Ontario will not be safe." In the House of Commons militant Protestants and Francophobes demanded the disallowance of the Act. Macdonald bluntly refused and reprimanded his supporters, as did the leaders of the Liberal party. Nevertheless, thirteen English-speaking Canadians, variously described as the "Noble Thirteen" or the "Devil's Dozen," broke party lines to vote for disallowance. By this time the leading spokesman for the anti-French and anti-Catholic element was D'Alton McCarthy, who split with Macdonald on the issue.

Thwarted in his demand to secure disallowance of the Jesuit Estates Act, which would serve as a symbol of English and Protestant supremacy in Canada, McCarthy announced his intention of carrying on a crusade for the abolition of French language rights and Roman Catholic separate schools outside Quebec. "Now is the time," he informed the Orange Lodge at Stayner, Ontario, "when the ballot box will decide the great question before the people, and if that does not supply the remedy in this generation bayonets will in the next." In the fall of 1889, he carried his campaign into Manitoba and the Northwest Territories, where the English-speaking majority gave him a more than sympathetic hearing and ultimately adopted his views.

In 1890 the province of Manitoba abolished French as an official language and virtually abolished separate schools, guaranteed in the Manitoba Act of 1870, by withdrawing all public funds from their support. The question was immediately taken before the courts to test the constitutionality of the legislation and, as a result, was not an issue in the election of 1891. As the old chieftain knew only too well, however, here was an issue that could divide the nation as it had never been divided before, and it was an issue that he had not been able to destroy at birth.

2. CONSERVATIVE FAILURE

As the Manitoba School Question wound its way through the courts, the Conservative party disintegrated in the face of conflicting views about the racial and religious conflict. Its lack of leadership both contributed to this and reflected the divisions within the party. When Macdonald died there were three logical candidates for the succession: Sir Hector Langevin, Sir Charles Tupper, and Sir John Thompson. But Langevin was then deeply implicated in a scandal that was to end his career; Tupper had no desire to leave the pleasant and apparently lucrative office of the Canadian High Commissioner in London; and Thompson was rejected by the McCarthy wing of the party because he was a convert to Roman Catholicism. The mantle therefore fell on old Sir John Abbott who rightly declared: "I am here because I am not particularly obnoxious to anyone." Eighteen months later Abbott resigned because of ill-health and Thompson, clearly the ablest man in the party, was selected to succeed him, despite rumblings of discontent from anti-Catholic elements in the party. Two years later, with the Manitoba School Question still before the courts, Thompson died at fifty, at Windsor Castle. With Tupper, Macdonald's old warhorse, still preferring the sidelines, the party seemed bereft of leadership. Responsibility for selecting a new Prime

Minister fell on the Governor-General, Lord Aberdeen, whose wife summarized their views of the contenders in the following manner:

> This has come so suddenly that there has been no preparing for any successor & Mackenzie Bowell was only appointed acting premier in Sir John's absence quite in a temporary way. Mr. Foster the Minister of Finance is an able man, a good speaker and a good man, but he has no power over other men and showed no power for leading in the House once before when Sir John was away. And then that clique against him and his wife because they married in the United States, after she had divorced her husband makes a difficulty. And Mr. Haggart who is the strongest man is admittedly a Bohemian & also idle. . . . Mr. Mackenzie Bowell himself is 75, rather fussy, & decidedly common place, also an Orangeman, at one time Grand Master of the Orangemen of N. America & also presided at one of the tip-top grand Orange affairs at Belfast—but he is a good & straight man & he has great ideas about the drawing together of the colonies & the Empire. . . .

In the end Bowell, as the senior cabinet minister, was chosen, but he lacked the qualities of strength and judgement needed by his party in a time of crisis.

Bowell was hardly settled in his new office when the crisis over the Manitoba schools came to a head. As early as 1892 the courts had decided that Manitoba was within her constitutional rights to abolish separate schools. But the further question remained whether the federal government had the power to take remedial action. Section 93 of the British North America Act provided that if a province interfered with the educational rights that a minority possessed at the time of union, an appeal could be made to the federal government to remedy the grievance. Once it was decided that the Manitoba legislation was constitutional, the minority therefore, fully supported by the Roman Catholic Church and the people of Quebec, petitioned the federal government for remedial legislation. And in January 1895 the

QUEBEC GETS A SHOW.

SIR ADOLPHE CARON—" Me and Joe Ouimet will now exhibit Sare Mackenzie. Bowell in the act of forming his heroic resolve to protect ze rights of ze menoritee."

Most people suspected, in many ways unfairly, that Bowell, the Orange-man, had no intention of passing remedial legislation. The unfortunate Prime Minister was under strong pressure from both sides. This con-temporary cartoon shows two of his Quebec cabinet ministers gently persuading Sir Mackenzie to go ahead with remedial action.

Judicial Committee of the Privy Council declared that the federal government had the power to act. The legal question was solved; the political question remained. Could or should the Conservative government pass remedial legislation?

For a year the Conservatives drifted. There were repeated threats of resignations in the cabinet and in January 1896 seven men actually did resign, only to return later. On one hand the government begged Manitoba to amend its legis-lation and on the other threatened and blustered. Cabinet meetings were orgies of dissension and argument, and ministers attacked and counter-attacked each other in the Commons and in the press. Sir Joseph Pope, Macdonald's former secretary, wrote that these were days "I never recall without a blush, days of a weak and incompetent administra-tion by a cabinet presided over by a man whose sudden and unlooked-for elevation had visibly turned his head, a ministry without unity or cohesion of any kind, a prey to internal dissensions until they became a spectacle to the world, to angels, and to men."

Finally in February 1896 the government decided to introduce remedial legislation to force the government of Manitoba to restore separate schools. But with the natural five-year life of parliament due to expire in the spring, the opposition saw an ideal opportunity for obstruction. For weeks the bill was before the House of Commons. Liberals and anti-remedialist Conservatives debated each of the one hundred and twelve clauses at length. Members slept in committee rooms, at their desks, and in the corridors as the debate continued day and night. The more boisterous filibusters provided their own entertainment as they waited their turn to speak, with Nicholas Flood Davin, the colourful bard from Regina in the Northwest Territories, delighting the members with a Blackfoot dance which he ended by springing onto the long table in the smoking room and "jigging down the centre, kicking over bottles and tumblers and plates at every step." After a solid month of debate, only fifteen of the one hundred and twelve clauses had been passed, and the government withdrew the bill. Soon afterwards the House of Commons was dissolved and an election called for June 11, 1896. Before the campaign got under way, Bowell was replaced by the aging Tupper who had finally returned from England in a last desperate attempt to save the party he had helped Macdonald create.

The Conservative party entered the election divided. Some candidates openly denounced remedial legislation, while Tupper and his colleagues argued that it was an act of justice to the minority. Realizing that their appeal would fall on stony ground in Ontario, the Conservatives counted on the support of the Roman Catholic Church in Quebec to bring them an overwhelming victory there. They hoped too that while Laurier would be denounced as a French-Canadian Roman Catholic in the English-speaking provinces, he would be denounced by the Roman Catholic Church in Quebec for opposing the remedial bill.

MAKING THE GREATEST SHOW ON EARTH OF THEMSELVES.

Liberal cartoonist J.W. Bengough on the Conservative platform in the 1896 election

Laurier, who had become leader of the Liberal party in 1887, found himself in a very difficult position. He opposed the remedial bill, but he did not object to the restoration of separate schools; indeed, he promised that if elected he would secure justice for the minority in Manitoba. The answer, he said, was not threats and the coercion of a province, but a policy of "sunny ways," of peaceful and amicable negotiations with the government of Manitoba. The Conservatives, he claimed, have "blown and raged and threatened and the more they have raged and blown, the more that man Greenway [the Premier of Manitoba] has stuck to his coat. If I were in power I would try the sunny way. I would approach this man Greenway with the sunny way of patriotism, asking him to be just and to be fair, asking him to be generous to the minority, in order that we may have peace among all the creeds and races which it has pleased God to bring upon this corner of our common country."

Laurier's objection to the coercion of a province and his policy of sunny ways won favour in English-speaking Canada. But in Quebec the leaders of the Roman Catholic Church grimly supported the Conservatives. One influential priest publicly warned Laurier that "the episcopacy, like one man, united with the clergy, will rise up to support those who have fallen in defending us." But with the spectre of a religious war before him, Laurier clung steadfastly to the principles he had enunciated in 1877 when he had denied the Church's right to interfere in politics and appealed for politics free from religious strife. "So long as I have a seat in the House," he said in March 1896, "so long as I occupy the position I do now whenever it shall become my duty to take a stand upon any question whatever, that stand I will take not upon grounds of Roman Catholicism, not upon grounds of Protestantism, but upon grounds which can appeal to the consciences of men, irrespective of their particular faith, upon grounds which can be occupied by all men who love justice, freedom and toleration."

With religious education and French culture at stake, the bishops regarded Laurier's statement as little short of heresy and cultural betrayal. Remedial legislation appeared to be the only action guaranteed to restore separate schools and, after much discussion and argument, the bishops issued a *mandement* or statement to guide the electorate of Quebec:

> All Catholics ought to give their votes only to candidates who swear formally and solemnly to vote in Parliament in favour of legislation giving the Catholic minority in Manitoba the school rights which are recognized as theirs by the British Privy Council. This solemn duty is necessary for every good Catholic, and you would not be justified either before your spiritual guides or before God himself if you fail to fulfil this obligation.

Although the *mandement* was not explicit, it was clear that the bishops endorsed Conservative candidates. Equally emphatic clerical statements were issued from the other side. The Protestant Churches were opposed to remedial action and separate schools. One Methodist minister informed his congregation that support of remedial action "would stare the voter in the face at the Judgement Day, and condemn him to eternal perdition."

When the ballots were counted, Laurier and the Liberals had emerged with a clear majority. Five years of Conservative bungling, economic distress, and lack of leadership had destroyed Macdonald's old party. In Quebec, the electors rejected the appeal of the Roman Catholic Church, and gave Laurier a resounding victory, while in Ontario he won half the seats despite the attacks on his race and religion.

In office, Canada's first French-Canadian Prime Minister at once adopted the policy of sunny ways. Laurier's emissaries persuaded the government of Manitoba to grant concessions to the minority, such as provisions for instruction in French where ten students spoke the language, and religious instruction at the end of the day. Like most compromises, this satisfied no one, but it did, for the moment at least, end the cultural strife that had threatened to destroy the nation. With this question out of the way, Laurier was able to turn to the tasks of national development that Macdonald had left unfinished.

11 LAURIER AND NATIONAL DEVELOPMENT

THE Liberal ministry that Laurier formed in 1896 has been called the "government of all talents." Its greatest strength was the Prime Minister himself. Like Sir John A., Laurier was a master of the art of party management and could direct the efforts of men with strong and sometimes diverse opinions towards a common goal. His immense personal charm and his oratorical power in both English and French made him very popular in all sections of the country. Though determined and steady of purpose, he was willing to compromise when the nation's welfare demanded it. He enjoyed politics and the exercise of power and, like Macdonald before him, he was determined to build a stronger, more united Canada.

Macdonald had laid the framework for the Canadian nation. Laurier knew that to complete the structure he would have to heal the sectional and racial conflicts that had divided and weakened the country. His main aim was always to bind French- and English-speaking Canadians together in a common nationality, by following a path that was neither narrowly English nor French, Roman Catholic nor Protestant, but broad enough to win the acceptance of all groups. As he told a friend:

> My object is to consolidate Confederation and to bring our people, long estranged from each other, gradually to become a nation. This is the supreme issue. Everything else is subordinate to that idea.

In his first cabinet, Laurier included the men he thought were best qualified to assist in the tasks of uniting and developing the country. To the important post of Minister of Finance he appointed W. S. Fielding, the former Premier of

Hon. W. Laurier

Nova Scotia. Here was a clear indication that the Liberals had abandoned unrestricted reciprocity, for Fielding, unlike Richard Cartwright who had expected to become Finance Minister, was not a free trader. Oliver Mowat, who gave up his position as Premier of Ontario to become Minister of Justice, was also regarded as a "safe" man by central-Canadian businessmen. From the Manitoba government came the experienced politician and businessman, Clifford Sifton, the western representative in Laurier's cabinet. As Minister of the Interior, Sifton's main task was to fill the western plains with prosperous farmers. In Quebec, Laurier turned away from the old *parti rouge* elements in the party who were still suspected by the Church and chose Joseph-Israel Tarte, at one time a staunch Conservative, as Minister of Public Works. Tarte, who had once remarked that "elections are not won by prayers," had helped Laurier to win his victory over the Roman Catholic Church in Quebec in the 1896 election.

The new administration clearly indicated the changes which had taken place in Liberal thinking since 1878. Instead of Mackenzie's caution, there was now a confident acceptance of policies of national development very similar to those of Macdonald. But one very important circumstance had changed. Soon after Laurier took office in 1896 world prosperity returned. New markets opened up, money for investment flowed more freely, and immigrants looked to Canada as a land of promise. Thus, the Liberals had the opportunity to make their national economic developments a success, whereas depression had prevented Macdonald from achieving his goals.

1. LIBERAL ECONOMIC POLICY

The first indication of Laurier's willingness to accept the basic elements in Macdonald's National Policy was the Fielding tariff of 1897. In opposition, the Liberals had always been critical of the protective tariff, and in 1891 had proposed unrestricted reciprocity with the United States. But under the guidance of W. S. Fielding the Liberals in 1897 accepted the principle of protection, though with some reductions in duties on such items as binder twine, wire fencing and farm implements to meet the demands of their western supporters. Sifton summed up the Liberal government's view when he wrote: "The people decided some eighteen years ago to have the protective policy, and got it and have stood by it ever since. And the business of the country . . . has adapted itself to the tariff; and the introduction of a tariff from which the principle of protection would be entirely eliminated would be fraught with results that would be most disastrous to the whole Canadian people."

The Liberals did make one important change in the country's tariff policy: they introduced a preferential tariff which offered lower rates to countries which reduced their

In the field of economic policy, Laurier's chief lieutenant was W. S. Fielding, Minister of Finance. From 1884 to 1896 he had served as Premier of Nova Scotia, but he accepted a call to Ottawa in 1896 to become a member of Laurier's "Government of All Talents." In 1897 his first budget included an Imperial preference and in 1911 it was Fielding who negotiated the reciprocity agreement with the United States—the agreement which played such a large part in the defeat of the Liberals in 1911. When the Liberals returned to office a decade later, the new Prime Minister, Mackenzie King, once more chose Fielding as Minister of Finance, a post he held until 1925.

tariffs against Canada. Since Britain practised free trade, she was most affected by this policy. The result was that the Canadian tariff on British imports was reduced first by one-eighth and later by one-third. But even this measure did not seriously alter the basically protective character of the Canadian tariff. Although the Liberals made some minor alterations in the tariff before 1911, it was probably only pressure from the growing number of western agrarian voters that prevented them from adopting even higher tariffs.

Tariffs alone could not ensure prosperity and expansion for Canadian industry. W. S. Fielding found a more satisfactory method when he noted: "The best way you can help the manufacturers of Canada is to fill up the prairie regions of Manitoba and the Northwest with a prosperous and contented people, who will be consumers of the manufactured goods of the east." The filling up of the West was an object pursued vigorously by the Laurier government, and especially by Clifford Sifton.

In immigration as in most other respects, changed world economic conditions greatly aided the Liberal programme. The revival of prosperity and the growth of industry in Europe increased, just as transportation costs began to decline on the transatlantic steamships. This prosperity also lured settlers to western Canada from both eastern Canada and Europe, settlers who in earlier years might have gone to the United States. But by 1896 the American frontier was closed and many people who had left Canada for the United States in the earlier period now began to find their way back across the border, as did Americans themselves. With the good farmlands of the United States taken up, the Canadian prairies became "the last, best west," the last frontier of North American agriculture.

Railways and steamship lines assisted the government's immigration programme. The Canadian Pacific Railway had received large tracts of land from the government and hoped to sell it to settlers. But the government played the leading role in encouraging people to settle in Canada. The North Atlantic Trading Company, created by Sifton, spread information about Canada throughout Europe and arranged for immigrants to travel to new homes in the Canadian West.

This effort to attract European settlers, in addition to those from Britain and the United States, was one way in which Sifton's immigration policy differed from that of the Macdonald government. Sifton believed that the best pioneers for the Canadian West were not urban industrial workers, but hardy farmers. As he put it himself: "I think a stalwart peasant in a sheep-skin coat, born on the soil, whose forefathers have been farmers for ten generations, with a stout wife and a half-dozen children, is good quality." Between 1897 and 1912 some 594,000 people came to Canada from Europe. Another 961,000 came from the British Isles, while 784,000 crossed into Canada from the United States. But it was immigrants from Europe, with their new languages and cultures, that began to change the character of Canada. Although Mennonites and Icelanders had settled in Canada in the 1870's and 1880's, it was the new national and religious groups, the Germans, Ukrainians, Poles, Doukhobors and others, who gave the Canadian West a character similar to that of the "melting pot" of the United States. But because of Canada's smaller population, these groups were more slowly and less completely absorbed into the older English-Canadian culture.

Although many went to the urban factories, most of the new immigrants took up farming in the West. Soon new methods of cultivation and new types of grain transformed the dry, flat prairies into one of the greatest grain-growing areas in the world. Since rainfall was limited on the prairies, only large farms could produce enough grain to make farming profitable. To cultivate these large farms, machinery was necessary as well as numerous additional hands at harvest time. By the turn of the century, the development of new mechanized ploughs, binders and threshers made farming easier and more efficient. Each autumn thousands of young men from eastern Canada went West to find temporary employment in harvesting the crop. Many remained to establish their own homesteads.

Science was not only applied to machinery; it was also applied to developing new varieties of wheat. Because of the short growing season in the West it was essential to produce new types of grain that would mature between the late spring and the early autumn frosts. To promote the science of agriculture the government established several experimental stations. In 1904, Charles Saunders and his team of scientists produced the quick-maturing, rust-resistant Marquis wheat, which in due time extended the farming frontier north into the fertile Peace River country. Soon Canadian Number One Northern wheat was in demand throughout the world. New people, new lands and new varieties of grain, these were the elements which produced the "Wheat Boom" during the first decade of the twentieth century. This western boom spread prosperity throughout most of the country.

In 1895 only 66,000 people lived in the vast Northwest Territories between Manitoba and British Columbia. Ten years later the number leaped to 400,000, ample testimony to the vigour of Sifton's immigration policy. Although the Territories had had responsible government since 1897 the powers of their government were limited, but their growth in population inevitably brought demands for provincial status. In 1905 the Laurier government bowed to the views of the people and created two new provinces, Saskatchewan and Alberta.

Drawing the boundaries proved to be a far less difficult task than designing the new provincial constitutions. The most serious difficulty arose over the provisions to be made for education in the new constitutions, or Autonomy Bills. Roman Catholic and French schools had been established in the Territories in 1875, but these minority privileges had gradually been whittled down. In drawing up the Autonomy Bills, Laurier hoped to satisfy his Church and his people by including a clause which restored the school system that had existed in the Northwest in 1875. A storm of protest arose in the West and Ontario. The Toronto *Telegram* condemned Laurier's action as "fastening the dead hand of denominational control" on the western schools. The dispute split Laurier's cabinet and Clifford Sifton, who had been absent when the Bills were drawn up, submitted his resignation in protest. Sifton's resignation, and the obvious strength of English-speaking Canadian opposition to separate schools, forced Laurier to reverse his course and leave the western schools as he had found them.

WHY LAURIER STILL REIGNS

Laurier I: "Manuel of Portugal would have never lost his throne if he'd had the R. L. Borden Zouaves to take care of him like they've took care of me."

Laurier was constantly attacked by English Canadians for being closely allied with the Roman Catholic Church, particularly after his speech at the Eucharistic Congress in September 1910. A month later a critical cartoonist gave his version of Laurier's success. The figure of his opponent, Conservative leader R. L. Borden, dressed as a Zouave, those who guarded the Vatican, suggests that the cartoonist, like many Conservatives, believed that Borden's ineptness helped keep Laurier in power.

The growth of the West placed heavy demands on the country's railway facilities. At harvest time there were never enough railway freight cars to carry western grain to the seaports, and the prairie farmers soon began to demand more railways. Several groups of railway promoters, desiring to gain a share of the profitable traffic of the Canadian Pacific Railway, were eager to meet their demands. In 1902 the Grand Trunk petitioned the government for assistance in building a line from North Bay to the Pacific coast. This petition was followed by a counter-proposal from two western promoters, William Mackenzie and Donald Mann, who were laying plans for a transcontinental railway, the Canadian Northern. When efforts to persuade the two groups to combine in a single venture failed, Laurier agreed to charter both companies. "We cannot wait," Laurier claimed, "because at this moment there is a transformation going on in the conditions of our national life which it would be folly to ignore and a crime to overlook." That transformation was the enormous increase in the output of the western farmer.

The scheme adopted to aid the Grand Trunk Pacific and the Canadian Northern in 1903 was very similar to Macdonald's earlier combination of public and private enterprise. Both the Grand Trunk, which was to be built from Winnipeg to Prince Rupert, and the Canadian Northern, which planned a third transcontinental line, were granted large-scale government assistance. To Conservative criticism of the government's generosity, Sifton replied: "My own view is that twenty years ought to see at least twelve million people in Canada, but if this result is to be accomplished, small ideas of trying to cut off expenditures on railways and public works will have to be dropped. For myself, I am altogether in favour of going ahead." This was the same argument that Macdonald had used against his Liberal critics in the 1880's.

Laurier's optimism about the future of Canada, and his inability to resist the pressure from powerful railroad promoters, resulted in the construction of two new transcontinentals to compete with the Canadian Pacific Railway. The cost of each of the new systems exceeded expectations, while mismanagement and corruption brought further financial burdens. When the lines were completed they were forced into ruinous competition for traffic in areas like northwestern Ontario where one efficiently run railway would have been enough. Chronic financial problems time and again forced the promoters to seek further governmental

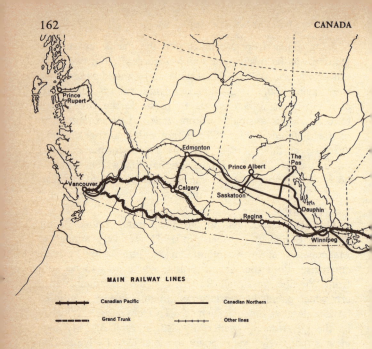

MAIN RAILWAY LINES

| | Canadian Pacific | | Canadian Northern |
| | Grand Trunk | | Other lines |

assistance. Finally, at the end of the First World War, and at great expense to the Canadian taxpayer, the government was forced to take over the railways and unite them into a single, publicly owned corporation, the Canadian National Railways.

But this result lay in the future. During Laurier's term of office the future of Canada seemed unbounded. The success of Sifton's immigration policy, the growth of business behind the protective tariff, and the massive capital investment represented by the railway schemes, brought prosperity to all Canada. With prosperity came a new, glowing optimism about the prospects of the country. This confidence was well summed up by Laurier's famous remark: "The nineteenth century was the century of the United States, the twentieth century will be the century of Canada."

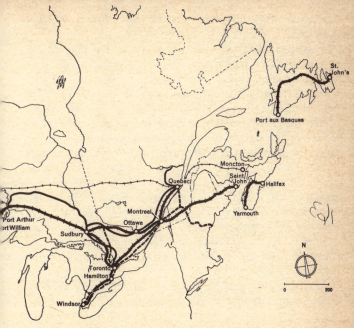

2. TRADE AND INDUSTRY

Laurier's optimism about Canada's future was, at least in
part, based on solid achievements. The growth of population, of primary importance to the rapid development of the
country, was remarkable. In the years between 1891 and
the outbreak of the First World War, the number of Canadians grew from four million eight hundred thousand to
nearly eight million. Production and trade also increased
substantially. In 1891 exports of Canadian wheat amounted
to about two million bushels a year; within twenty-five
years this figure had risen to over one hundred and fifty
million bushels. In the same period the export trade as a
whole rose in value from eighty-eight million dollars to
seven hundred and forty-one million dollars, while the value

of manufactured products showed more than a fourfold increase.

Important factors in this growth were the opening up of new areas of wealth and the diversification of the economy. The most spectacular development was in the northern Yukon Territory, where the discovery of the Klondike gold field brought a vast and colourful influx of fortune seekers in the years 1898-1903. But elsewhere there were more stable and substantial economic advances. In northern Ontario, the discovery of gold, silver, copper and nickel produced a mining boom. Similar developments were taking place in the interior of British Columbia. In addition, British Columbia, Ontario and Quebec were rapidly increasing their production of timber and wood pulp. To meet the needs of these new primary industries, as well as to add comfort to everyday living, the hydro-electric resources of Canada's great rivers were gradually being harnessed for use. The establishment of the Ontario Hydro-Electric Power Commission was only one example of the exploitation of natural resources for the public's benefit.

3. THE PROBLEM OF EXPANSION

The rapid growth brought problems in its wake. Unregulated business expansion brought about large concentrations of wealth and power which did not always place the public interest before private gain. The development of large corporations and monopolies, which was a distinctive feature of the business development of the United States during the last decades of the nineteenth century, was duplicated on a smaller scale in Canada. Between 1909 and 1911, one hundred and ninety-six firms were combined into forty-one corporations. Since 1889 there had been laws in Canada prohibiting monopolies which restrained free competition, but they had rarely been applied. Even the new Combines Investigation Act which the Liberals enacted in 1910 proved too weak to prevent the growth of monopoly. Apparently few people were worried about the dangers in this situation that were pointed out by a young Conservative Member of Parliament from Manitoba in 1911. This young man, Arthur Meighen, remarked: "At present our great industries are coming together, and more and more we are being brought industrially under the power of mergers and combines. If matters go on as they are, absolutely unhindered, absolutely uncontrolled, the powers of the corporations will be more absolute, more despotic than will be the powers of Parliament itself."

Most seriously affected by the growth of big business was the urban working class which turned increasingly to trade unions to protect their interests. The first labour unions in Canada dated back to the mid-nineteenth century, but these had been chiefly organizations of skilled craftsmen like printers and typographers. In 1885 the Knights of Labour spread into Canada from the United States, and for a few years succeeded in organizing unskilled workers. But the hard times of the 1890's made the extension of unionism difficult because labour was cheap and readily available. Nevertheless, the central organ of Canadian unionism, the Trades and Labour Congress of Canada, which had been established in 1886, grew in strength and laid the foundations for a great expansion of labour organization after the turn of the century.

In 1901 there were only 1,078 union locals in the country, but within ten years the number had nearly doubled and membership exceeded 175,000. For the most part the union leaders worked quietly to increase membership and win the right of collective bargaining, often against the determined opposition of employers. But strikes did occur and these were sometimes long, often bitterly fought, and usually won by the employers. Working-class leaders concluded from their repeated defeats that only direct political action could win the workers their just share of the nation's wealth. But political action was very slow in developing, for in the prosperous years before the First World War most wage earners were satisfied to give their support to one of the existing parties. Conscious of the growing strength of labour, the Liberals established a Department of Labour in 1900, and in 1907 provided for arbitration of disputes under the Industrial Disputes Investigation Act. These were small concessions which indicated that labour was not yet well enough organized to make its voice effectively heard at Ottawa.

The farming community was more vocal, effective, and better organized, and its demands won sympathetic attention from the Laurier government. In the early years of the century the chief demand of the farming community was for cheap transportation. This demand was at least partially met by the construction of new railways and lower freight rates under the Crow's Nest Pass agreement of 1897. In return for government assistance to aid in the construction of a railroad through the Crow's Nest Pass, the Canadian Pacific Railway agreed to reduce its freight rates on agricultural products and machinery carried for farmers. The farmers also believed that a railway to Hudson Bay would provide cheaper transport and further reduce freight rates. After much controversy, Laurier agreed to begin the project in 1910, though it was not until 1931 that the Hudson Bay Railway was finally finished.

The farmers' sharpest criticisms, even in these prosperous years, were directed against the protective tariff. The tariff, the farmer maintained, raised the cost of the manufactured goods he had to buy; his grain, on the other hand, was sold on the free international market and faced fierce competition. The tariff served to fatten the eastern industrialist, but swallowed the farmers' profits. It also encouraged the growth of cities which attracted farmers' sons, destroyed the family farm, and undermined the rural community. By 1910, Grain Growers' Associations, Farmers' Unions, and farmers' newspapers like the *Grain Growers' Guide* were all loudly demanding a downward revision of the tariff. In the summer of 1910 Laurier made his first tour of the West and heard farmers everywhere clamouring for tariff reductions, and in December a delegation of eight hundred farmers converged on Ottawa from the West and Ontario.

One of the main charges against the Canadian protective tariff was that it gave special privileges to the business interests at the expense of consumers and farmers who were forced to pay higher prices for the necessities of life. The Canadian government, so the proponents of tariff reductions maintained, was controlled by the business interests. A resolution passed by the United Farmers of Alberta in 1910 declared: "Having suffered for so many years under the bondage of a protective tariff which has been maintained by the Government and is but the levying of a tribute upon the people . . . and as in its practical operation the present Canadian tariff works unfairly in favour of the manufacturing industries and to the prejudice of the agricultural industries, we therefore ask for a general move towards freer trade."

The leaders of this "march on Ottawa" demanded that the government negotiate a reciprocity treaty with the United States and increase the British preference. Their petition concluded: "Believing that the greatest misfortune that can befall any country is to have its people huddled together in great centres of population, and that the bearing of the present customs tariff has the tendency to encourage that condition and realizing also that the constant movement of our people away from the farms, the greatest problem that presents itself to the Canadian people today is the problem of retaining our people on the soil, we come doubly assured of the justice of our petition."

The Canadian farmers' demand for freer trade coincided with a renewal of interest in the subject by President Taft of the United States. Early in 1911 Canada and the United States concluded an agreement which provided for a free exchange of a wide range of natural products like grain and raw materials and lowered rates on some manufactured products. The reciprocity agreement won the immediate approval of the farmers, but when the Liberals appealed to the country to support the agreement in the election of 1911, Laurier discovered, too late, that powerful business interests were completely opposed to any lessening of their tariff protection against their American competitors. In Toronto, eighteen influential Liberal businessmen led by Laurier's former colleague, Clifford Sifton, denounced reciprocity. Their number included the President of the Canadian Bank of Commerce, the Vice-President of the Canadian Northern Railway, department store presidents, food manufacturers, insurance company directors and others. The treaty, they claimed, would destroy the Canadian economy which had developed on an east-west axis, and lead eventually to Canadian absorption into the United States. After the Liberal defeat, one westerner wrote: "The moment he [Laurier] showed signs of putting real Liberal doctrine into effect, the interests combined and crushed him." In their attack on reciprocity, however, the industrial and financial community found powerful allies among those Canadians who differed with Laurier's Imperial policy.

12 CANADA, THE EMPIRE AND THE UNITED STATES

THE similarities between the domestic policies of Sir John A. Macdonald and Wilfrid Laurier showed that both men were guided by a desire to expand, develop and unite the nation. When their policies differed, the differences were in approach, and in the times in which they governed, rather than in the goals they hoped to attain. The same is true of their attitudes to Canada's relations with the outside world, for both Macdonald and Laurier were nationalists who wanted their country to develop as a strong self-governing nation within the framework of the British Empire.

1. CANADA AND NATIONALISM

Both men realized that a small nation like Canada needed outside support if it were to preserve its independence. Without such assistance, Canada would always be in danger of slipping into the control of the United States. Laurier expressed this fear in 1903: "I have often regretted . . . that we are living beside a great neighbour whose people I believe . . . are very grasping in their national actions, and who are determined on every occasion to get the best in any agreement which they make." Since Canada had developed out of a British colony, it was natural that outside assistance, whether military or financial, should come from Great Britain. Nevertheless, neither Macdonald nor Laurier allowed the British connection to limit the growth of Canadian powers of self-government. Since their years in office witnessed different types of external problems, some of the methods the two men used were different. But their aims remained the same: the development of a self-governing nation.

Macdonald had looked upon the United States as the

most serious threat to Canada's national existence. For him, Great Britain was a counterweight against the United States. He talked often of the need for a "permanent alliance" between Canada and Great Britain, a phrase which suggested some form of equality between Canada and the mother country. In 1880 he had created the office of Canadian High Commissioner to Great Britain, because he believed that Canada "had ceased to occupy the position of an ordinary possession of the Crown." The appointment of a High Commissioner implied a diplomatic status greater than that of a mere colony. While Canada had no direct diplomatic relations with foreign countries, Macdonald did secure for Canada the right to negotiate commercial treaties. Macdonald did not regard the Empire as a closely integrated organization that should have common trading policies or automatic mutual military obligations. His National Policy turned upon an independent tariff policy made in Canada for the benefit of Canadians. The Conservatives also guarded jealously Canada's right to make its own decisions in military affairs. In 1885 a suggestion that Canada be asked to give military aid to help the British Prime Minister Gladstone's government in a quarrel in the Sudan, received a sharp reply. "Why should we waste our men and our money in this wretched business?" Macdonald asked. "Our men and our money would be sacrificed to get Gladstone & Co. out of the hole they have plunged themselves into by their own imbecility." On the whole, however, external and Imperial affairs did not cause the Conservatives much difficulty during their years in office.

2. LAURIER AND THE NEW IMPERIALISM

Laurier faced more difficult problems, but his solutions followed the lines that Macdonald had already laid down. Laurier came to office when the great powers of Europe and the United States were competing with one another for new empires and new sources of power. After nearly a century of industrial supremacy and "splendid isolation"

Britain realized by the 1890's that the rapidly growing military and economic power of Germany and the United States threatened her position. Her Empire, long regarded with indifference, suddenly became a possible source of strength. The chief British advocate of Imperial consolidation and unity was Joseph Chamberlain who became Britain's Colonial Secretary in 1895. Chamberlain belonged to a new school of British politicians who looked upon the Empire as a valuable asset. With fanatical single-mindedness Chamberlain tried to bind the Empire into a military, economic and political federation.

Although some Canadians sympathized with Chamberlain's schemes for Imperial federation, the majority, and especially the French Canadians, opposed every plan that would limit Canada's freedom of action or increase her military obligations. As a French-Canadian Prime Minister, Laurier was caught between the powerful Imperial sentiments of English-speaking Canada, especially Ontario, and the vigorous opposition of Quebec to active participation in Imperial affairs. Thus he found it necessary to follow a cautious middle course which he hoped would satisfy a majority in both cultural groups. "I am neither an Imperialist nor an anti-Imperialist but a Canadian first, last and always." This middle course of compromise was neither easy nor heroic, but Laurier knew it was necessary. He wrote to a disgruntled supporter: "Our existence as a nation is the most anomalous that has yet existed. We are British subjects but we are an autonomous nation; we are divided into provinces, we are divided into races, and out of these confused elements the man at the head of affairs has to sail the ship onwards, and to do this safely, it is not always the ideal policy from the point of view of pure idealism which ought to prevail, but the policy which can appeal on the whole to all sections of the community."

The year after he became Prime Minister, Laurier was invited to attend an Imperial Conference in London which was to be part of the celebration of Queen Victoria's Diamond Jubilee. Ten years earlier at the Queen's Golden

A not too unfair view of Laurier's performance at the Imperial Conferences

Jubilee there had been an informal meeting of colonial leaders, but in 1897 these discussions were put on a formal basis. Joseph Chamberlain hoped to use this festive occasion to promote Imperial solidarity and to encourage the first step toward Imperial federation. The visiting statesmen were lavishly entertained; as Laurier wrote: "I am not sure whether the British Empire needs a new constitution, but I am certain that every Jubilee guest will need one." Chamberlain's plan of persuasion also included granting Laurier a knighthood, which the French-Canadian Prime Minister accepted with reluctance. But he refused to accept Chamberlain's proposal for the establishment of a permanent Imperial Council on the grounds that such an institution might limit Canada's powers of self-government. "Colonies are born to become nations," he told a British audience. "Canada is a nation. Canada is free, and freedom is nationality. Canada is practically independent; in a few years the earth will be encircled by a series of independent nations, recognizing, however, the suzerainty of England. The first place in our hearts is filled by Canada." Moreover, Laurier asked, how could Canada's devotion to the Empire be questioned when it had granted Britain a trade preference under the Fielding tariff of 1897? Imperial preference was the key to Laurier's attitude to the Empire; commitments must be voluntary, and not imposed by any outside body, whether it be the British government or an Imperial parliament in which Canada might be represented.

While Laurier escaped from the Imperial Conference of 1897 without accepting any new obligations, the Boer War, which broke out two years later, posed a more difficult problem, for it aroused the Imperial emotions of English-speaking Canadians, particularly in Ontario. Chamberlain tried to take advantage of this sentiment to promote his goal of Imperial unity. He suggested through Lord Minto, the Governor-General of Canada, that Canadian troops might be sent to fight in South Africa. While Laurier found it easy enough to resist the Imperial authorities, he found it impossible to withstand the pressure which built up in English-speaking Canada to send a Canadian contingent to South Africa. Yet while English-speaking Canada favoured sending troops to aid the Imperial cause, French Canadians were adamantly opposed.

As usual, Laurier attempted to find a compromise that would save the country from a division along cultural lines. He agreed to equip and transport one thousand volunteers to South Africa, where Britain would then assume full responsibility for them. But this action was not to be regarded as a precedent for a Canadian contribution to every

Our Honourary Colonel in Peace ; Leading the Colonial Contingent in the Jubilee Procession.

Hugh Graham, owner of the Montreal Star, led the movement to force the Laurier government to send troops to South Africa. This version of Laurier's policy was used to inflame public opinion—successfully, as it turned out.

British war. "Whilst I cannot admit that Canada should take part in all the wars of Great Britain," Laurier explained, "neither am I prepared to say that she should not

Honourary Colonel in War: Leading the Colonial Contingent in the Transvaal Trouble.

take part in any war at all. I claim for Canada this, that in future she shall be at liberty to act or not act, to interfere or not interfere, to do just as she pleases." In 1899 the government sent a second contingent of Canadian troops to South Africa, which, coupled with private enlistments in the British army, brought to seven thousand the number of Canadians who served in the Boer War.

Laurier's compromise was not completely successful in preventing conflict between Ontario and Quebec. In Ontario, Conservatives denounced him as an enemy of the Empire; in Quebec, some French Canadians criticized him as an Imperialist. One of Laurier's young supporters, Henri Bourassa, resigned his seat in Parliament in protest against Laurier's action and was triumphantly re-elected as an Independent by his constituents. Bourassa was a brilliant young French-Canadian politician who was sometimes regarded as Laurier's successor. But, as his resignation in 1899 indicated, Bourassa was not a party man. Consistently placing principle above party, he found it impossible to submit to the inevitable compromises that democratic politics demand. Like his great-grandfather, Louis Joseph Papineau, Bourassa was a staunch defender of French-Canadian rights. Yet he was also a Canadian nationalist who insisted that Canada should acquire full powers of self-government and remain aloof from Imperial wars unless her own interests were directly involved. After his protest against Canadian participation in the Boer War, he gradually became one of Laurier's sharpest critics. In 1907 Laurier wrote: "No one recognizes Bourassa's talents better than I do. But he has one capital defect: he does not know how to keep within bounds." However, in 1899 Bourassa's popularity in Quebec was a warning to Laurier against close involvement in Imperial affairs.

The election of 1900 emphasized that Laurier's compromise during the crisis over the Boer War had not entirely satisfied Ontario either, for the Liberals lost eight seats in that province. But most moderate Canadians, British and French, approved Laurier's compromise. At an Imperial Conference in 1902 he again refused to commit Canada to schemes that he feared would involve permanent military obligations and unified political direction of the Empire. Faced with the Canadian Prime Minister's persistent refusal to support any plan for Imperial consolidation, one frustrated Imperialist remarked that Laurier should change his name from Sir Wilfrid to "Sir Wont'frid."

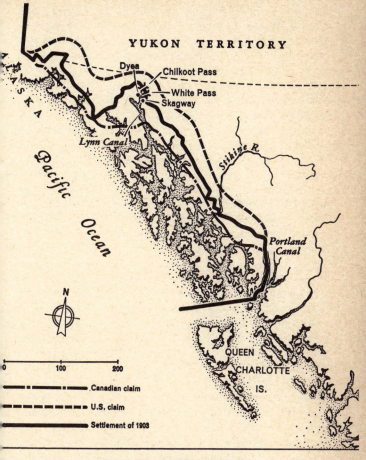

THE ALASKA BOUNDARY DISPUTE

3. THE BIG STICK

No sooner did the pressure for Imperial commitments temporarily relax than Laurier's government faced serious difficulties with the United States over the Alaska boundary. The Yukon Gold Rush in 1898 brought the long-standing dispute to a head, for both Canada and the United States wanted control of the Lynn Canal, which gave the best access to the Yukon. Canada wanted the matter to be submitted to a board of arbitration composed of impartial outsiders. But the United States refused to accept this proposal, and Canada reluctantly agreed to the American suggestion of a judicial tribunal composed of three jurists appointed by each side.

In 1903 the tribunal was established, and from the outset it was clear that it would divide along national lines. Even before it met, President Theodore Roosevelt bluntly declared that he would reject any decision that did not accept all the American claims and he brazenly appointed three men whose reliability was greater than their impartiality. Canada appointed two members to the tribunal and Britain selected the third, all "impartial jurists of the highest repute" as the agreement had demanded.

The two Canadian delegates were caught between the determined Americans and the unfortunate Englishman who was anxious both to preserve friendly Anglo-American relations and to see the boundary properly defined. As it turned out, the Americans had the sounder case, and, with the British member supporting it, the tribunal rejected Canada's arguments and granted almost all of the American claims.

Announcement of the tribunal's decision produced violent protests in Canada directed primarily against the British delegate who was charged with sacrificing Canada in Britain's interests. In the heat of the debate Laurier even suggested that the time had arrived for Canada to assume full control over her foreign affairs. "The difficulty, as I conceive it to be," he stated, "is that so long as Canada remains a dependency of the British Crown the present powers that we have are not sufficient for the maintenance of our rights." But once Canadian tempers had cooled, the suggestion was forgotten. Indeed, the Alaska affair seemed once more to underline the necessity of maintaining the British connection for fear that, without it, "Theodore Roosevelt's "big stick" might be used more often. Perhaps the most lasting result of the Alaska dispute was the hardening of anti-American sentiment in Canada, a sentiment which was to play an important part in Laurier's downfall in 1911.

4. IMPERIAL DEFENCE AND RECIPROCITY

Both the Boer War and the Alaska boundary dispute had shown Canada that the role of a young country in a world of great powers is a difficult one. As the powers of Europe moved along the road to the First World War in 1914, Canada found herself involved, sometimes willingly and sometimes unwillingly.

Laurier's personal inclinations were to remain outside what he once called "the vortex of European militarism," even though he knew that Canada derived benefits from her membership in the Empire and that if a serious crisis arose she would have to help in its defence. Naturally some English-speaking Canadians felt that Canada should commit herself wholeheartedly to policies of Imperial defence, while other Canadians, especially but not only, French Canadians, felt that Laurier was not firm enough in his opposition to Imperial commitments. This division of Canadian opinion was both a strength and a weakness for Laurier. If he could keep the extremists separated and preserve his hold on the moderates, his leadership would remain unchallenged. But if issues were to arise which united the extremists and shattered the confidence of the moderates in his government, Laurier's days would be numbered.

As competition between Britain and Germany increased in the years following 1902, Britain began to turn more often to the Dominions for assistance in the defence of the Empire. This policy seemed reasonable to the British for the colonies benefited both economically and militarily from membership in the Empire. Surely, it was argued, the British taxpayer should not have to bear the entire burden of Imperial defence. Many Canadians felt, however, that they could contribute best to the strength of the Empire by developing their own country and its defences. Since Laurier shared this view, he refused to make any direct military contribution to Imperial defence in peacetime. Moreover, although Canadian military plans and practices were designed to conform with Imperial needs, Laurier's policy was to place Canadian military services completely under Canadian command, and in 1904 the British commander of the Canadian militia was replaced by a Canadian.

The most controversial issue of Imperial defence arose over naval policy. As the naval competition between Britain and Germany intensified in 1909, pressure mounted both in Britain and in Canada for the establishment of a Canadian navy. In keeping with his policy of maintaining Canadian control over Canadian affairs, Laurier decided in 1910 to establish a small navy owned, manned and directed by Canada. At first the policy seemed to win unanimous approval, but suddenly serious opposition emerged. In English-speaking Canada the Conservatives cried that Laurier's plan would merely provide a "tin pot navy," and that the best way of assisting the Empire would be a direct financial contribution to the British navy. In Quebec, a group of French-Canadian nationalists led by Henri Bourassa opposed the establishment of any navy at all, claiming that having a navy would cause Canada to be dragged into every Imperial war. These two extremes united in opposition to Laurier's naval policy. But after a long battle against the Conservative opposition, the Naval Bill was finally made law.

The controversy over the Naval Bill joined the wrangle over reciprocity as the major issues in the 1911 election. Cloaking their economic interests in patriotic fervour, opponents of reciprocity charged that it was a sell-out to the United States and, like the naval policy, ample proof that the Liberals with their French-Canadian leader were betraying Canadian and Imperial interests. In Quebec, Henri Bourassa, supported by the Conservatives, led the campaign against Laurier. In his newspaper, *Le Devoir,* Bourassa condemned the Liberal naval policy as a victory for Imperialism: "It is time for the people of the province of Quebec to prove to M. Laurier that if they admired him

UNCLE SAM—"I CAN ALMOST HEAR THEM SINGING THE STAR SPANGLED BANNER' IN OTTAWA. BE GOSH."

A Conservative cartoon during the 1911 election

when he served the interests of the country well, today he has prevaricated, today he has duped us." In English-speaking Canada, on the other hand, the Conservatives maintained that Laurier's policy was not Imperialistic enough. They argued that the Liberal naval policy was a threat to the unity of the Empire, while reciprocity would break the Imperial connection by pushing Canada into the arms of the United States. Conservative orators made effective use of the indiscretions of some United States politicians, including a letter written by President Taft which noted that "the amount of Canadian products we would take would produce a current of business between Western Canada and the United States that *would make Canada only an adjunct of the United States. . . .* I see this argument made against Reciprocity in Canada, and I think it is a good one." The Liberals replied that rather than being a danger to Canada, reciprocity would make her stronger economically, and therefore more independent politically. But after fifteen years in office, the Liberals had lost their vigour, and were constantly kept on the defensive by the office-hungry Conservatives.

When the votes were counted on September 21, 1911, Robert Borden's strange coalition of Quebec nationalists and English-Canadian Conservatives had triumphed. Only in the Maritimes and the prairie provinces had reciprocity won the day. Defeated and despondent, Laurier summed up his position:

> I am branded in Quebec as a traitor to the French, and in Ontario as a traitor to the English. In Quebec I am branded as a Jingo, and in Ontario as a Separatist. In Quebec I am attacked as an Imperialist, and in Ontario as an anti-Imperialist. I am neither, I am a Canadian.

His policy had been one of moderation, an attempt to preserve unity by leading both his party and the nation along a middle course between the extremes. For fifteen years he and the Liberals had succeeded. Now it was Robert Borden's turn to struggle with the difficulties of governing a small power in the face of an increasingly critical international situation. The union of extremes which had made his victory possible now made more difficult the formulation of policy.

5. THE COMING OF WAR

Robert Laird Borden was a Nova Scotian, who in 1901 had succeeded Sir Charles Tupper as leader of the Conservative party. As a politician, Borden was quite unlike either of his two great predecessors, Macdonald and Laurier. He lacked the warm affability and shrewdness which had made Macdonald the master manager of men; nor did he have Laurier's brilliance as a speaker or his French-Canadian charm. Borden's strengths were those of a hard-working and careful lawyer. Although he was a good debater, his judiciousness made him somewhat uncomfortable in the rough-and-tumble of Canadian politics.

From the beginning Borden faced the problem of keeping English and French Canadians working together—the central problem of all Canadian Prime Ministers. Like Laurier before him, Borden soon discovered that events in the outside world, which by 1914 would sweep Canada into war, created his most difficult problems. Moreover, Borden was only in power a short time when the rosy glow of prosperity which had lasted through the years of Liberal government began to fade. Foreign investment in Canada declined, world wheat prices fell, business activity diminished, and unemployment increased. The war was to halt the recession temporarily, but while it lasted, the recession nourished the seeds of urban and rural discontent which were to flower in the post-war years.

Borden's immediate problem was to find a solution to the naval question. Before winning power, his party had taken the position in English-speaking Canada, that the Imperial emergency was so serious that Canada should make a direct financial contribution to the British navy. But Borden knew that this view was not held by his French-Canadian supporters and he therefore found it necessary to tread very carefully in devising a new naval policy.

In 1912 Borden visited England to discuss the naval question with the Imperial authorities. He returned home convinced that the European crisis was so grave that Canada must take immediate action to help Britain. While in Britain he had argued that if Canada were to contribute to the military strength of the Empire, she should have some control over its foreign policy, but the Imperial authorities had been unresponsive to the idea. On his return, Borden put forward a plan which called for a Canadian contribution of thirty-five million dollars to the British navy for the construction of three dreadnoughts. This, he insisted, was a temporary expedient. No permanent policy could be settled upon until there was further discussion in the matter of giving Canada a voice in the determination of Imperial foreign policy.

"When Great Britain no longer assumes sole responsibility for defence upon the high seas," Borden pointed out, "she can no longer undertake to assume sole responsibility for and sole control of foreign policy which is closely, vitally and constantly associated in that defence in which the Dominions participate."

Despite assurances that the direct contribution was merely a temporary policy to meet an emergency, some of Borden's French-Canadian colleagues refused to support it. Nevertheless, the bill passed the House of Commons, only to be rejected by the Senate, which contained a majority of Liberals. Thus it happened that when Canada entered the war in August 1914 her naval defence was composed of two old cruisers, the *Rainbow* and the *Niobe*. The long, bitter debate on naval policy had ended in a stalemate.

Few Canadians in the years before 1914 had taken much interest in world affairs. Even fewer had any clear understanding of the issues involved in the complicated events which preceded Britain's declaration of war on Germany. Even the government, with its tiny Department of External Affairs, set up in 1909, lacked the detailed information that independent states need in deciding such important issues as declarations of war. But in 1914 Canada was not an independent state and Britain's declaration of war was made on behalf of all the Empire, including Canada. Few Canadians resented this fact. If Britain declared war, most Canadians automatically accepted the view it was a just war. If the Empire was in danger, Canada must help to defend it. Sir Wilfrid Laurier summed up this feeling when he eloquently declared: "When the call goes out, our answer goes at once, and it goes in the classical answer of the British call to duty: 'Ready, Aye Ready'."

13 THE TRIALS OF WAR

"THERE are no longer French Canadians and English Canadians," declared the Montreal *La Patrie,* on August 3, 1914. "Only one race now exists, united by the closest bonds in a common cause." Unfortunately, the sense of common purpose evident at the outbreak of the war gradually weakened. As the national and personal sacrifices exacted by the war steadily increased, some sections of the Canadian community lost their enthusiasm for the war effort. By the summer of 1917 the national unity which had been so apparent in 1914 had almost completely disappeared, and Canada faced her most serious crisis since Confederation.

1. CANADA'S WAR EFFORT

In the autumn of 1914 these storm clouds had not yet appeared on the horizon. The Prime Minister, Sir Robert Borden, immediately summoned parliament and with no dissent the members approved the War Measures Act which gave the government broad powers to deal with wartime emergencies without the usual limitations of parliamentary debate and approval. Without hesitation the government then decided to raise a fighting force of twenty-five thousand men to bolster Canada's tiny regular army. Under the leadership of the energetic, if erratic, Sam Hughes, the Minister of Militia, the troops were recruited and trained. Within two months after declaration of war Canadian soldiers set sail for Britain. Soon afterwards the Canadian Corps was created by the addition of a further two divisions. By 1918 over six hundred thousand Canadians had served in the army, while the navy enlisted nine thousand sailors mainly to man a one hundred and thirty-four vessel fleet responsible

THE WAR IN FRANCE, 1914-1918

for patrolling the Atlantic coast. Canada had no air force
of her own, but Canadians took readily to the air and

contributed twenty-four per cent of the pilots in the Royal Air Force. Among the Canadian aces was "Billy" Bishop, who set a wartime record by destroying seventy-two enemy aircraft.

Canada's major military contribution, however, was in the brutal and costly trench warfare in France. In April 1915, shortly after arriving in France, Canadian troops among others were victims of the first German poison gas attack at Ypres. As the French troops on their flank broke and fled, the Canadians fought bravely and blocked the gap through which the Germans hoped to drive towards the English Channel ports. An American war correspondent wrote of this exploit: "The Canadians made a stand which was to be remembered as one of the heroic episodes of the war." A year later the Allies launched an offensive at the Somme where the Canadians again won honours but at the cost of many casualties. The Germans soon learned the fighting qualities of the Canadian infantry. The British Prime Minister, David Lloyd George, declared: "The Canadians played a part of such distinction that henceforth they were marked out as storm troops; for the remainder of the war they were brought along to head the assault in one great battle after another." Their most famous and costly single engagement was at Vimy Ridge in the spring of 1917, by which time the Canadian Corps was under a Canadian commander, Sir Arthur Currie. The victory at Vimy was followed by a bitter struggle at Hill 70. Then the Canadian forces moved into the bloody inch-by-inch, man-to-man struggle in the mud at Passchendaele. In 1918 the tide began to turn decisively in the Allies' favour. On August 8, at Amiens, the Canadian army, flanked by Australian and French troops, broke through the enemy lines on what was known as the "black day of the German army," and from then until the end of the fighting continued to spearhead Allied attacks.

Although the Canadian army was small in comparison with those of the British and French, and later the United States, it won a great reputation. "Whenever the Germans

found the Canadian Corps coming into the line," Lloy
George wrote, "they prepared for the worst." So respected
was their fighting quality that the Canadians were often
thrown into the bloodiest battles where casualties were the
heaviest. The loss of 60,661 killed was a price higher than
that paid by the much larger United States. With justice
Sir Robert Borden could write at the end of the war: "It
is a glorious history, and I am extremely proud of it."

The military contribution was matched by the economic
efforts at home. Agricultural produce, Canada's leading staple
product before the war, provided a large part of the food
consumed by Allied troops and civilian populations. The
heavy demand for Canadian grain caused the price to rise
so rapidly that the government in 1917 established a Board
of Grain Supervisors to handle grain sales and fix prices.
Lumber, another staple product of long standing, experienced a boom as a result of wartime demand. Even more
important for the future was the stimulus which the war
gave to the development of industry. Canadian metals,
copper, lead, zinc and especially nickel, were greatly in
demand. But instead of shipping these valuable minerals
abroad to be processed, as would have been done before
the war, Canadians developed their own heavy industry to
turn out finished products. New industrial plants were
designed to produce shells and guns which were manufactured under the direction of the Imperial Munitions Board.
The growth of industry during the war, and its retooling
for peaceful purposes afterwards, rapidly transformed Canada from an agricultural into an industrial nation.

The demands of war made it necessary for the federal
government to assume powers that would have been un-
thinkable in times of peace. The greatest difficulty faced by
Sir Robert Borden's government was to find sufficient men
to keep Canada's armed forces supplied with reinforcements;
the next was to finance the war effort. Before the war
Canadian development had always been heavily dependent
on British investment. The war cut this source of funds off.
While the American money market helped to fill the gap,

Imperial Officer:—And you Sir Sam and your Government insisted upon your soldiers using this rifle.

Against the wishes of the British, the Canadian army used the Ross rifle which was manufactured in Canada. The rifle was excellent for target practice, but, as many had predicted, it could not stand up to the wear and tear of the battlefield. At Ypres in 1915 when German infantry followed their gas into the Canadian trenches, the gasping troops desperately smashed the jammed bolts with their boots in an attempt to repel the enemy. As men in the field threw away the Ross and picked up Lee-Enfields from British casualties, Sir Sam Hughes, the Minister of Militia, stubbornly continued to defend the Ross. Finally, in 1916, the British Army Council forced Hughes to withdraw the rifle.

the Canadian government found it necessary to depend more heavily than ever before on domestic financial resources. This meant heavier taxes, and in 1917 the first Federal Income Tax Law was passed. In 1915 the government had turned to the people for loans in the form of Victory Bonds. The more then two billion dollars raised in this fashion during the war was a clear indication of the growing financial strength of the country.

The economic prosperity brought about by the demand for Canadian products was accompanied by rising prices and food shortages, but it was not until 1916 that growing public discontent forced the Borden government to introduce measures for control by the appointment of Cost of Living Commissioners, and later the establishment of a Food Controller and a War Trade Board. None of these agencies was really effective, for the government was reluctant to depart from the traditional Canadian view that government controls and restrictions were an unjustified interference in the lives of citizens. But as a result of wartime inflation, farmers and wage earners suffered severely and stored up discontents that were to explode in strikes and political radicalism after the war.

Although both Liberals and Conservatives had united in 1914 to commit Canada to active participation in the Great War, by 1916 party politics were again growing bitter. The Liberal opposition, anticipating an election in 1916, charged that the Conservative party, riddled with corruption, was collapsing. They pointed to the defeat of Conservative provincial governments in British Columbia, Manitoba and Nova Scotia. In fact, by 1916 the Liberals had great hopes of driving Sir Robert Borden's government from office. By the spring of 1917, however, the question of conscription for overseas service swept all other questions aside, providing the basis for a coalition Union government, and the defeat of the anti-conscriptionist, anti-coalition remains of the Liberal party in the wartime election of 1917.

2. CRISIS 1917

By 1917 Borden faced a manpower problem which was far more serious in its implications than an inflationary economy; for it was a problem whose solution demanded very drastic interference with the rights of private citizens. The army and war industries absorbed Canada's manpower on a scale for which there was no precedent. Until the spring of 1917, when casualties on the battlefields of Europe rose to unexpected heights, the government had managed to find enough reinforcements. But by the middle of 1917 declining enlistment figures and mounting casualties showed that new recruiting methods would have to be adopted if reinforcements were to be found to fill growing gaps at the front. All efforts to stimulate voluntary enlistment failed and the government was compelled to revoke its promise not to introduce compulsory military service. When this decision was announced the always uneasy relations between French- and English-speaking Canadians took a turn for the worse. At the beginning of the war Quebec, like the rest of Canada, supported the Allied cause. Even the nationalist Bourassa stated that it was Canada's duty "to contribute within the bounds of her strength and by means which are proper to herself, to the triumph, and especially to the endurance, of the combined efforts of France and England." But Bourassa and most other French Canadians believed that Canada's contribution to the war should be a voluntary one. No one suggested in 1914 that the conscription of men would be necessary to win the war.

Unfortunately for the country and for the war effort, the revival of the controversial school question in the early years of the war undermined the goodwill and co-operative spirit that had existed in Quebec in 1914. This time the centre of the dispute was in Ontario where a rule known as Regulation 17 confined teaching in the French language to the early grades and appeared to restrict the establishment of new French-language schools. The French Canadians immediately attacked the regulation as an attempt to limit minority rights, and once the argument over language rights had begun the eyes of most people in Quebec turned away from the battlefields of Europe towards the cultural conflict in Canada. Bourassa put the French-Canadian view in its most extreme form when he wrote: "In the name of religion, liberty and faithfulness to the British flag, the French Canadians are enjoined to fight the Prussians of Europe. Shall we let the Prussians of Ontario impose their domination like masters, in the very heart of the Canadian Confederation, under the shelter of the British flag and British institutions?" In the end, the courts found the Ontario language regulations valid, but this did nothing to dispel the French Canadians' belief that an injustice had been done to them, particularly when Manitoba also abolished bilingual schools in 1916.

By 1917, as the Ontario school controversy reached its peak, the need for manpower became critical. English-speaking Canadians pointed to low enlistment figures in Quebec as the cause of the manpower shortage. To some extent the charge was true. The French Canadians as a whole were never as deeply committed to the war as were most English-speaking Canadians. They had no strong emotional tie with either Britain, which had conquered them, or with France, which had deserted them. However, when the enlistment record was carefully examined, it was obvious that the largest number of recruits from English-speaking Canada came from among the most recent British immigrants. Native-born English-speaking Canadians, like French Canadians, were somewhat more reluctant to volunteer for overseas service. Finally, the French Canadians were still largely an agrarian people, and farmers in *both* sections of the country had been slower to join the military services than had urban dwellers.

It was not merely the habits of an established way of life, however, that kept French Canadian enlistments lower than those from English-speaking Canada. The inept handling of recruiting by the Borden government also discouraged French-Canadian volunteers. The government showed little understanding of the language difficulties faced by French-Canadian recruits in training camps commanded by English-speaking officers and was slow to create French-Canadian regiments and to promote French-Canadian officers. Moreover, the appointment of at least one Protestant clergyman as a recruiting officer in Quebec did nothing to soothe the uneasiness of the French Canadians. At the centre of this problem was the Minister of Militia, Sam Hughes. Ever since the bitter debates of the 1890's, Hughes had been in the forefront of the anti-French and anti-Catholic crusade. During the war he suppressed his real opinions, although in an unguarded moment in his home town of Lindsay, Ontario, in 1916 he declared that Quebec "has not done its duty as it should and would if the young manhood of the Province had been taken in hand by the proper people, who have benefited so much from British institutions in days gone by." Such statements did nothing to remove the French-Canadian suspicion that Hughes was a prominent Imperialist, anti-French and anti-Catholic Orangeman.

As complaints and criticism of the French-Canadian contribution became more intemperate in English-speaking Canada, the stubbornness of the French Canadians increased. Prime Minister Borden returned from a visit to the Western Front in the spring of 1917 convinced that a policy of compulsory enlistment would have to be adopted, if Canada's fighting men were to be adequately reinforced. To the French Canadians, conscription was unacceptable. To avoid a disastrous racial division, Borden proposed that Laurier and the Liberals join a coalition government.

Laurier enthusiastically supported the war effort and had many times appealed to his countrymen to volunteer for service. In August 1916, he declared:

> There are many people who say we will not fight for England: will you then fight for France? I speak to you of French origin. If I were young like you and had the same health that I enjoy today, I would join those brave Canadians fighting today for the liberation of French territory. I would not have it said that the French Canadians do less for the liberation of France than the citizens of British origin. For my part I want to fight for England and also for France. For those who do not want to fight either for England or for France I say: will you fight for yourselves?

But Laurier had repeatedly promised that he would oppose conscription. In 1917 he realized that if he joined a coalition government whose purpose was to impose conscription he would give control of Quebec to Bourassa and the

Nationalists. Moreover, he believed that conscription would split the country and so harm the war effort.

Despite Laurier's refusal to join a coalition, Borden and many Liberal leaders in English-speaking Canada were determined to form a union government that would enforce conscription. The temper of English-speaking Canada had been roused, and much of the anger was directed against Quebec. One Liberal newspaper announced:

> The authentic voice of Quebec today is that of Bourassa. He has been stating his views with perfect frankness. He says Quebec is against the war. Laurier is at best a moderating, not a controlling power in Quebec. If he came into a coalition government he would leave Quebec behind him. This is why the problem now before the people of Canada must be solved, if there is any solution, without the assistance of Laurier or Quebec.

Under the leadership of Sir Clifford Sifton, N. W. Rowell, the Liberal leader in Ontario, and a number of western Liberals, the movement for coalition government gained widespread support in English-speaking Canada. Pushing Laurier aside, these Liberals began negotiations with Borden. Before the negotiations were completed the Conservatives enacted two new electoral laws giving votes to the soldiers overseas and their female relatives at home (women in 1914 had not the right to vote) and disfranchising all immigrants who had come to Canada from enemy countries after 1902. This legislation helped to ensure an electoral victory for supporters of conscription and no doubt helped to bring the negotiations for coalition government to a successful conclusion. In October 1917, Prime Minister Borden announced the formation of a Union government of Conservatives and English-speaking Liberals.

Before conscription was enforced an election was called for December 1917. The campaign was a bitter one. In English-speaking Canada election posters warned that "Laurier is the tool of Bourassa," and that "a vote for Laurier is a vote for the Kaiser." In Quebec, conscription

Women of Canada
Remember Your Sisters in Belgium

THE KAISER and his war lords have repeatedly said: "We must leave nothing to the women in the countries we vanquish but their eyes to weep with."

Yet Laurier and Bourassa say we must QUIT the fight against these inhuman monsters.

Our boys in France are giving their lives to save the women and children of France, Great Britain,—yes, and of Canada—from the same brutal violence with which the Huns violated Belgium.

To hold back the Germans our boys send an urgent call for reinforcements. Union Government is pledged to raise the reinforcements at once, and is actually doing this now under the Military Service Act, 1917. Women of Canada, now is your opportunity to revenge your sisters in Belgium and help your boys in France.

Vote for the Union Government Candidate

When women were enfranchised posters such as these appeared soliciting their votes. The caption under the picture urged women to make good use of the weapon put into their hands and, by supporting the Union government, to defend themselves against the fate of their Belgian sisters.

was denounced in equally vigorous terms. But the result of the election was never in doubt. Laurier and his followers won eighty-two seats, all but twenty of which were in Quebec. The Unionists swept English-speaking Canada, carrying one hundred and fifty constituencies, but won only three in Quebec. Canada was split along cultural lines as never before, and was governed by a cabinet which, for the first time since the achievement of responsible government, included none of the recognized leaders of French Canada.

Following the election, which left Quebec almost completely isolated from the rest of Canada, Mr. J. N. Francoeur, a Liberal member of the Quebec legislature, proposed, more in despair than in anger, a motion which declared, "This Chamber is of the opinion that the Province of Quebec would be disposed to accept breaking of the Confederation pact of 1867 if in the other provinces it is believed that she is an obstacle to the union, progress and development of Canada." The motion never came to a vote but most of the members agreed with the Quebec Premier, Sir Lomer Gouin, who concluded the debate by declaring: "It is to preserve my country's greatness, to cherish in the hearts of our children all their hopes, to hand down to them, in a word, the heritage which we received from our fathers, that we should struggle fearlessly against the passing storm, that we should labour ceaselessly and untiringly to develop and maintain the Canadian Confederation."

Gradually tempers cooled, but it was a long time before French Canadians were willing to forgive English-speaking Canada, and especially the Conservatives, for conscription. The conscription policy raised about 120,000 men, of whom about 47,000 were sent overseas before the war ended. The disruption of national unity was a high price to pay for these reinforcements, but in the spring of 1918 the war was in its most critical phase and neither Borden nor anyone else realized that Germany would collapse in November. Furthermore, like Macdonald and Laurier, Borden was a nationalist. He regarded Canada's war effort not only as an expression of maturing Canadian nationalism, but as an opportunity to advance her national status. If he were ever to convince Great Britain and the world that Canada deserved to be recognized as a nation, he could not allow his country's war effort to slacken.

3. IMPERIAL DEVELOPMENT AND PEACE

In 1914 Canada was automatically at war because Great Britain had declared war. Canada had played no part in pre-war diplomacy, since direction of the foreign policy for the Empire was entirely in the hands of the British government. Yet Canada suffered the consequences of policies which she had played no part in making. Prime Minister Borden and many other Canadians found this situation most unsatisfactory. As the war dragged on the feeling grew stronger that Canada should have a larger measure of influence and control over policies that touched Canadian interests.

Canadian subordination to British control was most evident in military affairs. From the beginning of the war, Borden and Hughes insisted that Canadian soldiers should be kept together as a Canadian army, rather than being divided up and dispersed among British troops. Although a Canadian Corps was formed, it was at first commanded by a British officer, Sir Julian Byng. By 1917 Borden's insistence compelled the British to appoint a Canadian commander, Sir Arthur Currie. But Borden was not content with this small concession. He was anxious to gain some voice in the determination of policy. The British authorities were unwilling even to keep the Canadian government fully informed about military policy, but Borden was a stubborn fighter and did not give up easily. "It can hardly be expected," he warned, "that we should put 400,000 or 500,000 men in the field and willingly accept the position of having no more voice and receiving no more consideration than if we were mere toy automata. Any person cherishing such an expectation harbours an unfortunate and even dangerous delusion." Towards the end of 1916 Borden's complaints won a more sympathetic hearing in London. David Lloyd

George, the new British Prime Minister, saw the justice of these complaints and established the Imperial War Cabinet, a body composed of the chief British ministers and the Prime Ministers of the Dominions. Since the Prime Ministers of the Dominions could only spend a small amount of time in London, this method of consultation was not entirely satisfactory. For the first time, however, Canada had a seat in the inner circle of the policy makers.

Borden hoped that the new status of the Dominions as equal partners in the Empire would receive formal recognition after the war. At the Imperial War Conference of 1917 he introduced a motion known as Resolution IX, which recommended that a conference should be called after the war to draw up a declaration which would recognize the self-government of the Dominions in domestic affairs, and their position as "autonomous nations" with "an adequate voice in foreign policy." Resolution IX expressed Borden's belief that Canada and the other Dominions had reached a position of equality with Britain as members of the Empire.

Sir Robert Borden's objective was not merely to have Canada's status as a nation recognized by Britain. That was only the first step. Equally important was his desire to have nations outside the Empire accept Canada as an independent nation. This aim was made clear in Borden's attitude when it came time to draw up a peace treaty at the end of the war. He believed that since Canada and the other Dominions had made large contributions towards the Allied victory, they should be allowed to participate individually in drawing up the terms of peace. Once more Borden had to overcome British opposition, but in the end each of the Dominions took part in the Peace Conference at Paris in its own right, and as members of the British Empire delegation. Moreover, each Dominion signed the treaty for itself and, again on Borden's insistence, each Dominion parliament ratified the treaty separately. Thus Britain was no longer acting alone in implementing the foreign policy of the Empire. Each Dominion now had a voice in determining the collective policy of the Empire. This was not the same as each Dominion having its own foreign policy, but it was a step beyond the pre-war position when Imperial foreign policy was the exclusive responsibility of Britain.

While Canada had asserted and obtained a right to take part in the peace negotiations, she played a very small part in deciding the precise terms that would be imposed on the defeated powers. Borden's main concern was with the new international organizations, the League of Nations and the International Labour Organization, which were created by the peace treaty. Borden insisted again that the Dominions should be given separate representation in these bodies. This struggle for international recognition of Canada's new status was Borden's greatest battle, for he had to fight the United States and France, both of whom suspected that votes for the British Dominions in these international bodies would be nothing more than additional British votes. The usually mild Borden argued that "the Dominions have maintained their places before the world during the past five years through sacrifices which no nation outside Europe has known" and were entitled to full recognition. The justice of this claim was difficult to deny, and in the end Canada and the other Dominions were accepted as independent members of the League of Nations.

Canadian nationalism had been given a sharp stimulus by the war. When peace returned, the country was no longer ready to accept a position of subordination either within the Empire, or Commonwealth as it was now being called, or in international affairs. Borden's greatest achievement was that through dogged persistence he was able to win for his country a new status in the eyes of the world. At home, however, serious problems awaited the attention of Canada's political leaders at the end of the war. The economic and cultural strains which the war had produced meant that national development would be more difficult than it had ever been before.

14 THE TRIUMPH OF MACKENZIE KING

THE First World War had a powerful impact on every aspect of Canadian life. Not least important was its effect on politics. By 1919 there was no truly national party in the country that could claim support from all sections of the Canadian community. The Union government, which continued in office after the war, was without support among the French Canadians, and was losing ground among Ontario and western farmers who hated its high tariff policy. The Liberal party was strong only in Quebec, because it had opposed conscription in 1917. It had some followers in the Maritimes, and hoped that Liberals who had supported the Union government in 1917 would return to their old party when the war ended. In western Canada and rural Ontario no party held the allegiance of the voters, who opposed the tariff policies of the Unionists and the anti-conscription policy of the Liberals in 1917. With neither of the old parties able to gain a following, the way was clear for a new party, the Progressives, to win the support of Canadian farmers.

1. NEW LEADERS AND A NEW PARTY

Immediately after the war three new political leaders competed for the support of the electorate. Following the death of Sir Wilfrid Laurier in February 1919, representatives of the Liberal party met in Ottawa in August to select a new leader. The chief contenders for the position were two former cabinet ministers: the elderly, experienced W. S. Fielding, and the young, ambitious William Lyon Mackenzie King. Fielding had been one of Laurier's most trusted colleagues, but in 1917 he had broken with Laurier and had supported conscription. King, the grandson of the rebel leader of 1837, had become Canada's first Minister of Labour in 1909, after spending many years studying economics and sociology and working in the civil service. Only forty-five years old in 1919, King knew that he had one distinct advantage over Fielding and the other candidates. As he wrote in his diary: "All the Liberal members of the Union government failed in a moment of crisis, at a time of great need. They left their leader when the popular tide was rising against him." By standing with Sir Wilfrid in the conscription crisis, King had ensured himself of the support of Quebec in his quest for the party leadership. After three ballots, the Ottawa Liberal convention elected Mackenzie King.

Dumpy and undistinguished in appearance, King lacked the personal grace and warmth of Laurier, but he possessed the patience and capacity for compromise that were necessary for a leader whose first task was to mend a party shattered by the conscription issue in 1917. On the surface King was calm, and his manner ponderous, but in times of crisis he could act with deliberation and ruthlessness. Since he remained a bachelor and developed few non-political interests, he devoted his life almost entirely to managing his party and governing the country. His personal life was lonely and marked by a deep devotion to the memory of his mother. He possessed a strong religious conviction which, in later life, included a mystical belief in spiritualism. King never lost the conviction that the hand of destiny guided his actions. On his election to the party leadership he wrote: "My thoughts were of dear mother and father and little Bell all of whom I felt to be very close to me, of grandfather & Sir Wilfrid also. I thought: it is right, it is the call of duty. I have sought nothing, it has come. It has come from God."

By the summer of 1920 the Unionist, or Conservative party as it was again being called, also required a new leader, for Sir Robert Borden had seriously undermined his health during the trying war years and now retired from political life. The new Conservative leader, Arthur Meighen, was

selected, not by a convention, but by the Conservative members of parliament. Like King, Meighen was born in Ontario and the two men had attended the University of Toronto together. But here the similarity ended. While King did post-graduate studies in the United States, Meighen went West to set up a law practice in Portage la Prairie, Manitoba. In 1908 Meighen was elected to parliament where he soon impressed the members with his great abilities as a parliamentary debater. When war broke out he held only a minor post in the government, but rose rapidly to become Borden's chief lieutenant. His quick mind, his sharp tongue and his superb skill in detailed argument won the admiration, though seldom the affection, of many members of parliament. Recognizing his ability and industry, Borden made him responsible for some of the heaviest tasks that the government had to perform. Meighen was the government's chief defender of conscription in 1917, and also the architect of the complex and controversial legislation authorizing the nationalization of the nearly bankrupt Grand Trunk Railway in 1919.

Meighen was straightforward, direct and sometimes arrogant. He enjoyed debate and argument, but did not work easily with men whose minds moved more slowly than his. He was a formidable foe for Mackenzie King, and attacked the Liberal leader with characteristic sarcasm in a speech in 1919:

> I have one suggestion to offer to the fair rose of expectancy of His Majesty's loyal Opposition; it is that when we have a concrete subject before the House for debate he would be good enough to offer some remarks which really bear upon the issue and leave out of consideration, if he possibly can, these old hackneyed phrases "democracy," "autocracy of executives"—all of the rest of it which have no more relevancy to the discussion than were he to discuss the merits of the government of Japan.

It was no wonder that King feared and even hated Meighen! But the new Conservative leader suffered from two serious handicaps: in Quebec his name was associated with the conscription policy, while in the West his high tariff views made him unpopular.

The most popular politician in the West at this time was Thomas A. Crerar, the leader of the new Progressive party that sprang up among the farmers immediately after the war. Crerar was a natural leader for the farmers' political movement. He had business experience gained as the president of a farmer-owned grain-buying organization, and political experience as a member of the wartime coalition government. His popularity among the farmers increased greatly when he resigned from the Union government in 1919 in protest against the continuation of a high tariff. In January 1920, when the National Progressive party was launched, Crerar's political experience as well as his knowledge of western problems made him the obvious choice as leader.

The appearance of Crerar and the Progressive movement on the Canadian political scene was one of many signs that the country was in a state of economic dislocation and social discontent in the years immediately after the war. It was this disturbed situation which made the three-cornered struggle for power among King, Meighen and Crerar a vigorous and exciting one.

2. POST-WAR PROTEST MOVEMENTS

The earliest and most dramatic signs of discontent came from the urban working class. Conscription had never been popular among this group, for they felt that wealth as well as manpower should have been conscripted. There seemed to be rank injustice in a system that sent a worker to the front while his employer fattened on lucrative war contracts. The attack on these "war profiteers" gave an edge to the growing tension between capital and labour. Moreover, the cost of living had raced far ahead of wages, despite the government's attempts to control prices. Trade union membership doubled between 1914 and 1918 and once the war ended union leaders attempted to gain the right of collective bargaining. The end of the war also brought servicemen home to find jobs, at a time when the end of wartime demands caused a business recession, wage cuts, and unemployment. In Canada, as in the United States, the year 1919 was marked by a wave of fierce strikes and new and alarming talk of socialism, the formation of One Big Union of all workingmen, and a general strike to reveal its power.

The main centre of urban discontent in Canada was Winnipeg. In May 1919 the Winnipeg Trades and Labour Council called a general strike to display sympathy and solidarity with the members of the metals trades union who had been denied the right to bargain collectively by their employers. The strikers' success in paralyzing the economic life of the city brought a strong reaction from businessmen and professional people. By the end of May the latter were describing the strike as "a serious attempt to overturn British institutions in this western country and to supplant them with the Russian Bolshevik system of Soviet rule." It

Headlines from the strikers' newspaper provide a graphic outline of the course of the Winnipeg General Strike.

should be recalled that the Russian Revolution had occurred only two years earlier. Sympathetic strikes broke out across Canada, and, as hysteria mounted in the business community, provincial and federal authorities intervened. On June 17 the Royal Canadian Mounted Police arrested key men among the strikers on very slim evidence. Among those arrested was James Shaver Woodsworth, a former Methodist minister who, as temporary editor of the *Western Labour News,* had quoted a Biblical text which the authorities considered subversive. On June 21, "Bloody Saturday," armed policemen broke up a peaceful parade and troops dispatched by the federal government guarded the street corners.

By such tactics, the back of the strike was broken. Many strikers had been reduced to near starvation. When the Manitoba government promised to appoint a Royal Commission to investigate labour grievances, the strike was called off. The Royal Commission later reported that the strike had not been called with revolutionary intentions, however radically some of the strikers had talked, but had sought only the right to collective bargaining and an improvement in what the Commission agreed were deplorable working conditions.

While labour's immediate grievances disappeared with the return of prosperity, later in the 'twenties, the bitterness engendered by the strike had lasting effects. Labour leaders were convinced that direct political action was necessary to protect their interests. Woodsworth was elected to the House of Commons as a Labour member soon after his release from jail, while four others were elected to the Manitoba legislature as Labour spokesmen.

Unrest among the farmers in Ontario and on the prairies erupted in a less violent fashion, but it was no less startling, and brought more immediate results. The Union government had broken its promise not to conscript farmers' sons, and this, together with wartime profiteering and corruption, high prices, indifferent incomes, and rural depopulation, shattered their confidence in both the economic order and the traditional political parties. J. J. Morrison, an Ontario farm leader, wrote in 1919:

> We have passed through an orgy of corruption that is a disgrace to true Canadians and was only made possible by the utter failure of machine party politics to defend the rights of the people. I have followed partisan politics long enough and am disgusted. Something better must be found.

To many farmers the only solution to the uncertain economic situation was a farmers' political party. As one agrarian leader said: "Go into politics, or go out of farming." Ever since Confederation, the farmers believed, the country had been governed by men who supported economic and tariff policies which benefited only the industrial East. Their basic grievance was the tariff which, by protecting industry, forced the farmers to pay high prices for farm machinery and other essential manufactured goods. Yet their agricultural products had to be sold on a free and competitive international market. Since both the Liberals and the Conservatives supported a high tariff policy, the farmers concluded that they would have to form their own political party. In 1916 the Canadian Council of Agriculture issued a programme, The *New* National Policy, which by 1919 was accepted as a statement of aims for an agrarian political movement. Its main demand was for a lower tariff, but it also advocated political reforms such as the initiative, referendum and recall, all demands for direct democracy similar to those advocated earlier by the American farmers. The New National Policy also demanded public ownership of railways and lower freight rates. The platform was in effect a vigorous denunciation of the old National Policy, which encouraged tariff-protected industries, restricted railway competition, and nurtured monopolies and combines, and of the political parties that supported it. The *Winnipeg Free Press* explained the farmers' platform in this way: "It is the common acceptance of an economic policy which makes the encouragement of the basic industries of Canada—agricultural, mining, forestry, fishing—the first charge upon the interest and sympathy of the state."

By 1919 the farming community was organized and optimistic, as their battle song "The Day of Right" (sung to the tune of "The Battle Hymn of the Republic") suggests:

> The farmers of the prairie lands are massing in their
>   might,
> Exulting in a Principle, a Cause for which they fight,
> The sacred cause of Justice, the establishment of Right,
> And Equal Rights to all.

Their confidence was justified. In 1919 the United Farmers of Ontario swept into power in the most industrialized province in Canada. Two years later the United Farmers of Alberta began a fourteen-year tenure of office, while the farmers of Manitoba were catapulted into office in 1922. Federally, these provincial farmers' movements gave vigorous support to T. A. Crerar and the National Progressive party.

These events provide the background for the exciting

federal election of 1921, in which all women of voting age were permitted to vote for the first time as a result of the Election Act of 1918. Prime Minister Meighen asked the electors to approve not only the government's wartime record but also the nationalization of the Grand Trunk and Canadian Northern railways. This railway policy was based on the report of a commission appointed in 1916 to examine the financial problems of the two railways. Rather than allow the railways to flounder in bankruptcy, the Union government had decided in 1919 to combine the two systems under government ownership. This decision drew criticism both from the businessmen who opposed the principle of government ownership, and from others who believed that the government had paid too large a price for the near-bankrupt railways. As an issue in 1921 the tariff was more important than any other single question because of the farmers' intense interest in it. Meighen believed that Canada could only thrive and grow with the aid of "a tariff system . . . made on a clear, sound, impregnable principle, and that system must not rest on the insecure foundation of arrangements with the United States." Meighen's view was in complete contradiction to the farmers' demand that the tariff should be lowered.

Mackenzie King's viewpoint was not so clear-cut. He argued that it was "time for a change," and criticized the Conservatives' railway policy. On the crucial tariff question, however, his position was vague, for King was unwilling to adopt any policy that would alienate either the low-tariff westerners or the high-tariff eastern industrialists and financiers. Meighen was right when he charged that King's statements on the tariff were "just the circular pomposity of a man who won't say what he means."

Like Meighen, Crerar believed that the tariff was the main issue in the election. "I stand opposed to the principle of protection," he said, "and I trust I ever shall. Our policy rests on this consideration: that the wealth of Canada can best be developed or added to by developing the natural resources of the country."

The result of the 1921 election clearly revealed the divisions within the nation. Mackenzie King's Liberals won the largest number of seats, one hundred and seventeen, nearly half of which were in Quebec. Arthur Meighen's following was reduced to a mere fifty members, thirty-seven of them from Ontario. The surprise was the election of sixty-five Progressives, forty-one from the West and twenty-four from Ontario. Mackenzie King had won a narrow victory in the first round of the three-cornered fight with Meighen and Crerar.

3. KING, THE PROGRESSIVES, AND THE DEFEAT OF MEIGHEN

The new Liberal Prime Minister's natural caution was increased by the narrowness of his majority in the House of Commons. During the four years after the 1921 election his major objective was to win the support of the Progressives, whom he chose to regard as "Liberals in a hurry." "This is a moment for great generosity," he wrote in 1921, "and all the conciliation that is possible towards those who, believing in ideals which are strongly Liberal, have nevertheless been a powerful opposing force in the campaign just concluded. I want, if I can, to have the West feel that I am its friend." To the westerners King offered some slight tariff reductions and attempted to meet their demands for lower freight rates on shipments of western grain. But his main strength was the Progressives' realization that if they defeated King they would return Meighen to office, and with him high tariffs.

Moreover, internal divisions weakened the federal Progressive party. Most members, especially those from Ontario and Manitoba, were moderate in their demands for reform and concentrated almost exclusively on the tariff and freight rates. Many of them looked forward to an alliance with those members of the Liberal party who also favoured a lower tariff. But one wing of the farmers' movement had more radical ideas. The strength of this group lay in Alberta where Henry Wise Wood guided the United Farmers organization. Wood attacked the basic structure of the party system and parliamentary government, for he believed that

Winnipeg Free Press cartoonist Arch Dale comments on the success of King's policy of wooing the Progressives. In 1926 King secured a promise from J. S. Woodsworth and the Progressives that they would support his minority government if he promised to introduce old-age pensions. The promise was kept in 1927.

representation should be on an occupational basis. Within the parliamentary party Wood's followers carried on a running battle with Crerar and the moderates, and denounced every suggestion of co-operation with the Liberals. In 1922 Crerar resigned from the leadership of the Progressive party. His successor, Robert Forke, was another moderate but he lacked Crerar's strength and after Crerar's resignation the Progressive movement began to disintegrate.

By 1925 these internal divisions had weakened the party, while the return of prosperity and higher wheat prices had taken the edge off agrarian discontent. Only twenty-four Progressives, mainly of the radical wing, were returned to parliament in the election of that year. Mackenzie King's conciliatory policy enabled him to capture Progressive seats in the West, but his party suffered heavy losses in Ontario and the Maritimes and won only one hundred and one seats. Meighen and the Conservatives made a comeback in the East and increased their standing to one hundred and seventeen seats to make them the largest party. The stage was set for the last round of the political struggle of the 'twenties. Crerar had withdrawn from the fight, leaving only King and Meighen in the ring.

Although Prime Minister King's government was defeated at the polls in 1925, no party had won a clear majority. King therefore decided to meet parliament rather than resign. Thus began one of the most complicated episodes in Canadian political and constitutional history. King had hoped to carry on government with the support of the twenty-four Progressive members. But early in the parliamentary session of 1926, a committee uncovered evidence of serious corruption in the Customs Department. This revelation made it impossible for the Progressives to continue supporting the Liberals, for it confirmed their worst suspicion of corruption in the two old parties. Before a motion of no confidence could be passed against his government, King asked the Governor-General, Lord Byng, for a dissolution and a new election. Since it was less than a year since an election had been held, and because the Conservatives actually had more seats in parliament than the Liberals, Lord Byng rejected King's advice. King resigned and Byng called upon Arthur Meighen to form a government.

In asking the Conservative leader to form a government, Lord Byng had acted in a completely constitutional manner. But he may have been unwise, for Meighen's prospects of holding office for any length of time were very small since to do so he would have to depend upon the support of the Progressives who had never trusted him. The expected defeat came within four days. Now there was no alternative but to call another election. In the campaign that followed the Liberals charged that Lord Byng's refusal to grant King a dissolution in the first place was unconstitutional, and that Meighen was responsible for the situation, since he had agreed to form a government. "If that is not anarchy and absolutism in government, I should like to know what category political philosophy would assign government carried on under such conditions. I know of nothing in British history comparable to this since the days of Charles the First," Mackenzie King maintained. Moreover, claimed King, the refusal of a British official to obey the advice of his Canadian Prime Minister was an infringement on Canadian autonomy or national status. Arthur Meighen rightly argued that the Governor-General's action was entirely constitutional and had nothing to do with autonomy or status. "It is ridiculous to assume that he [the Governor-General] sought in any way to establish gubernatorial autocracy, or to menace self-government," Meighen stated. Moreover, he added, the Liberals had attempted to create a constitutional issue to cover up the mismanagement and corruption that had been revealed in the Customs Department.

But the Canadian electorate, which suspected that Meighen had been over-anxious for office when he attempted to form a minority government, accepted King's appeal to their nationalism and returned a large Liberal majority in the election of 1926. In this election the Progressives were almost completely wiped out as the West joined the Liberal fold. The election of 1926 marked the triumph of Mackenzie King over his bitter enemy, Arthur Meighen. Though possessed of a sharp mind and brilliant debating skill, Meighen had appeared as a cold and sometimes arrogant politician. The colourless and cautious Mackenzie King proved more to the electorate's liking. In 1927 Meighen resigned from the leadership of the Conservative party, and was replaced by a millionaire lawyer from Calgary, Richard Bedford Bennett.

4. ECONOMIC GROWTH, SOCIAL CHANGE AND DEPRESSION

In the late 1920's Canadian politics resumed a more normal course as the nation's economy expanded and prospered. The rapid development of new staples like gold, nickel, copper, pulpwood and newsprint gave better balance to an economy that had formerly depended so heavily on grain exports. This development altered the pattern of Canadian trade which before the war had been carried on largely with Britain and Europe. The new staples fed the developing Canadian industries and supplied the enormous United States demand for raw materials.

In the post-war decade, pulp and paper mills expanded in northern Ontario, British Columbia, Quebec and New Brunswick. Asbestos from eastern Quebec; copper and nickel from Sudbury and Copper Cliff in Ontario; oil from Alberta's Turner Valley fields; lead, zinc, and copper from Trail in the Kootenay Mountain regions of British Columbia provided new sources of wealth and new areas for employment and settlement. The processing of these metals increased the demand for electrical energy, and several provinces, including Saskatchewan and Manitoba, followed the pattern established in 1905 by Ontario in setting up publicly-owned power commissions.

The prosperity brought by these new economic developments was not evenly distributed across the country. Ontario and Quebec benefited most from the mining developments, with Toronto and Montreal providing the finances necessary for the development of new mineral deposits. The prairies and the Maritimes were less favourably affected by the surge of prosperity. Grain, and especially wheat, remained the great source of western wealth, and competition on the international market was keen. The farmers' political protest movements in the 1920's were in part a reflection of economic problems which resulted from the gradual shift in the Canadian economy from agriculture to industry, from the country to the city. In their battle for lower tariffs and lower freight rates, the farmers were attempting to save the agricultural way of life that was being displaced by the growth of cities and industry.

The new prosperity almost completely by-passed the Maritime provinces, which had never fully recovered from the late nineteenth-century decline in their shipbuilding industry. Like the farmers, the Maritimers also felt that Canada's tariff structure was designed primarily to benefit people living in the central provinces. While increased federal subsidies to the Maritime provinces and assistance to the coal industry in Nova Scotia eased economic difficulties temporarily, the Atlantic provinces remained economically poorer than the other parts of the country.

The years of prosperity came to an abrupt end in the autumn of 1929, with a great crash, when the world-wide economic depression began. In Canada the impact of the depression was severe. Not only were there weak spots in the economy, especially in the important agricultural sector, but Canada's prosperity depended heavily upon foreign trade. The impoverishment of international markets as the world succumbed to the depression meant economic disaster for Canada.

Though the depression affected the whole country, it was most serious in those areas that had gained least in the economic boom of the late 1920's. Such regions as the western provinces were also those most heavily dependent upon declining world markets. Although the same was true of some of the newly opened mining areas, the hardships were particularly severe in western Canada where the economic depression was aggravated by natural disaster. In the 1930's few prairie crops escaped the ravages of drought or grasshoppers, and many farmers saw their only source of income disappear under the destructive attacks of one or the other or both. In Saskatchewan the average personal income fell from four hundred and seventy-eight dollars to one hundred and thirty-five dollars, and Alberta and Manitoba were little better off.

The impact of the depression and the collapse of the prairie farm economy was soon felt throughout the Dominion. In eastern Canada, factories began to close their doors or reduce production. Thousands of men had no means of supporting themselves or their families.

The plight of the unemployed can be seen in two case histories. John McKinnon told a *Toronto Star* reporter in 1930: "I have tried every means to get a job—but no luck. I have tried to keep straight, but I had to bum money from people in the streets to get something to eat. . . . The police gave me a ticket for a night's lodging at a King Street lodging house and I changed my name three times to get more, so I could have shelter. . . . Last Friday night I went to the hostel again, but at three o'clock I had to get up. The place is running with bed-bugs." Six years later, Raymond Wandless told the *Star:* "We have been all over Ontario and a good bit of Quebec. By hitch-hiking, riding freights, and just tramping, we have covered hundreds of miles, but steady work just seems as far away as ever." His young wife, Alice, was clad in a cheap, threadbare cotton dress, no stockings; her red swollen feet stuck out between the uppers and soles of an old pair of shoes. The man was as poorly clothed—no socks, battered shoes.

Since there was no unemployment insurance in these years, men without work were forced to depend on direct government relief or local charities. Some "hopped freights" and "rode the rods" across the country hoping to find some kind of work that would enable them to become self-respecting citizens again. Few succeeded, and as the ranks of the unemployed reached half a million, people looked for new political means of solving their economic problems. The depression struck while Prime Minister King was still in power in Ottawa. The Liberal government insisted that unemployment was temporary, and that the depression would soon yield to the traditional policies of cutting government expenditures and balancing the budget. The Conservative opposition claimed that the economic collapse was serious, demanded that jobs should be provided by public works projects and that tariffs be raised to stimulate Canadian industry. In the spring of 1930, the argument was carried out onto the hustings when Prime Minister King called an election.

R. B. Bennett launched a vigorous campaign to convince the people that the Conservatives had a solution to the country's economic difficulties. The major Conservative campaign plank was a demand that Canada should raise the tariff in order to make it plain to other countries, especially the United States, that Canada would reduce its tariff only if other countries did so. Canada should "blast her way

THE SPECTRE AND ITS WARNING

into the markets of the world," Mr. Bennett declared. The Conservative campaign found a sympathetic response throughout the country, for many people felt that the Liberals had failed and that the Bennett party should be given a chance to try to restore the country to prosperity. When the votes were counted the Conservatives were elected by a majority of thirty-one seats. J. W. Dafoe, editor of the *Winnipeg Free Press,* wrote after the Conservative victory: "No doubt what beat the government was the very feeling that something better might come out of a shake-up. . . . I don't think the bolters, whose defection beat the government candidates, gave a thought to the effect of their vote on policy—what they wanted was to hit someone in the eye, in retaliation for hard times, low prices of grain, disappointment at the failure of the wheat pool to deliver the goods, losses suffered through speculation, lack of cash, the indignity of having to put up with the old car, and for a hundred other causes, just as profound."

In the autumn of 1930 R. B. Bennett was sworn into office as Prime Minister, and the country awaited his magic solution to the hardships and difficulties that the depression had brought.

15 DEPRESSION DECADE

SPEAKING to a radio audience in January 1935, Prime Minister Bennett pointed out that "in the last five years great changes have taken place in the world. The old order is gone. It will not return. We are living amidst conditions which are new and strange to us." Most Canadians agreed that great changes had indeed taken place since the "Great Crash" of 1929. The depression had brought unemployment, worsened living conditions and frustrated ambitions. It had also raised fundamental questions about the traditional political and economic institutions of the country. Why had such a serious economic collapse taken place? Why had it not been prevented? Why was so little being done to cure it? Probably the most disturbing question was why there was such obvious poverty in a nation so rich in human and natural resources as Canada.

By 1935 even Prime Minister Bennett was remarking: "Canada on the dole is like a young and vigorous man in the poorhouse. The dole is a condemnation, final and complete, of our economic system. If we cannot abolish the dole, we should abolish the system." But not everyone was satisfied that either the Conservatives or the Liberals could really find the answers to Canada's economic problems. Thus there developed a series of unusual political movements, offering new answers to the problems of a country where poverty existed in the midst of plenty.

1. BENNETT AND THE CONSERVATIVES

During the first four years of his term of office, Prime Minister Bennett attempted to meet the hardships of the Canadian people by following traditional policies. He was not the kind of man from whom radical policies were expected. Born in modest circumstances in New Brunswick, Bennett had gone west to Calgary where he had rapidly prospered as a corporation lawyer. He had always regarded his business career as a first step towards entering public life. In 1911 he was elected to the federal parliament as a Conservative; in 1927 he was chosen leader of his party. His great capacity for hard work raised him to the top in both business and politics, just when the kind of society that had produced him was on the edge of collapse.

As Prime Minister, Bennett immediately called a special session of parliament to pass emergency measures increasing federal unemployment relief, and establishing a public works programme to create employment. But the government's most important proposal to cure the depression was the traditional Conservative one, a higher tariff. The Conservative argument was that since Canadian trade had been seriously injured by foreign tariff barriers like the American Hawley-Smoot Tariff of 1930, Canada should retaliate. Higher Canadian tariffs, Bennett believed, would at least protect the domestic market for Canadian manufacturers and perhaps force other countries to lower their tariffs against Canada.

The new Canadian tariff law of 1930 established the highest tariff in Canada's history. It protected not only goods already being produced in Canada, but goods that might be produced in the future by Canadian manufacturers. With this tariff as a lever, Prime Minister Bennett hoped to persuade the other countries of the Commonwealth to set up an Imperial preference which would turn the British Commonwealth into a trading area protected against the rest of the world. In 1932 Prime Ministers from all the Commonwealth countries met in Ottawa to draw up trading agreements. Though the British government, which had followed a policy of free trade for nearly a century, was reluctant to adopt the Bennett plan for a tariff ring around the Commonwealth, agreement was finally reached. Britain promised to allow a large number of Canadian manufac-

FACING BOTH WAYS.

A Liberal view of Mr. Bennett's economic policy

tured and agricultural goods to enter Britain duty-free in
return for a reduction of the Canadian tariff on British
goods. In addition, bilateral agreements providing for special tariff treatment were worked out among all the members of the Commonwealth.

The Bennett tariff policy had some worth-while results.
It protected Canadian manufacturers against foreign competition and thus created some new jobs in Canadian factories. More important, Imperial preference increased Canadian trade both with Britain and with the other members
of the Commonwealth. But two facts remained unchanged
by the tariff revisions. Domestic purchasing power, the

money that Canadians had to spend, remained too limited to allow them to buy all the goods produced at home, for tariff protection also increased the cost of these goods. Moreover, Canada could not survive without access to the enormous markets of the United States and Europe. These markets remained largely closed to Canada, partly because the United States and many European countries had high tariffs, and partly because Canadian tariffs prevented foreign nations from selling goods in Canada. Thus, while Canada suffered from the strangulation of world trade caused by high tariffs in the 1930's, she also contributed to it by her own trade policies.

By 1932, when the Imperial economic agreements were coming into effect, depression conditions were growing more serious in Canada. J. S. Woodsworth, a Labour member of parliament, described the situation when he pointed out:

> For two generations we had an outlet in western Canada but that outlet is not only closed, the people are drifting back to the East from that country. In the old days we could send people from the cities to the country. If they went out today they would meet another army of unemployed coming back from the country to the city; that outlet is closed. What can these people do? They have been driven from our parks; they have been driven from our streets; they have been driven from our buildings, and in this city [Ottawa] they actually took refuge on the garbage heaps.

With unemployment increasing and drought destroying the crops in the West, a mood of despair seized many Canadians. In the West, farmers rode in automobiles drawn by horses, because gasoline was too expensive, and derisively called them "Bennett buggies." In the cities, the tar-paper shacks that housed evicted families were christened "Bennettburghs." It was in this atmosphere that new parties of political protest made their appearance.

2. THE NEW PARTIES

The main centre of political discontent in the 1930's, as

in the 'twenties, was western Canada where the depression hit hardest. The first new group to appear was the Social Credit movement in Alberta, organized and led by a school teacher and fundamentalist preacher, William Aberhart. A man of immense energy, Aberhart was gifted with powers of oratory and the ability to dramatize issues in a manner that quickly attracted a mass following. Moreover, he was one of the first Canadian public men to recognize the value of radio in political campaigning. He learned this first as a revivalist radio preacher, and his name and voice were well known throughout Alberta before his political movement was founded. In 1934 he began applying the same technique to politics.

Aberhart's political views were based on the writings of an English engineer, Major Douglas, who had evolved the doctrine of Social Credit. The theory, reduced to its simplest form, was expressed in the "A + B = C" equation. In this crude mathematical formula "A" equals wages and dividends paid to producers, "B" the other costs of production, including raw materials, bank charges and profits, and "C" the total cost of the product. Douglas maintained that since the cost of production (C) always exceeds the producer's buying power (A), "poverty in the midst of plenty" was bound to exist, for there would never be enough money available to buy the available goods. His solution was for the government to issue a "social dividend" or cash payment to all citizens. Aberhart read Douglas' book, and was convinced.

Before long Aberhart was mixing Social Credit and religion in his Sunday morning radio talks. His growing legion of supporters willingly listened to his vigorous attacks on the country's financial system, for many Alberta farmers were experiencing difficulties in obtaining credit or meeting mortgage payments. Climaxing his campaign in 1935, Aberhart declared: "You remain in the depression because of a shortage of purchasing power imposed by the banking system. If you have not suffered enough, it is your God-given right to suffer more." But he added, "We have still one free hand with which to strike—to mark our ballot on election day. Let us strike then with all our might at this hideous monster that is sucking the very life-blood from our people." This was the kind of spell-binding oratory that brought the people flocking to Social Credit meetings in the summer of 1935.

An Alberta farmer described the appeal of "Bible Bill" Aberhart: "Us farmers, being the producers of real wealth, were the first to feel the pinch and we felt it the hardest as the years went by. When we were all feeling down and out, Mr. Aberhart began to show the link between the economic injustices of today and the economic injustices of Christ's time. He linked these two up and showed how Christ had cleared the money changers out of the Temple. Then he showed us how the money changers of today had everything cornered ... the tie-up between religion and economics made me realize that Social Credit was the answer to all our problems. Once I realized this, I went out and talked up Social Credit and organized groups among farmers all through our district."

From the meetings, the people of Alberta carried their enthusiasm to the voting booth. In the provincial election that summer, Social Credit, previously without a seat in the legislature, won power. But Social Credit was easier to preach than to practise. Aberhart soon discovered that most of his ideas and promises, especially those that had to do with the field of banking and finance, lay outside the constitutional powers of the provincial government to make good. Attempts to control banking, finance and credit were rejected by the courts because they interfered with the federal power over banking and currency, and after several unsuccessful experiments with "social dividends," Aberhart was content to give the province good government while his followers dreamed of the day when Social Credit would capture Ottawa.

Social Credit was not the only new party born during the depression. The apparent collapse of free enterprise created new interest in the socialist movement which had possessed a small following for many years. Since the days

"The shortage of purchasing power which results from the operation of the money system would be made good by putting new money directly into the hands of the people." To fulfil this plank in its platform Premier Aberhart's government in 1936 issued "prosperity certificates" or "funny money," as the opponents of Social Credit called them. In taking this unusual step the Alberta government was found by the Supreme Court to have exceeded its powers and the certificates, which had been received suspiciously by most Albertans, were withdrawn from circulation.

of the Winnipeg general strike in 1919, J. S. Woodsworth had led a small Labour party in the House of Commons. A former Methodist minister, Woodsworth had come to believe that the principles of Christianity could only be applied to politics and economics through some form of democratic socialism. A vigorous critic of Marxian communism, he nevertheless believed that the capitalist system gave too much power to too few men. The solution, he and the socialists declared, was to increase government authority over economic life.

Woodsworth had found few converts in the prosperous 1920's. His most important achievement lay in convincing Mackenzie King in 1926 that the country needed government-sponsored old age pensions. But when the 1929 depression struck, Woodsworth's views about the weaknesses of the capitalist system found a much more sympathetic

HE LETS US SUFFOCATE
IL NOUS LAISSE ETOUFFER

Les trusts nous pressurent. Chacun de nous est victime de leur emprise. Mais M. Taschereau-les-Trusts s'en lave les mains, en refusant de nous en délivrer. Quand secouerons-nous le joug de cet hypocrite?

The trusts squeeze us. Each of us is caught in their grip. But
Mr. Taschereau-the-Trusts washes his hands and refuses to
save us. When will we shake off the yoke of this hypocrite?

The depression in Quebec brought widespread attacks on the trusts,
which were largely controlled by English-speaking Canadian or American
capitalists. The alliance of the Taschereau government and big business
was both known and condemned.

audience. Farmers, labour leaders and some middle-class
intellectuals agreed that the time had come to establish a
socialist party.

In 1932 representatives of these groups met in Calgary
where they established the Co-operative Commonwealth
Federation, or C.C.F. A second conference at Regina in the
following year approved a platform which came to be known
as the Regina Manifesto. The aim of the party was summed
up in part of the platform which read: "We aim to replace
the present capitalist system with its inherent injustice and
inhumanity by a social order from which the domination
and exploitation of one class by another will be eliminated,
in which economic planning will supersede unregulated

private enterprise and competition, and in which genuine democratic self-government based upon economic equality will be possible." Woodsworth appealed to the delegates to support the new policy. "The C.C.F. believes in bringing about the changes our country needs through orderly and peaceful means. I believe that in Canada we must work out our own salvation in our own way. There are all kinds of socialism—Christian Socialism, Utopian Socialism, Russian, Marxist, German, American Socialism. Why not a Canadian Socialism?" Woodsworth's "Canadian Socialism" advocated government planning of the economy through nationalization of the railways, banks, insurance companies and other industries of large-scale economic importance. These policies gained greatest acceptance in Saskatchewan. By 1944 the C.C.F. had come to power in that province under the leadership of the popular T. C. "Tommy" Douglas.

In Quebec in the 1930's political unrest combined social radicalism with French-Canadian nationalism. Since the war, Quebec had been passing through an industrial revolution which transformed the province from an agrarian to an industrial society. Most of the capital which financed this transformation came from English-speaking Canadian, British and American investors. Many French Canadians became concerned about the domination of their economy by English-speaking capitalists. When the depression threw thousands of French Canadians out of work, smouldering resentment exploded into anger against "foreign" employers.

Two groups sought to take advantage of these disturbed social conditions in Quebec. One was the tiny Conservative party which hoped to regain office by appealing to the nationalism of the French-Canadian voters. A second group, composed of radical Liberals who were dissatisfied with the provincial Liberal government, devised a programme which called for the nationalization of some industries owned by English-speaking investors, and the introduction of social welfare measures. These two groups united to form a new party called the *Union Nationale* led by a former Conservative, Maurice Duplessis.

SWEEPING BACK THE SEA

Mitchell Hepburn, who led the Liberal party to victory in Ontario in 1934 on a platform of social and economic reform, had, by 1937, developed a strong opposition to labour unions, especially labour unions with affiliations in the United States. When the United Automobile Workers, backed by the Committee for Industrial Organizations in the United States, called a strike at the General Motors plant in Oshawa in 1937, Premier Hepburn unequivocally voiced his support for the company against the union. Messrs. Croll and Roebuck, later Canadian Senators, resigned from Hepburn's cabinet on the issue, saying they "would sooner walk with workers than ride with General Motors." While most Ontario voters sympathized with the Premier's opposition to American-sponsored unions, the efforts of the province's workingmen to organize themselves into unions proved nearly irresistible. Premier Hepburn found he could no more prevent union organization than he could sweep back the sea!

By 1936 Duplessis and his radical allies succeeded in driving the corruption-ridden Liberal party from power. But once in office Duplessis outmanœuvred the sincere reformers and quickly forgot the promised reforms. The government provided assistance for farmers, but ignored the needs of the working people and did nothing to restore control of Quebec's economic life to the French Canadians. Instead, Duplessis cleverly turned the eyes of his compatriots away from local problems by declaring war on the federal government which, he claimed, was trying to undermine provincial autonomy, and was therefore threatening French-Canadian rights. This appeal to nationalist sentiment was successful, for, in the troubled atmosphere of international affairs in the 1930's, many French Canadians were reminded of the conscription crisis of 1917, and exhibited a strong hostility toward the government at Ottawa.

Ontario also produced a radical who, like Duplessis, rose to power on promises of reform. In 1934 Mitchell Hepburn brought the Liberals back to power in Ontario, after twenty-nine years in the Opposition, with promises to fight the depression by a reduction of government expenditures and by aid for the farmer, the worker and the unemployed. In his first years as Premier he introduced legislation to raise agricultural prices for farmers and to provide legal protection for the growing trade-union movement in the province. But within a few years he, too, began to lose his zeal for social reform. In 1937 he attempted to prevent the United Automobile Workers union from gaining recognition during a long and bitter strike in Oshawa and declared that the American labour organization, the Committee for Industrial Organizations, would enter Ontario only over his dead body! Like Premier Duplessis, he was soon to carry on a bitter battle against the federal government and Mackenzie King.

In British Columbia T. D. Pattullo's Liberal party had won the provincial election of 1933 with a promise of "Work and Wages," which echoed Roosevelt's New Deal. Unemployment was especially heavy in the Pacific coast province not only because it depended on exports, but also because, as Pattullo himself wrote, "by reason of its diversity of interests, its salubrious climate and general attractiveness [British Columbia] is the mecca of those who suffer from misfortunes, mischance or ill health." After his victory, Pattullo raised the level of relief payments, set maximum hours of work and minimum wages, provided financial assistance for the mining and fishing industries, and began public works projects to create employment. While Premier Pattullo's reforms helped to revive the economy, they also cost a great deal of money. To meet the rising deficit Pattullo appealed to Ottawa for financial assistance, and by 1935 was engaged in a bitter quarrel with the federal authorities over financial policies.

The appearance of new parties and leaders willing to use the power of government to fight the depression was a clear warning to Prime Minister Bennett that more vigorous action by the federal government was necessary. In 1934 he attempted to bring some order into the country's financial system by establishing the Bank of Canada, whose purpose was to regulate currency and credit, to provide financial services to private banks, and to act as a financial adviser to the government. To aid the farmers, Bennett re-established the Canadian Wheat Board, first used during the First World War, to regulate the sale of grain. Bankrupt provinces were given federal loans. The Canadian National Railways, which had suffered serious financial losses during the depression, was reorganized. In air transport, Bennett laid the basis for the establishment of the government-owned Trans-Canada Airlines. In the field of broadcasting, the Conservative government in 1932 established the Canadian Radio Broadcasting Corporation, which four years later became the national radio network known as the Canadian Broadcasting Corporation.

Some of Bennett's colleagues pressed him to more radical adventures in government regulation. By 1934 H. H. Stevens, the Minister of Trade and Commerce, was insisting that the government should control business practices.

Stevens was especially concerned about the way large retail stores used their buying power to force small manufacturers to sell to them at low prices, with the result that the manufacturers had to pay low wages to their employees. Stevens also believed that farmers received prices too far below those charged by meat packers and canners for the retail product. In short, he felt that large profits were being made by some large retailers who were underpaying producers, overcharging consumers, and forcing small businessmen out of the market. After Stevens had made his views public, Bennett agreed to establish a Royal Commission on Price Spreads with Stevens as Chairman. Unfortunately, Stevens was somewhat indiscreet in his public speeches on the price spreads problem, and some of his colleagues, closely connected with large companies, complained. Stevens resigned from the cabinet and in 1935 created the Reconstruction party, whose platform included a demand for stricter government regulation of business.

The price spreads investigation and Stevens' resignation were further warnings to Bennett that unless his government stepped up the pace of reform, its defeat was certain in the 1935 election. Meanwhile, from Washington, his brother-in-law, W. D. Herridge, Canadian Ambassador to the United States, urged Bennett to imitate Roosevelt's New Deal. He wrote: "Declare for the new Toryism, for it means government in business [which] is the only fulcrum powerful enough to lift us from the wreck of capitalism ... [the people] want action, and if government does not give it to them, action they will nevertheless have, and it will be action of their own making." By January 1935, Bennett had decided that the time had come for action. In a series of radio addresses he announced his plans for a Canadian "New Deal." "The economic system must be reformed," he told the people. "Great social and economic changes have taken place in the life of all the nations, and these have gravely disturbed the operation of the system. What we call the crash of 1929 was simply the crash of the system." This was radical talk coming from a Conservative

They Won't Fit Him Very Well

Arch Dale's comment on Prime Minister Bennett's sudden swing to the left.

Prime Minister. The measures which followed were designed to reduce farm debt, control the export trade, regulate business practices, set up a system of unemployment insurance and establish minimum wages and maximum hours of work.

Bennett's "New Deal" caused great excitement. Within his own party there was opposition to this radical departure from traditional Tory principles. But it was accepted. The Liberals, too, were shocked. In parliament they argued that the measures were beyond the powers of the federal government and that they should be tested in the Supreme Court before being put into practice. But Bennett could not delay his programme, for an election was due in the summer of 1935.

In the election campaign the Conservatives defended the "New Deal." The Liberals accepted the need for social reform but on platforms across the nation insisted that the Bennett legislation was a farce because it went beyond the powers of the federal government. The Liberals also argued that the government's high tariff policies harmed the Canadian economy by stifling international trade. Finally, the Liberals charged that Bennett was a dictator and ran a "one-man government" in which ministers were mere puppets, and parliamentary rights ignored. "What the country needs is not the fist of the pugilist but the hand of the physician," declared Mackenzie King, although his prescription for curing the sick nation was not clear.

The election results showed that Bennett's decision to adopt drastic measures had come too late. Most people were disillusioned with Conservative government and wanted a change. However, the results also showed that the Liberals, who won one hundred and seventy-one seats, had gained very few supporters, for their popular vote was almost unchanged from 1930. Bennett's defeat was largely due to the million voters who decided to support the three minor parties. The Conservatives won only thirty-nine seats, while Social Credit gained seventeen, the C.C.F. seven, and the Reconstruction party one—for its leader, H. H. Stevens. It remained to be seen whether King had any effective plans to meet the country's continuing economic difficulties.

3. KING AND THE ROWELL-SIROIS COMMISSION

The first action of Mackenzie King's new government in 1935 was to refer Bennett's "New Deal" legislation to the courts. While awaiting the courts' decision, King was able to take action in the field of trade with the United States. Bennett had already begun negotiations with Washington before his defeat. The King government resumed these negotiations and successfully concluded a bilateral trade agreement which gave Canadian agricultural, mining and industrial products freer access to the American market, while the Canadian tariff against goods from the United States was also reduced.

Success in finding new markets for Canadian products was

important but it had little immediate effect on the hardships created by the depression. In 1936 the Supreme Court ruled that the most important parts of the Bennett "New Deal" were unconstitutional. This left the federal government almost powerless to adopt measures to fight the economic and social disaster that lay all around. Obviously, if this were due to the constitution, the constitution needed to be amended. In 1937 Prime Minister King announced the appointment of a Royal Commission on Dominion-Provincial Relations to investigate the constitutional and financial relations between the federal and provincial governments. Five Commissioners and a host of assistants were given the enormous task of studying the history of the Canadian federation and of recommending solutions for the constitutional obstacles that stood in the way of any effective action to remove the worst hardships of the depression. This Commission, usually called the Rowell-Sirois Commission after its two chairmen, worked for three years before submitting its conclusions to the government.

From its extensive investigations the Commission concluded that since Confederation in 1867 two developments had taken place in Canadian life which affected the constitution. First, a series of court judgements handed down by the Judicial Committee of the Privy Council had restricted the legislative authority of the federal government to the enumerated powers of Section 91 of the British North America Act, and had completely undermined the effectiveness of its residual authority except in periods of "national emergency" such as wartime. At the same time, the responsibilities of the provinces had been expanded beyond the limits originally contemplated by the Fathers of Confederation, as education, highway construction and social services became the responsibility of the provincial governments. Yet the major powers of taxation remained with the federal government, so that the provinces had wide responsibilities, but lacked the funds necessary to fulfil them.

The second point emphasized by the Rowell-Sirois Commissioners was that since Canada was gradually changing from an agricultural to an industrial nation, it was desirable that the federal government should have broader powers over the economic life of the country and authority to enact social security measures that would be uniform for the whole country. "Canada's present and prospective economic condition," the Commission reported, "makes it clear that we can neither continue to afford the friction and waste of conflicting policies, nor the greater loss due to paralysis of policy arising from a possibly obsolete division of governmental responsibilities and powers."

After a thorough examination of the existing conditions the Commissioners recommended that the Dominion government should be given exclusive powers of direct taxation, in return for which the Dominion would pay the provinces national adjustment grants to provide a minimum standard of government and social services throughout the country. The purpose of this recommendation was to ensure a more equitable distribution of the national wealth among the provinces. It was particularly designed to meet the needs of the Maritimes and the prairie provinces, which, because of their lack of industry and natural resources, had not the sources of revenue that were available to the wealthier provinces. This was an admission that the national policies, which successive Canadian governments had followed, had not benefited all the sections of the country equally. Central Canada had grown rich at the expense of the Maritimes and the West. The national adjustment grants were designed to rectify these inequalities. A further important recommendation was that the federal government assume responsibility for unemployment relief and insurance, and that a system of social security be established by the provinces aided by financial grants from the Dominion government.

The Commission believed that these recommendations would bring the Canadian federal system into line with the developments and changes that had taken place since 1867. As the Report remarked: "The financial proposals are, in terms of the economic conditions of 1939, very similar to what the provisions of the British North America Act were in terms of the economic life of 1867."

The Commissioners hoped that the recommendations would find general acceptance throughout the country, and argued that they preserved the basic structure of a federal system in which both the Dominion and the provincial governments had important roles to play. "The Commission does not consider," the Report concluded, "that its proposals are either centralizing or decentralizing in their combined effect, but believes that they will conduce to the same balance between these two tendencies which is the essence of a genuine federal system and, therefore, the basis on which Canadian national unity can most securely rest."

Unfortunately, the Commissioners were too optimistic in their expectations. While the poorer provinces were heartily in favour of a plan which would give them a larger share of the national income, the richer provinces, Quebec, Ontario and British Columbia, felt that they would lose by the suggested redistribution of powers and revenue. The government of Quebec, led by Maurice Duplessis, had opposed the Commission from the beginning, while Hepburn in Ontario and Aberhart of Alberta had been reluctant to co-operate. This staunch provincialism meant that the Commission's recommendations would be difficult to implement.

When the Rowell-Sirois Commission presented its report to the King government in the spring of 1940, Canada was again at war. Clearly the war effort would require increased federal authority if Canada were to contribute its share to allied victory. Prime Minister King called a meeting of the leaders of all the provincial governments in January 1941 to consider the recommendations of the Commission. By the time the Dominion-Provincial Conference met, Premier Duplessis had been turned out of office by the Quebec Liberals, and there was reason to believe that the new government of Adélard Godbout would be willing to accept a reorganization of the financial structure of Confederation. But vigorous opposition came from three other provincial premiers. Led by Mitchell Hepburn, Ontario, Alberta and British Columbia refused even to discuss the recommendations of the Rowell-Sirois Report. After two days of wrangling, the Conference ended and three years of hard work by the Commission was set aside. Nevertheless, the strains of war made it necessary for the federal government to conclude with each of the provinces separate taxation agreements which allowed federal government access to the largest proportion of their tax revenues. This provided the federal government with the additional sources of revenue necessary to pay for the costly war effort. Thus the Conference of 1941 had not been a complete failure. Prime Minister King noted in his diary: "While to appearances it has been a failure, in reality it has served the purpose we had in view, of avoiding attack for not having called the Conference, and particularly what would certainly have followed, invasion of provincial sources of revenue. We have now got the pledge of the Provinces to let us take their revenues if we need them—a tremendous achievement." Moreover, even before the Dominion-Provincial Conference met, the federal government had secured a constitutional amendment giving it power to establish unemployment insurance.

By 1940, of course, all eyes were turned to the terrible events which were convulsing Europe. Although the demands of war soon had the Canadian economy working at full strength again, the strains imposed on the country by the depression were not easily overcome. In addition, the war also caused the reappearance of old tensions and conflicts and illustrated once more the difficulty of governing a geographically and culturally divided nation like Canada.

16 NATIONALISM AND ISOLATION

CANADA'S entry into the Second World War on September 10, 1939 ended a twenty-year period of intense debate about the Dominion's relations with the outside world. Despite the divisions which existed among races, classes and sections in 1919, participation in the First World War had given Canadians a new sense of national identity. This national feeling was difficult to define, except as a sense of belonging to a separate nation, and a desire that that nation should exercise all the powers of an independent state. There were still some Canadians who felt that the country should continue to follow Britain's policy in international affairs, and there were others who felt that Canada should be completely independent of the mother country. But these groups represented the extremes. The majority of Canadians felt that Canadian independence should be worked out within the structure of the British family of nations.

1. THE ROOTS OF CANADIAN FOREIGN POLICY

As Canada gradually moved towards full nationhood, it became evident that there were enduring factors in public opinion which guided the formation of Canadian foreign policy, regardless of which party was in power. In the first place, there was a strong sentiment which opposed any step that would increase Canadian commitments to the outside world. Some groups even wished to reduce the responsibilities that Canada had assumed as a result of her membership in the Commonwealth and the League of Nations. The groups which most firmly opposed an active Canadian role in international affairs were of a kind with the isolationists in the United States. French Canadians were especially isolationist in their outlook because they feared that foreign responsibilities would result in another crisis like the one that had split the country in 1917. Many Canadians of both races were isolationists because they believed that Canada was secure in North America and had no reason to get involved in what appeared to be other people's quarrels. Senator Raoul Dandurand, a Liberal, expressed this sentiment when he told the League of Nations in 1924 that Canadians "live in a fireproof house far from inflammable materials." Every Canadian government in the inter-war period had to consider this isolationist sentiment when formulating policy.

There were two other groups in Canada whose views were also important in influencing foreign policy. There were those people, though their numbers were decreasing, who supported the idea of a common Imperial foreign policy. Then there were the internationalists who gave vigorous support to the League of Nations and held that the peace of the world depended upon the successful implementation of collective security through the League. The most influential spokesman for this group was John W. Dafoe, editor of the *Winnipeg Free Press*.

Although no Canadian government in the inter-war period adopted completely the point of view of any one group, it was the widespread isolationist sentiment that came nearest to controlling government policy, especially in the late 'thirties.

In addition to these domestic considerations there were also three constant external factors that played a role in shaping Canadian foreign policy. First, there was Canada's membership in the British Commonwealth. While membership involved no specific commitments or responsibilities, it did at least imply that if any member were threatened with war, the other members would come to its aid. Secondly, there was Canada's close relationship with the United States. Since the United States had refused to join the League of Nations, Canada had to tread carefully in its international activities in order to avoid upsetting Canadian-

OPERATION SUCCESSFUL, BUT THE PATIENT DIED

—*Winnipeg Free Press*

From the foundation of the League of Nations in 1919 Canada had been critical of the institution as a means of coercing aggressor nations. As Europe began to slip down the road to war in the 1930's, Canada's desire to be free of League commitments grew stronger. Speaking before the Assembly of the League of Nations in 1936, Prime Minister King defined the Canadian position when he said there was "a widespread conviction, born of experience, that at this stage in the evolution of the League, emphasis should be placed upon conciliation rather than upon coercion. There is a general unwillingness of peoples to incur obligations which they realize they may not be able in time of crisis to fulfil, obligations to use force and to use it at any place, at any time, in circumstances unforeseen, and in disputes over whose origin or whose development they had little or no control."

American relations. Finally, there was Canada's membership in the League of Nations. Canada had fought for membership because it would bring further recognition of nationhood. But few Canadians believed that membership in the League should involve Canada in heavy responsibilities for preserving the peace of the world.

No sooner had Canada joined the League than the government began to wonder whether the commitments it had made were too binding. The "heart" of the League Covenant, Article X, called upon the member nations to "undertake to respect and preserve as against external aggression the territorial integrity and existing political independence of all the members of the League." This article meant that if a League member were attacked, the other members would be obliged to come to its assistance. Even at Paris, while the Covenant was under discussion, the Canadian delegation attempted to have Article X weakened so that Canada could not be drawn into international disputes everywhere in the world.

When the Liberals came into office in 1921, their attitude towards the League and Article X was the same as Sir Robert Borden's had been when the Covenant was being framed. In 1924 the Liberals succeeded in securing an interpretative resolution concerning Article X which stated that in asking for military assistance the League would take into account the size and geographical position of member states. This really meant that Canada would be involved only if aggression occurred in the Americas. Henceforth, Liberal spokesmen, including Prime Minister King, repeatedly informed the League that while Canada favoured and supported the League as an instrument of arbitration and conciliation, it had strong doubts about the League as a body for enforcing peace by coercion. In 1936 King told the League Assembly: "Our attachment to this idea is as strong today as it was at the inception of the League. At the same time there is general concurrence in the view which has been expressed by leaders of all political parties since the beginning of the League, that automatic commitments to the application of force is not a practical policy." In effect, Prime Minister King was saying, as others had said before him, that Canada was no more willing to commit herself to supporting a common foreign policy devised by the League of Nations, than she was to a common foreign policy set out by the members of the British Commonwealth. A belief that Canada should assume no binding commitments whatsoever was the essence of Canadian foreign policy between the wars.

2. THE GROWTH OF NATIONAL STATUS

After the First World War, the first task in external affairs that the Canadian government faced was to define the relations between Great Britain and the Dominions. This family of nations which, before the war, had been called the British Empire, was by 1919 in the process of changing its name and its structure and was soon to emerge as the British Commonwealth of Nations. In 1919 the question before Canadians was how to increase Canadian independence without destroying the bonds which held the family together. Since Canada had already largely achieved self-government in domestic matters, the problem in the inter-war period centred mainly on whether Canada should have an independent foreign policy, or whether there should be a common foreign policy for all the members of the Commonwealth.

Both the supporters of a common Imperial foreign policy and of an independent foreign policy had an opportunity to test their views in the 1920's. Prime Minister Meighen's Conservative government followed the procedures which had been established by Sir Robert Borden during the war and at the peacemaking. At Paris in 1919 Borden had represented Canada as part of the British delegation. Moreover, he had insisted that Canada should be given individual representation in the League of Nations. The implication of Borden's policy was that the Dominions would have separate representation at international conferences, but that there would be a common Imperial policy worked out beforehand. After Borden's retirement in 1920, Meighen, Borden's successor, and his Conservative supporters continued to look upon Borden's approach as a satisfactory solution to the problem of allowing Canada a share in formulating foreign policy without breaking the united front that the British nations would present to the world. As Borden suggested in Resolution IX of the Imperial War Conference, "continuous consultation" would provide the machinery to devise a common foreign policy. "By tradition, by the sense of common inheritance and of common ideals, the Dominion of Canada aspires to one destiny, and one only—a destiny than which there is no nobler—a nationhood within the British Empire," declared Arthur Meighen in 1921.

Mackenzie King and the Liberals agreed that Canada should aspire to nationhood within the British Empire; but they disagreed about the means of attaining this end. They felt that nationhood meant that Canada should have complete freedom to formulate her own foreign policy, even if that policy differed from the policy of the other members of the Empire. As the *Winnipeg Free Press,* an independent Liberal newspaper, put it: "The only system that will work is one by which each British nation will attend to its own foreign affairs and accept responsibility therefor; reserving for a common policy only those questions—relatively few—in which we are all interested. When these questions arise there will be no difficulty about securing common action, as in war." Thus the Liberals believed that Canadian foreign policy should be primarily concerned with Canadian interests. The Conservatives believed that Canada's interests were the same as the interests of the Empire and that therefore there should be a common foreign policy for all the members of the Empire.

The Conservatives under Arthur Meighen were in power when the first opportunity arose to test their views of a common Imperial foreign policy in a practical fashion. The most important issue facing the Imperial Conference in 1921 was the renewal of the Anglo-Japanese alliance originally negotiated in 1902. Fearful of the rising power of Japan in the Pacific, Australia and New Zealand were determined to have the alliance renewed. Realizing that she could no longer maintain a fleet in every theatre of war equal or superior to any other nation, Britain also wished to keep the alliance with Japan. With the United States withdrawing from world affairs, Britain felt that the alliance was the only alternative to a ruinous naval armament race in the Pacific and a disruption of the balance of power.

The United States, however, was adamantly opposed to renewal. The Anglo-Japanese alliance, the Americans felt, could only be directed against them, for there were no other important powers in the Pacific. Moreover, renewal of the alliance would encourage the Japanese to expand in the

Pacific, a course of action which alarmed the United States as much as it did Australia and New Zealand. To the United States non-renewal was viewed as the acid test of Anglo-American goodwill.

Canada was deeply affected by American feeling. Situated as she was in the North Atlantic Triangle, Canada was convinced that good relations between Britain and the United States lay at the foundation of her foreign policy. Thus when Meighen went to London he was determined to prevent renewal of the alliance at all costs. During the debates he spoke powerfully and eloquently of the need for good relations between the Empire and the United States. He explained the American position so well and so forcefully that the irate Prime Minister of Australia exclaimed that he was really speaking for the United States and not for Canada. Meighen answered that in any matters affecting the United States Canada's voice must be heard. "It has developed through the years, not as a matter of sudden departure or acquisition, but as a matter of growth out of the very necessities of the case," he said, "that in the determination of questions affecting not the Empire as such and the United States, but affecting the United States and Canada, the Dominion should have full and final authority." While this was a matter affecting the whole Empire, it was also a question that bore directly on Canada, whose position would be extremely uncomfortable if serious trouble arose between neighbour and mother country. Meighen's determination and logic prevented the alliance from being renewed. His suggestion of a multi-power discussion of Pacific affairs and naval disarmament in the Far East was grasped as an alternative. And at that precise moment President Harding of the United States, who had watched the proceedings of the Conference with great interest, invited the Pacific powers to a conference at Washington, where a disarmament treaty was signed and the Anglo-Japanese alliance was allowed to lapse.

The Imperial Conference of 1921 revealed that the members of the Empire had widely divergent interests in foreign policy. These fundamental differences had been overcome in 1921 when an alternative that all could accept, however reluctantly, was found. But such an alternative would not always be available. What would happen if no agreement could be reached? Would the Empire break up? Such were the questions that remained unanswered in 1921.

3. KING AND AN INDEPENDENT FOREIGN POLICY

The 1921 Imperial Conference was the only meeting of the leaders of the British nations that succeeded in formulating a common foreign policy. Shortly after the Conference the Conservative government in Canada was defeated at the polls. The victorious Liberals had never made any secret of their opposition to the principle of a common foreign policy for all the Commonwealth. Moreover, the Liberals were the party most strongly influenced by the attitudes of the French Canadians, and to French Canadians a common Imperial foreign policy meant Canadian involvement in Imperial wars.

The first opportunity for the new King government to give practical expression to these views came in September 1922, when the British government publicly appealed to the Dominions for assistance in a crisis at Chanak in Asia Minor where it appeared that Britain might be drawn into a war with Turkey. Prime Minister King read of the request in a newspaper before he received the official message from the British government. Understandably, the Prime Minister was furious. His cabinet agreed that most Canadians had no desire to engage in a war in Asia Minor that had no connection with Canadian interests. In his private diary King wrote: "Surely all that has been said about equality of status and sovereign nations within the Empire is all of no account if at any particular moment the self-governing Dominions are to be expected, without consideration of any kind, to assume the gravest responsibility which any nation can assume, solely and wholly upon an inspired dispatch from Downing Street." King was extremely suspicious of the motives of the British government. The British request, he wrote, "is drafted designedly to play the Imperial game, to test our centralization vs. autonomy as regards European wars. I have thought out my plans. No contingent will go without parliament being summoned in first instance." King had no intention of asking parliament to send a contingent. No doubt his suspicion was exaggerated, for the British were only acting on the theory of a common foreign policy which had been accepted at the 1921 Imperial Conference. But the Chanak crisis, and Canada's reaction to it, indicated that the theory was a weak one.

When a crisis like Chanak arose there was no time for consultation and the formulation of a common policy. As a result, British policy would have to become the policy of the Empire. Prime Minister King, however, did not believe that a common policy was desirable. But even those who did were faced with an insoluble problem in circumstances similar to the Chanak crisis. The Canadian Conservatives argued that Canada should have agreed to the British request and sent troops. "When Britain's message came, Canada should have said, 'Ready, Aye Ready',", stated Arthur Meighen, who now led the Conservative Opposition in Parliament. Perhaps Meighen's proposal was the more heroic, but in 1922 the Canadian people were not in a heroic mood. With the Great War still vivid in their memories, they wanted no part in any war and agreed with Mackenzie King that Canada must decide issues for itself.

The Chanak crisis and Canada's refusal to send troops to Asia Minor really killed the idea of a united foreign policy for the Empire. The next steps in asserting Canada's right to formulate her own foreign policy came in quick succession during the next ten years. In 1923 Ernest Lapointe, the Canadian Minister of Justice, signed the Halibut Treaty with the United States. This treaty, which governed United States fishing rights in Canadian coastal waters, was significant because it marked the first time that Canada had signed an international treaty alone. Previously, a British representative had always taken part in the negotiation of diplomatic treaties affecting Canada and signed the document on Britain's behalf. After 1923 this was no longer done. Four years later Canada took a further step in asserting her diplomatic independence when she appointed a Canadian representative to Washington to take charge of the relations between Canada and the United States, which, until then, had been handled by the British Embassy.

The most important step in Canada's gradual achievement of complete independence in foreign affairs was taken at the Imperial Conference of 1923. At this Conference the members of the Commonwealth agreed to the principle that each member nation should have the right to negotiate its own international treaties. Moreover, the Conference struck another blow at the idea of a common Imperial foreign policy, and again it was Mackenzie King who wielded the axe. He strongly objected to a suggestion that the meeting should issue a statement indicating that the Conference had arrived at agreement about a common foreign policy. The Canadian Prime Minister insisted that he could not agree to a policy that did not have the sanction of the Canadian parliament. "We believe that the decision of Great Britain on any important public issue, domestic or foreign, should be made by the people of Britain, their representatives in Parliament, and the Government responsible to that Parliament," King told the Conference. "So the decision of Canada on any important issue, domestic or foreign, we believe should be made by the people of Canada, their representatives in Parliament, and the Government responsible to that Parliament." In short, King's policy was one of no commitments, and his method of stating that policy was to say that "Parliament will decide in the light of existing circumstances."

The practical result of the Imperial Conference of 1923 was the acceptance of the view that each Dominion had the right to complete control over its own foreign policy. This view was not written into any constitutional document, but it was admitted in a section of the Report of the Conference that had been included to satisfy Prime Minister King. This section declared: "This Conference is a Conference of the several Governments of the Empire; its views and conclusions on Foreign Policy, as recorded above, are necessarily subject to the actions of the Governments and Parliaments of the various portions of the Empire and it trusts that the result of its deliberations will meet with their approval."

Two years later the control of the Dominions over their own foreign policy was further emphasized when the Locarno Agreements were negotiated. By these treaties Germany and France promised not to use force in settling any disagreements that arose between them, and Britain guaranteed to aid either against aggression by the other. The Locarno Treaties were important in Imperial relations, too, for there was a clause inserted into the agreements, largely at Canada's insistence, which exempted the Dominions from their terms unless the Dominions accepted them by their own decision. The fact that none of the Dominions did so indicated that while Britain had one policy the Dominions had another, and that the Dominions did not share responsibility for Britain's policy. Thus the idea of a common Imperial foreign policy was completely undermined.

The Imperial Conference of 1923 and the Locarno Agreements of 1925 clearly revealed that a united Empire with a common foreign policy had been transformed into a Commonwealth of Nations in which each member had its own foreign policy. This development was formally recognized in 1926 when another Imperial Conference issued a famous declaration named after its author, Arthur Balfour, a former Prime Minister of Great Britain. The Balfour Declaration described the Commonwealth as an association of "autonomous communities within the British Empire, equal in status, in no way subordinate to one another in any aspect of their domestic or external affairs, though united by a common allegiance to the Crown and freely associated as members of the British Commonwealth of Nations."

A number of legal anomalies remained to be removed before Dominion autonomy was as complete in law as it had become in practice. This was done by the Statute of Westminster in 1931, the final coping-stone on the development of self-government. The Statute gave the Dominions power to enact extra-territorial legislation, repealed the Colonial

Laws Validity Act of 1865, which had declared British law supreme in any conflict with colonial law, and declared that no British law would extend to the Dominions. Britain retained some authority over Canada after 1931, for the Judicial Committee of the Privy Council was still the final court of appeal for some Canadian cases, and amendments to the Canadian constitution still required the approval of the British parliament. But Britain retained these powers only because Canadians were unable to agree on a more satisfactory way of dealing with judicial appeals and constitutional amendments.

Thus, in 1931, the British Commonwealth obtained legal definition as an association of self-governing or autonomous nations. Canada had not been alone in effecting this transformation for strong support had come from other Dominions, especially from South Africa and Ireland. Moreover, it was not just one party in Canada that had favoured this evolution. Although there had been differences of opinion between the parties on matters of detail, the gradual growth of Canadian powers of self-government received support from all. Macdonald, Laurier, Borden, Meighen and King had each played his part, and it was the Conservative government of R. B. Bennett that accepted the Statute of Westminster. "We are all autonomists now," one Canadian nationalist rightly claimed in 1931.

4. ISOLATION AND WAR

As war clouds gathered over a world compressed by technological and military advances, Canadians, like Americans, continued to believe that they could hide their heads in the sand like ostriches and remain untouched by explosions in Europe and Asia. One Canadian politician summed up the view of most of his countrymen in the 1930's when he wrote: "The more I see of the whole thing, the more I am certain that our destiny is on the North American continent and that if Europe is going to insist on destroying itself, it is no part of our mission to destroy ourselves in attempting to prevent it."

In 1931 the military dictators of Japan put the League of Nations to its first critical test when they launched an attack on the Chinese province of Manchuria. The attack was well timed, for most League members including Canada, were giving their undivided attention to the domestic effects of the economic depression and had no desire to rush to China's assistance. At Geneva, the representative of R. B. Bennett's government to the League left no doubt that Canadians were unwilling to go to war over Manchuria. "I had to tell them," he explained to the House of Commons later, "that I did not believe that under the then existing circumstances the parliament of Canada would appropriate a single dollar toward maintaining a single company of troops in the Far East for that purpose." That was exactly the position taken in private by the governments of England and France and by the governments of the chief European states.

The failure of the League members to act against Japan gave a green light to other would-be aggressors. In 1935, the Italian dictator, Benito Mussolini, sent his Fascist battalions into the nearly defenceless country of Ethiopia. Here was an opportunity for the League to redeem itself. The League Assembly condemned Italy for aggression and imposed economic sanctions by which League member nations were forbidden to supply Italy with goods she required. But these sanctions did not include oil, a product essential to Mussolini's mechanized army. Despite the Italian dictator's warning that the imposition of oil sanctions would mean war, the Canadian delegate at Geneva, Dr. W. A. Riddell, acted without instructions and proposed that oil sanctions should be imposed. Riddell's action caused a sensation, particularly in Ottawa. Within a few days Mackenzie King's government repudiated Dr. Riddell. Most Canadians preferred King's caution to Riddell's courage. King accurately measured their temper when he asked: "Do honourable members think it is Canada's role at Geneva to attempt to regulate a European war?" They did not, and from the repudiation of Riddell to the outbreak of war in September 1939, King continued to avoid international commitments.

The Canadian government objected to the initiative taken by its representative, Dr. W. A. Riddell, in suggesting that League sanctions against Italy should include coal, oil, iron and steel. Ernest Lapointe insisted that the Canadian government refused to take the initiative in proposing the extension of the measures with regard to the prohibition of exportation to Italy and did not propose to take the initiative in such measures. While most Canadians agreed with this stand, some believed that Lapointe was guided by pressure from Quebec. The Toronto **Evening Telegram** remarked: "If Canada's attitude is that this country is entitled to contract out of the League's collective efforts when it suits Quebec, that it is bound only to agree to sanctions that are agreeable to the aggressor, and that it is satisfied to have a spokesman at Geneva who does not speak for the Canadian government, then Mr. Lapointe's position is readily understandable. But that position is not, we think, the position of the Canadian people."

Mackenzie King was obsessed with the nightmare that foreign affairs could sharply divide Canadians again as in 1917 and he believed that the only way to prevent the country from splitting in two was to avoid positive actions.

"A strong and dominant national feeling is not a luxury in Canada, it is a necessity," King claimed. "A divided country can be of little help to any country, least of all to herself." Probably the majority of Canadians agreed with their Prime Minister. Only a few, like John W. Dafoe in Winnipeg, realized that if the League were to fail Canada would inevitably be drawn into war.

In Germany, the dictator Hitler rearmed in defiance of the Treaty of Versailles and moved to expand his country's borders by force. Prime Minister King's chief hope was that somehow the German dictator's demands would be satisfied without provoking a war. In September 1938, at Munich, Hitler won the acceptance of Prime Ministers Chamberlain of Britain and Daladier of France for his plan to help himself to most of Czechoslovakia. Prime Minister King, and with him most of Canada, hoped that with this territorial acquisition the savage German dictator's appetite had been satisfied. From Ottawa the Prime Minister cabled Chamberlain: "The heart of Canada is rejoicing tonight at the success which has crowned your unremitting efforts for peace." In the columns of the *Winnipeg Free Press* John Dafoe's solitary voice cried out, "What's the cheering for?" He realized that Hitler's appetite for conquest was insatiable and that world war was just around the corner.

Throughout the inter-war years, while successive Canadian governments were rejecting commitments to the League and to the Commonwealth, the unity of the country which had been shattered by the events of the First World War was gradually being restored. But this unity was only achieved at the cost of avoiding steps which might have helped to prevent another war. At no times in these dangerous years was Canada's military budget raised to a level that would have placed the country in a state of preparedness. It was only in 1937, when warnings of war were already obvious, that Prime Minister King took steps to add to the country's defences. Even then the Canadian government refused to co-operate with the British in the establishment of an air-training plan for the Commonwealth countries. It was only after the war broke out that this plan was put into effect and the task of serious rearmament began.

Canada's course in foreign affairs during these years had been cautious and even shortsighted, but it was of a kind with the policy of her closest friends and allies, Great Britain and the United States. Like Canada, the United States refused to be drawn into world affairs, even rejecting membership in the League of Nations. As the war clouds gathered in Europe in the late 1930's, relations between Canada and the United States grew closer. Since Canada was a member of the League of Nations and of the British Commonwealth, her possible involvement in a European war was more likely than that of the isolationist United States. This situation was watched carefully by President Roosevelt who told an audience at Queen's University in August 1935: "The Dominion of Canada is part of the sisterhood of the British Empire. I give you an assurance that the people of the United States will not stand idly by if domination of Canadian soil is threatened by any other Empire."

When war finally came, Canada's position was different from what it had been in 1914. In the earlier world conflict, Britain had declared war for all the members of the Empire. In 1939 Canada controlled her own foreign policy and therefore declared war independently. On September 10, one week after Great Britain, the Canadian government, with parliament's approval, declared war on Nazi Germany. Although there were some opponents, including J. S. Woodsworth and some groups in Quebec, the country seemed united. The years of caution and careful avoidance of issues and actions that might have divided the country ended in solemn, but united, support of the war. Concern to preserve the country's unity had always been Mackenzie King's justification for his unheroic course in international affairs. In supporting the declaration of war in 1939, he pointed out: "I have made it the supreme endeavour of my leadership of the Government of this country, to let no hasty or premature threat or pronouncement create mistrust and divisions between the different elements that compose the population of our vast Dominion, so that, when the moment of decision came, all should see the issue itself that our national effort might be marked by unity of purpose, of heart and of endeavour." It remained to be seen whether this carefully nurtured unity would survive the test of another war.

17 CANADA AND THE SECOND WORLD WAR

"IF today, I am prepared to continue to lead a Government charged with the awful responsibility of prosecuting a war, it is because, contrary to every hope and wish I have ever entertained, I have been compelled to believe that only by the destruction of Naziism, and the resistance of ruthless aggression, can the nations of the British Commonwealth hope to continue to enjoy the liberties which are theirs under the British Crown, and the world itself be spared a descent into a new and terrible age of barbarism." This was the message that Mackenzie King delivered to the Canadian people in October 1939. It was a message that only hinted at the terrible years of warfare that lay ahead.

Few Canadians realized in the autumn of 1939 that the new conflict would be longer and more costly than the First World War. The Second World War eventually spread from Europe to Africa and Asia and took Canadians to every battlefront in the world on land, on sea and in the air. At first, Canadians thought that their role would be limited mainly to providing materials and machines necessary to ensure the victory of the British and French fighting forces in Europe. But it soon became apparent that Canadian troops would be required too. By the end of 1939 the first Canadian contingent had been established in the military camps which transformed Great Britain into an island fortress. The "phony war" ended in the spring of 1940, with the German invasion of Denmark and the Low Countries followed by the fall of France in June. It now became clear that the war would be long and bitter and that every Canadian resource would be needed if Hitler's massive, well-trained armies were to be defeated.

The magnificent prose of the British Prime Minister,

Winston Churchill, best indicated the hard road that lay ahead. On June 4, 1940, in the House of Commons at West-minster, his defiant message steeled the spirit of his country-men and buoyed up the hopes of free men everywhere.

> We shall go on to the end, we shall fight in France, we shall fight on the seas and oceans, we shall fight with growing confidence and growing strength in the air, we shall defend our Island, whatever the cost may be, we shall fight on the beaches, we shall fight on the land-ing grounds, we shall fight in the fields and in the streets, we shall fight in the hills; we shall never surrender, and even if, which I do not for a moment believe, this Island or a large part of it were subjugated and starving, then our Empire beyond the seas, armed and guarded by the British fleet, would carry on the struggle, until, in God's good time, the New World, with all its power and might, steps forth to the rescue and liberation of the old.

But as Churchill's inspiring words emphasized, the defeat of Hitler would not be easy.

1. CONSCRIPTION IN THE SECOND WORLD WAR

The realization that the war would be long and difficult recalled to Canadians the disagreements that had split the nation during the last years of the First World War. Al-though the memory of these events was especially vivid among the French Canadians, they supported the declaration of war in 1939. But they made it clear from the outset that they opposed any form of military conscription for over-seas services. To French Canadians conscription was much more than a military matter; it emphasized their minority position in a bicultural society. If the majority of English-speaking Canadians united against Quebec, as they had in 1917, they could force their decisions upon the French-speaking minority as effectively as if they had been a con-quering army. Thus the conscription question was a harsh reminder to French Canadians that the country explored

LAPOINTE'S POINT

This cartoon was taken from publicity issued by the National Government party for the 1940 election. In an attempt to revive the Conservative party and to enlist the support of anti-Mackenzie King Liberals, the Conservative leader, Dr. Manion, changed the name of his party to the National Government party before the 1940 election. Dr. Manion, who had succeeded R. B. Bennett, also promised that if elected he would draw his cabinet from all parties and form a truly national government to fight the war. Only thirty-nine Conservatives were elected. The cartoon was an example of their campaign, with the Liberals being attacked for raising the conscription issue. In fact, conscription had been raised throughout Canada long before, and was an issue.

and settled by their ancestors had been conquered by the British in 1759. To defend their native soil, the French Canadians were prepared to submit to any measures, including conscription. But they insisted that the war overseas be fought on a voluntary basis.

Fully aware of Quebec's attitude towards conscription, Ernest Lapointe, Minister of Justice and the leader of the

French Canadians at Ottawa, stated the position of the Liberal government, and especially of his French-speaking colleagues: "The whole province of Quebec will never agree to accept compulsory service or conscription outside Canada. I will go farther than that: When I say the whole province of Quebec I mean that personally I agree with them. I am authorized by my colleagues in the Cabinet for the province of Quebec to say that we will never agree to conscription and will never be members or supporters of a government that will try to enforce it." Having made this position clear, Lapointe then concluded by noting that "we are willing to offer our services without limitation and to devote our best efforts for the success of the cause we all have at heart." Thus Quebec's position, and the position of the Liberal government, was defined: complete support for the war effort, with the provision that military service overseas would be kept on a voluntary basis.

The pledge to fight the war on a voluntary basis came none too soon, for Premier Duplessis of Quebec called an election in October 1939. The campaign focused on the question of participation in the war. The Union Nationale leader claimed that Canadian participation in the war would lead to conscription. Duplessis' campaign was denounced as "an act of national sabotage" by Ernest Lapointe and the federal Liberals, who appealed for the defeat of Duplessis as a vote of confidence in themselves as men strong enough to prevent the introduction of conscription. The provincial Liberals were victorious, but their victory was based on a reiteration of the "no conscription" pledge. In the spring of 1940 a federal election was held. Once more the Liberal party was victorious; and once more it had repeated its pledge to fight the war without adopting conscription for overseas service.

It was fortunate for the government that the federal election had taken place before the gravity of the European situation was fully apparent. The disastrous defeat of France in the summer of 1940 immediately revived the conscription question in Canada. Naturally, it was from English-speaking

Canada that the demand for compulsory enlistment came, and some Conservatives took up the cry. To silence the agitation for conscription, the Liberal government passed a law, which provided for conscription for home service only. For a short time the conscription issue slept, until the entrance of the United States into the war on December 8, 1941, once again brought the matter to a head. The United States had adopted a policy of compulsory military service and many Canadians felt that Canada could not play its part in fighting the war on the basis of voluntary service alone. Because of the mounting pressure for conscription in English-speaking Canada, the government decided to submit the question to the people. In a national plebiscite, in April 1942, the government asked the voters to release it from its promise not to apply conscription for overseas service. The plebiscite was not a vote on conscription, but a request by the government for a free hand in dealing with the problem. The vote showed that most Canadians were in favour of releasing the government from its pledge. But, equally important, the returns revealed that while English-speaking Canada had voted eighty per cent in favour of giving the government a free hand, seventy-two per cent of the voters in Quebec opposed the motion. The racial split of 1917 had reappeared. Mackenzie King wrote in his diary: "As I looked at the returns, I thought of Durham's report on the state of Quebec when he arrived there after the Rebellion of 1837-38 and said he found two nations warring in the bosom of a single state. That would be the case in Canada, as applied to Canada as a whole, unless the whole question of conscription from now on is approached with the utmost care."

Prime Minister King did not interpret the result of the plebiscite as a demand for the immediate enactment of conscription, but rather as a decision to allow the government to enact compulsory service whenever it was thought necessary. "Not necessarily conscription, but conscription if necessary," was the cautious way that King described his government's policy after the plebiscite. By adopting this noncommittal attitude, King hoped to prevent, or at least to postpone, the crisis.

While the government's cautious policy completely satisfied no one, it did at least have the virtue of partially satisfying everyone. But the end had not yet been reached. The government made every effort to keep Canadian troops at the front reinforced, but the invasion of France in 1944 created a new manpower crisis. When it became clear in the autumn of 1944 that voluntary enlistments were not providing enough reinforcements, Colonel J. L. Ralston, the Minister of Defence, insisted that conscription was now necessary. But King was still convinced that more vigorous recruiting efforts could produce the needed men; Ralston resigned from office.

To succeed Ralston, King chose General A. G. L. McNaughton, the recently retired commander of the Canadian army overseas. McNaughton, who had at first believed that conscription was unnecessary, soon realized that voluntary enlistment could not provide the necessary recruits. In November 1944, King and his cabinet, which was on the verge of breaking up, decided that a measure of limited conscription for overseas service was necessary. Sixteen thousand men who had already been conscripted for home service only were now placed on the general duty rolls and became eligible for overseas service.

Although this policy of limited conscription threatened to divide the Liberal supporters of the government, the danger soon passed. Some French-Canadian members of parliament voted against King, but there was no permanent division either in the party or in the country. Mackenzie King's moderation and caution paid dividends, for by trying to understand the French-Canadian point of view he had won their trust. Moreover, he had obtained the support of strong leaders from Quebec. When his close colleague, Ernest Lapointe, died late in 1941, King had appointed a relatively obscure Quebec lawyer, Mr. Louis St. Laurent, as Minister of Justice, and to him must be given a great deal of the credit for the harmonious solution to the conscription crisis of 1944. St. Laurent stood by King throughout the crisis and accepted conscription when he saw that it could no longer be avoided. As he told the House of Commons: "The will of the majority must be respected and it must prevail. But I trust that, here in Canada, the majority will always, as it is doing in this case, assert that will only after giving due consideration to the feelings and views of the minority." Thus, by the end of 1944, the spectre of conscription had at last been faced and successfully laid. With a sense of satisfaction and pride, Prime Minister King could write: "I shall never be able to say how grateful I was and ever will be to my colleagues of French origin who kept so close to my side as we ran into and safely beyond the cataract which threatened to engulf us all."

2. THE WAR EFFORT AT HOME AND ABROAD

Though the conscription issue was the most dramatic problem in Canadian politics during the war, it was not the only difficulty that Canadians faced. The government's main task was to mobilize the nation's resources for war. Many of the country's natural resources were of the kind necessary for the manufacture of war weapons. Iron and steel production was greatly increased to feed the factories that were turning out guns, munitions and ships. These activities in turn increased the pace of hydro-electric development which was necessary to run not only the older industries but the new ones like the giant aluminum industry that grew up in Quebec. By the end of the war, Canada's industrial exports were exceeding the export of staple products for the first time in the country's history. The war had transformed Canada into a major industrial nation.

Mining and manufacturing were not the only industries that flourished because of the war. Increased demand for food products raised wheat prices, and, blessed by years of high rainfall, the prairie farmer once more produced bumper crops. British Columbians prospered on wartime de-

AND THE COST OF LIVING SOARS MERRILY UPWARD

Not everyone was satisfied with the government's attempts to establish adequate price controls.

mands for their timber and mineral resources, while the Maritimes benefited from shipbuilding and the great use made of east-coast ports by the Atlantic convoys carrying men and materials to the war fronts.

The government supervised much of the economic development of the war period. Under the guidance of C. D. Howe, who earned the title "Minister of Everything," the economic production drive was highly successful. Where private industry could not meet the demands of the war effort, the government stepped in to provide publicly-owned and operated corporations. Scientists employed by the government in war agencies and at the National Research Council developed new materials, such as synthetic rubber, to meet the multiplicity of demands made by modern warfare. The government controlled prices and rationed foods, to ensure that the men at the front were properly fed and equipped and to prevent war profiteering. These controls, and heavy wartime taxation, affected all Canadians.

But the war's most immediate effect was on the thousands of young men and women who served in the armed services on the battlefronts of the world. By the end of the war Canada had raised a military force of over a million persons from a population of only twelve million. At the beginning of the war Canadian troops sailed for England where they played an important, if undramatic, role in deterring the Germans from attacking the British Isles. Once the threat of Nazi invasion of Britain passed, Canadian troops settled down to await the day when they were needed to take part in the invasion to liberate the European continent. Canadian troops had lost heavily in the fruitless attempt to defend Hong Kong against the Japanese in 1941, but it was not until August 1942 that Canadian troops first saw action in Europe. To test the German defences and to divert the enemy's attention while preparations were being made for landings in North Africa, five thousand troops of the Canadian Second Division landed at Dieppe on the French coast. It was a costly experiment. The Canadians held their ground for ten hours against heavy German fire, but were forced to retreat after suffering over three thousand casualties, of whom about half were taken prisoner.

In 1943 a Canadian division in the Mediterranean theatre assisted in the hard-fought conquest of Sicily and Italy. Then, on June 6, 1944, the long-awaited D-Day appointed for the invasion of Europe across the English Channel arrived. Canadian, British and American forces, all under the supreme command of United States General Dwight D. Eisenhower, stormed the Normandy beaches to begin the liberation of France. Led by General G. D. H. Crerar, the Canadian troops distinguished themselves in a year of long, hard fighting against some of Hitler's crack divisions.

Sweeping through France, the Allied forces cut off the Germans in the Falaise Gap in Normandy, and moved into Belgium and the Low Countries. In the Scheldt estuary, where the Germans were well dug in, the Canadian troops played a major role in freeing this important entrance to Europe from the enemy forces. When the Allied victory came in May 1945 it was the Canadian command that accepted the surrender of the Nazi forces in the Netherlands.

Six years of war had cost Canada 41,700 men, dead or missing. While Canada's contribution to the victory was naturally smaller than that of her allies, Britain, France, the Soviet Union and the United States, the quality of her armed forces had been high. In the words of the official historian of the Canadian Army, Canada's record "might command respect even by the standard of the greater powers."

It was not only the Canadian Army that emerged from the war with a proud record. The Royal Canadian Navy played an heroic and efficient role in the supremely important task of protecting Allied convoys from the Nazi submarines that lurked beneath the cold Atlantic. At the beginning of the war the Canadian naval service was only five thousand strong, but by 1945 it had increased to nearly one hundred thousand men. By the end of the war, the Royal Canadian Navy had assumed the main responsibility for ensuring the safe passage of Atlantic supply convoys to Britain. It was cold tedious work, often punctuated by an encounter with a Nazi U-boat. But its work was of the greatest significance for neither Britain, in the early years of the war, nor the Allied armies after the invasion of Europe had begun, could have survived without the supplies shipped from North America.

Canadians also won distinction in the air. The air force increased from four thousand to two hundred thousand men. Forty-five Royal Canadian Air Force squadrons fought in Europe, the Mediterranean, India and Burma. The Arctic Command aided the Canadian Navy in convoy activities. As important as the actual engagements of the fighter and bomber squadrons was the air training programme carried out in Canada under the British Commonwealth Air Training Scheme. From 1939 to the conclusion of the war men from all parts of the Commonwealth and Allied nations came to Canada to receive their training before departing

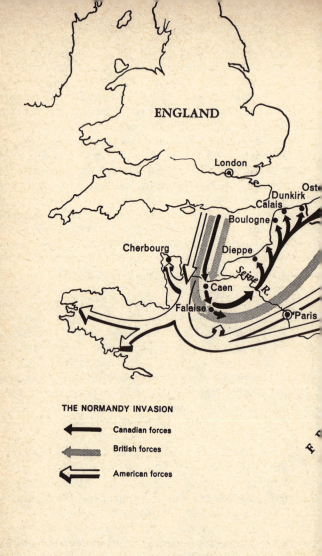

ENGLAND

London

Oste

Dunkirk

Calais

Boulogne

Cherbourg

Dieppe

Seine R.

Caen

Falaise

Paris

THE NORMANDY INVASION

Canadian forces

British forces

American forces

THE OCCUPATION

British zone

American zone

French zone

Russian zone

for the war theatres. The Air Training plan gave practical expression to the value of the Commonwealth association in defence matters. In this and many other ways the Commonwealth, which had faltered in the face of the German menace in the inter-war period, gave definite proof of determination to prevent the spread of totalitarianism.

It would be a mistake to overestimate the importance of Canada's contribution to the defeat of the Axis Powers, Germany, Italy and Japan. Canada was still a small country compared to her mammoth southern neighbour, or even to the heavily populated British Isles. Yet, in co-operation with these two countries, the rest of the Commonwealth and the Soviet Union, Canada played a role of more than minor importance. During the dark days after the collapse of France and before the Japanese had forced the United States into the conflict, Canada was Britain's major ally. At the level of diplomacy Canada was particularly important in working as a link between Great Britain and the United States, helping to ensure, even while the Americans remained neutral, that necessary materials and weapons were obtained by the hard-pressed British. This role held important political implications as the years of defeat began slowly to turn into victory.

3. PREPARATIONS FOR THE POST-WAR WORLD

During the war Canada's relations with her two powerful allies, Britain and the United States, were always close, but not always uncomplicated. Prime Minister King believed that Canada had a special role to play as the mediator between Britain and the United States, but he did not find it an easy one. Nor did he feel that the two big countries were properly appreciative of the contribution that Canada was making to the winning of the war. In 1943 he wrote in a somewhat irritated mood: "It was perfectly clear to me that, so far as Britain and United States were concerned, there was little thought of giving credit except in very general terms to what was being done by Canada."

But despite these momentary irritations, King worked very hard at his self-imposed role of mediator between Britain and the United States. By the end of the war Canada had probably come to deserve the description that Winston Churchill had earlier given when he wrote that Canada was "a magnet exercising a double attraction drawing both Great Britain and the United States towards herself, and thus drawing them closer to each other. She is the only surviving bond which stretches from Europe across the Atlantic ocean." The war made this bond more important than it had ever been, for it is unlikely that Hitler could have been defeated without the military and economic resources of the United States.

During the late 1930's relations between Canada and the United States had begun to grow closer. As Europe moved towards war, both Canada and the United States began to give serious thought to the defence of North America. When war came the United States remained a neutral, but a neutral interested in the outcome, especially as it might affect North America. In August 1940, Prime Minister King and President Roosevelt decided that the defence of North America required careful examination and mutual policies between the two neighbours. The result was the signing of the Ogdensburg Agreement which established the Permanent Joint Board on Defence. The purpose of this Board was to work out plans for the co-operative defence of North America in the event of any attack. This agreement was followed quickly by the announcement of an arrangement that had been worked out between Britain and the United States, with Canada as the go-between, whereby the United States was given permanent leases on a number of British naval bases in North America, including three in Newfoundland, in return for fifty over-age but badly needed destroyers. This agreement, King believed, vindicated his "whole life's work for better international relations, particularly between the United Kingdom and the United States." Thus Canada was playing the role of mediator, and at the same time moving closer to the United States. The construction of the American military road through Canada to Alaska, begun in 1940, also demonstrated the strengthening of the physical links between the two countries.

One of the Canadian government's problems from the outset of the war was a serious shortage of American dollars with which to pay for materials purchased from the United States. To find a solution, Prime Minister King paid an official visit to the American President in April 1941. The result of this meeting was the Hyde Park Declaration which provided for increased American purchases of war material in Canada and defence production sharing. In this way the economies of Canada and the United States were tied more closely together, just as North American defence was established on a co-operative basis. The growing friendliness between Canada and the United States was revealed by the informal manner in which President Roosevelt signed the original draft of the Hyde Park Declaration. He scrawled across the document, "Done by Mackenzie and F.D.R. at Hyde Park on a Grand Sunday, April 20, 1941." When the Japanese attack on Pearl Harbor on December 7, 1941, brought the United States actively into the war, co-operation between the neighbours grew even closer.

Some Canadians feared that their country was moving too readily into the well-intentioned but overpowering embrace of the United States. The enormous population, industrial might and material wealth of the United States could be a serious threat to Canada's independence. Was not the Canadian economy becoming too dependent on the United States? Was not Canada too closely tied to defensive arrangements in which the United States was the dominant partner? Was not the culture of English-speaking Canada becoming only a pale image of her neighbour's to the South?

These were questions which remained unanswered at the end of the war. During the war itself, when every effort was concentrated on defeating the Axis Powers, there was little time to worry about long term problems. Although Prime Minister King was aware of the dangers that threatened Canada through too close an association with the

United States, he felt that the dangers were counterbalanced by the benefits that would result from close co-operation between the nations of the English-speaking world. At the time of the Hyde Park Declaration he wrote in his diary: "I, personally, would be strongly opposed to anything like political union. I would keep the British Commonwealth of Nations as intact as possible. Canada, in time, and sooner than we expect perhaps, will become its centre. It is better to have two peoples and two governments on this continent understanding each other and reciprocating in their relations as an example to the world, than to have anything like continental union." Not even Mackenzie King could foresee that the events of the post-war world would push Canada even further along the road of co-operation with the United States.

When the surrender of Japan in August 1945 brought the war to an end, Canada was a greatly altered country. She had become a fully-fledged industrial and urban nation. Moreover, most Canadians were now convinced that their country would have to play an active role in the affairs of the world if future wars were to be prevented. And the prevention of war now seemed more necessary than ever, for the dropping of the atom bomb on two Japanese cities in the summer of 1945 gave support to the fear that man could invent a weapon powerful enough to destroy himself. It was with good reason that the Canadian parliament passed a resolution in the spring of 1945 which emphasized that "the establishment of an effective international organization for the maintenance of peace and security is of vital importance to Canada, and, indeed, to the future well being of mankind."

18 CANADA IN A WORLD OF SUPER POWERS

CANADA emerged from the Second World War far more united than it had from the First. Mackenzie King's careful handling of the explosive conscription issue in 1944 avoided the dangerous racial crisis of 1917. More thorough-going and rigid government controls prevented the serious regional and occupational grievances which had existed during and immediately following the 1914-18 period. The war lifted the country from the miseries of depression by prompting full mobilization of the economy to feed and supply the Allied forces. By 1945 Canadians were anxious to turn their energy to the constructive task of national development and reconstruction.

1. ECONOMIC GROWTH

The steady and insistent demands of war had given a tremendous stimulus to the expansion of the Canadian economy and this continued after the war. Between 1941 and 1962 Canada's population increased from 11,500,000 to 18,500,000. This increase was partly due to a high birth-rate, but it was also the result of renewed efforts to attract European immigrants to help meet the labour needs of an expanding economy. As usual, the heaviest inflow came from Great Britain, which provided nearly a third of the total number. Italians, Germans, Americans, Hungarians who fled their country during the 1956 rebellion, and many others from western, northern and central Europe brought the total immigration to 1,500,000 by 1957.

The newcomers, or "New Canadians" as they were soon being called, seldom went into agriculture as they had during the great immigration boom prior to 1914. Instead, they found opportunities for their skills in the growing industrial cities. By 1962 almost sixty per cent of the population of Canada lived in cities, thus marking the final and unmistakable transformation of Canada from an agricultural to an urban and industrial nation.

The nation's productive capacity increased with its population. Between 1939 and 1962, the Gross National Product leaped from five billion, seven hundred million dollars to over thirty-six billion dollars. This rapid economic expansion after 1945 was partly due to the fact that Canada was particularly attractive to foreign investors; the nation's political stability and economic potential together gave investors assurances of security and growing profits. Foreign capital financed the exploitation of natural resources like oil, natural gas, iron and uranium, and financed expansion of steel production, pulp-and-paper milling, aluminum processing, and secondary manufacturing of all kinds. By the 1950's aluminum from Kitimat, British Columbia, oil from Leduc, Alberta, and iron from Steep Rock, Ontario and Ungava, Quebec, found ready sales on domestic and world markets.

The agricultural sector of the economy also expanded and flourished. Wartime demands and the return of favourable food-growing conditions had already revived the wheat economy before 1945. In the post-war years Canadian farmers raised their wheat output to an average of five hundred million bushels annually. Until 1952, when a seven hundred million bushel wheat crop was harvested, there was no serious difficulty in finding markets for Canadian grain. But by 1952 the revival of European farming, combined with high Canadian prices and the disposal of United States agricultural surpluses at low prices, left a growing quantity of unsold grain in Canada in the years 1952-57. This situation produced dissatisfaction among western farmers who, by 1957, were ready to turn against the Liberal government in Ottawa.

The extensive economic developments of the post-war period created a demand for new transportation and communication facilities. A complex system of pipelines reached out from the oil wells in Alberta west across the Rockies, east across the prairies, and south into the United States, carrying crude oil to refineries and natural gas to feed industries and homes far from the western oil fields. As usual in Canada the construction of new methods of transportation brought public money and private enterprise into co-operation. The decision of the Liberal government to provide public money to aid in the construction of the trans-Canada pipeline in 1956 occasioned a political quarrel that added to the growing unpopularity of the Liberal administration.

The largest and most adventurous enterprise in the field of transportation and communications during the post-war decade was the construction of the St. Lawrence Seaway and hydro-electric project. Designed to transform the inland cities of the Great Lakes into major oceanic trading centres, the enterprise had been in the planning stages for many years. In 1932, Canada and the United States had negotiated a treaty for the joint construction of the inland waterway. But lobbies, or pressure groups, representing railway, coal and coastal-port interests had been able to prevent ratification of the treaty in the American Senate. By 1950, however, Canada felt strong enough to construct the Seaway alone and her threat to do so was sufficient to overcome objections in the American Senate. As President Truman told Congress in 1952: "The question before Congress now is whether the United States shall participate in the construction and thus maintain joint operation and control over this development, which is so important to our security and our economic progress." Finally, in 1954, the last details were arranged and five years later this vast oceanic highway was opened to traffic. But, as Lester Pearson, at that time the Minister for External Affairs in the Liberal cabinet, told an American audience, "to be perfectly frank, many Canadians didn't think too highly of this last-minute participation—either of its timing or of its nature."

This slight feeling of resentment at the attitude of the United States to the Seaway was part of a growing anxiety

Balance (?) Of Trade

"No fundamental change in our import curbs appears practicable at present. Now how about you taking some nice turkeys?"

Doug Wright's cartoon appeared in the Montreal **Star** in 1960. But it expressed a view of Canadian-American commercial relations that has existed since the end of the Second World War.

in Canada about the degree of influence which the United States seemed to exercise in Canadian affairs. Canada was, of course, a close ally of the United States in international affairs. But of more immediate concern to many Canadians was the increasing dependence of the Canadian economy on that of its southern neighbour. Not only was the United States Canada's most important market for exports and source of imports, but it was the source of a large proportion of the foreign investment which had financed Canada's economic expansion. This latter state marked a great transformation in Canadian economic life. Before the First World War, about sixty per cent of all foreign capital invested in Canada came from Great Britain. But during the inter-war years Britain's economy declined, and American capital gradually replaced British. In 1956 non-residents, mainly American, controlled fifty-seven per cent of the total investment in Canadian manufacturing, and sixty-six per cent of the total in mining, smelting and oil. By 1959, seventy-five per cent of all foreign investment in Canada came from the United States.

There was no doubt that the economic advances of the post-war years would not have taken place without the large inflow of American money. But many people were disturbed by the degree of control that foreign capital had gained over Canadian economic life. Moreover, there was a growing feeling that the United States often ignored Canadian interests. A committee of the United States Congress summed up this feeling when it reported in 1959: "The United States and its citizens have frequently adopted a patronizing assumption that Canada, like a poor relation, would remain at our beck and call, and that no matter what the provocation, Canadians would not object to any step we might take. This lack of interest, this ignorance of the Canadian heritage and Canadian problems, and this patronizing air have been displayed by the people, the press and the Government of the United States." Although there were obviously no easy solutions to these problems, many Canadians believed that methods should be found to encourage increased Canadian investment and more frequent employment of Canadians in managerial positions in foreign-controlled industries.

Despite such misgivings and fears, most Canadians enjoyed a high degree of material well-being in the prosperous decade after the Second World War. More homes were built, more domestic comforts purchased, more automobiles sold, and higher wages paid than in any comparable period of the country's history. And while the economy boomed, the non-material side of Canadian life was also expanding. Schools and universities bulged with students seeking every variety of education. Signs of a developing Canadian tradition, or rather traditions, French and English, in the arts, music and theatre began to appear. The Massey Commission, established in 1949 to investigate Canadian culture, reported: "We were conscious of a prevailing hunger existing throughout the country for a fuller measure of what the writer, the artist and the musician could give." The opening of the annual Shakespearean Festival at Stratford, Ontario, in 1953 was one sign of the new cultural awakening. Such government-sponsored agencies as the National Film Board and the Canadian Broadcasting Corporation continued to support artistically creative Canadians. But the main aid for these activities came in 1957 with the establishment of the Canada Council, whose one hundred million dollar endowment was to be used to aid universities and to provide scholarships and grants to Canadian students, writers and artists. Thus the dozen years following the war were years of expansion and progress in many areas of Canadian life. The darkest cloud on the Canadian horizon was the tense international situation, for Canada was now involved in world affairs as it had never been before.

2. CANADA AND THE COLD WAR

The Second World War was a harsh warning to countries like Canada and the United States that the peace of the world could only be preserved if all nations worked together to provide collective security. Despite their isolationist policies in the inter-war period, both Canada and the United States had become involved in the struggle to defeat the Axis Powers. Neither country wanted to see a repetition of these events. Both nations, therefore, became founding members of the United Nations Organization that succeeded the old League of Nations. As Louis St. Laurent, the Canadian Minister of External Affairs, put it: "The choice we face today is the choice between isolationism and its certain weaknesses, and the hope through collective action of preventing another war."

Canada's role in the post-war world was a minor one compared with that of such powerful nations as the United States. Still, it was the view of the Canadian government that small and middle powers had much to contribute. "Power is not exclusively concentrated in the hands of any four or five states," Prime Minister King claimed in 1945. "Experience has shown that the contribution of smaller powers is not a negligible one, either to the preserving of peace or to its restoration when peace has been disturbed." With the assistance of the Minister of External Affairs, Louis St. Laurent, and later through the work of Lester B. Pearson in the same office, the Liberal government formulated a foreign policy designed for the needs of a middle power like Canada.

The United Nations was the chief hope of all those who believed that world peace could best be preserved through an organization that had a world-wide membership. But the success of the United Nations, like that of the League before it, required the co-operation of the great powers who held permanent seats on the Security Council. On these nations, especially on the United States, Britain and the Soviet Union, rested the heaviest responsibility for the enforcement of United Nations' decisions. Shortly after the founding of the world organization it became tragically clear that the wartime allies, and especially the United States and the Soviet Union, who dominated the Security Council, rarely agreed on issues that disturbed the world's peace. In fact, the effectiveness of the United Nations was often nullified by the use of the veto power which had been given to the major powers. Although the Soviet Union was rarely able to muster a majority of votes in the General Assembly where all the member nations were represented, its use of the veto in the Security Council prevented the United Nations from playing the part in world affairs that its founders had hopefully assigned it.

By the late 1940's, the activities and growing hostility of the Soviet Union caused the nations of western Europe, the Commonwealth and the United States to investigate additional means of mutual protection and collective security. In 1946 Canadians were shocked to learn from Igor Gouzenko, a cipher clerk in the Soviet embassy in Ottawa, who deserted his post, of the operation of a Russian spy ring in Canada. When the Russian position in eastern Europe was further consolidated by a Communist seizure of power in Czechoslovakia in February 1948, the western powers determined to form a new defensive alliance to prevent further expansion by the U.S.S.R.

The western response to the growing fear that the Soviet Union intended to use her military strength to gain control of western as well as eastern Europe was the North Atlantic Treaty signed in 1949. Canada was one of the founding members of N.A.T.O., the organization that grew from this treaty. In suggesting such an organization Louis St. Laurent, the Canadian Minister of External Affairs, emphasized the need for "the creation and preservation by the nations of the Free World under the leadership of Great Britain, the United States and France, of an overwhelming preponderance of force over any adversary or possible combination of adversaries." But Canada also insisted that the organization should be more than a military alliance. "It must be economic; it must be moral," St. Laurent stated. As a result the treaty contained a clause providing for the social, cultural and economic co-operation of the member nations. However, the ideal of an Atlantic Community has proven easier to describe than to achieve. Since 1949 nothing has been achieved in transforming this section of the treaty of alliance into a reality.

Canada's membership in N.A.T.O. has meant the assumption of far-reaching military responsibilities. The scope of the alliance, originally limited to western Europe, was later expanded to include Greece and Turkey. In 1954 West Germany was permitted to rearm and join the Western Alliance. Under the N.A.T.O. agreement Canada has provided a brigade of infantry for service in Germany, twelve air squadrons, and some forty ships.

It was not only in Europe that Canada assumed military commitments in the 1950's. Under the authority of the United Nations, Canadian troops served in the Korean War which broke out in June 1950 when North Korean

forces moved against the American-sponsored government
of South Korea. During three years of war Canada suffered
one thousand six hundred and forty-two casualties, including four hundred and six dead. Canadian diplomats and
soldiers also served on an international commission super-
vising the 1954 ceasefire agreement between warring Communist and non-Communist forces in Indochina. In 1958 Canada
supplied the largest contingent for a United Nations' observer
group in Lebanon and in 1960 sent signallers and air force
personnel to the Congo when civil war erupted in that country.

Canada's willingness to join N.A.T.O. and to assume
widespread military and diplomatic responsibilities reflected
her awareness of the dangerous position of a country sand-
wiched between the Soviet Union and the United States.
One result of this situation was the growth of an increasingly close relationship between Canada and the United
States. The two governments not only continued the wartime
arrangements for continental defence; they organized new
measures for mutual defence which included three lines
of radar stations reaching into the Canadian north to detect any attack that might be launched over the northern
wastelands. In addition to this warning system the governments in 1957 signed a new defence arrangement known
as the North American Air Defence Agreement (N.O.R.-
A.D.) which placed Canadian and American air defence
in North America under a united command.

As well as reflecting the pressures of the Cold War, the
growing military dependence of Canada on the United States
revealed the declining influence of Britain in world affairs.
Having born the heaviest responsibility for fighting two
major wars in the twentieth century, Britain was on the
verge of economic exhaustion in 1945. Nevertheless, the
Commonwealth remained an important factor in the formulation of Canadian foreign policy. It was not the same
Commonwealth that had existed in the interwar years, for
in 1947 the first Asian members were admitted to membership. One of these members, India, insisted on becoming a
republic, and it was only after long negotiations, in which
Canada played a leading role, that a formula was worked

out whereby a republic could join an organization composed of monarchical states. The inclusion of India, Pakistan, Ceylon, Ghana, Nigeria and other non-white nations transformed the Commonwealth into a multi-racial organization. Moreover, since most of these new states were heavily populated and economically underdeveloped, Commonwealth members organized the Colombo Plan in 1950 to give them economic and technical assistance. By 1962 Canada had provided almost $400,000,000 in foreign aid under the Colombo Plan. These funds helped to finance a wide variety of developments: massive dams for power and irrigation, cement plants, an atomic reactor in India, fishing vessels, locomotives, raw materials and schools. The Colombo Plan also supplied teachers and technical experts.

Commonwealth relations were sometimes complicated in the post-war years. The most serious crisis occurred in 1956 when British and French troops invaded the Suez Canal zone in Egypt to prevent the government of Colonel Nasser from taking over full control of this vital communications artery. Britain's action in Suez, unquestionably a violation of the United Nations Charter, placed Canada and other Commonwealth nations in a difficult position. India and other former British colonies regarded the action as blatant imperialism and contemplated withdrawal from the Commonwealth.

At the United Nations, Canada agreed with the United States and Russia in condemning the Anglo-French action. But with the aid of Lester Pearson, the Canadian Minister of External Affairs, the United Nations reached a settlement which brought the intervention to an end and prevented the break-up of the Commonwealth. The solution involved the establishment of a United Nations Emergency Force, which included Canadian troops and was under a Canadian Commander, Major-General E. L. M. Burns; the duty of the force was to supervise the evacuation of the invading armies from the canal zone. This successful action by the United Nations prevented what might easily have been an outbreak of more general hostilities. For his contribution towards this peaceful solution, Lester Pearson was awarded the Nobel

Peace Prize in 1957. Although Commonwealth feelings ran high over the Suez episode, the trouble was finally smoothed over without any of the Asian members withdrawing from the organization.

Thus the post-war years saw Canada moving closer to the United States, while at the same time preserving and strengthening relations with the members of what was now a multi-racial Commonwealth. New leaders were to emerge in Canadian domestic politics to guide the country through these years of change and international tension.

3. THE END OF THE KING ERA

When the war ended in Europe in the spring of 1945 Mackenzie King's Liberal government was nearing the end of its five-year term of office. There were signs that the C.C.F., which had won power in Saskatchewan in 1944, and the Conservatives, who had taken office in Ontario in 1943, were both serious challengers to replace the Liberal government in Ottawa. But the Liberals had prepared for the post-war years, anticipating the need for social reform and economic planning to prevent the return of the conditions of the 'thirties. A Liberal brain-trust drew up a programme including price supports to guarantee stable prices for agricultural products, children's allowances, hospital insurance, government-sponsored housing developments, rehabilitation allowances for veterans and a scheme of public works projects to provide employment and counteract an economic recession. It was this programme that the Liberals offered the country in the election campaign of June 1945.

The election showed that the majority of the Canadian people approved the wartime policies of the King government and were prepared to entrust the Liberals with the tasks of post-war reconstruction. The Liberals had been particularly worried about their ability to retain the support of Quebec, for the French Canadians had resented the conscription policy of 1944. One sign of Quebec's distrust of the federal government had been the re-election of Maurice Duplessis and the Union Nationale in 1944. But in 1945 the

THE CHIEF COOK COMES THROUGH

As the Second World War drew to a close, many people expected that the King government would suffer the same fate that the Conservatives had experienced after the First World War. The question was whether the electorate would turn to M. J. Coldwell and the C.C.F. or to the Progressive Conservative party, now led by John Bracken. Prime Minister King's greatest fear was that the voters, anxious for measures of social security, would turn to the C.C.F. To meet this threat to his power, the Prime Minister began to plan for post-war social security measures.

French Canadians once more supported Mackenzie King. The French-Canadian newspaper, *Montréal-Matin*, gave the best explanation of the King victory when it pointed out that the Liberals' "policy has been sufficiently elastic to adapt itself to the wishes of the people, while other parties sought to impose their programme and doctrine."

Back in office the Liberals found that most of their plans for post-war reconstruction could not be implemented. Post-war prosperity weakened the popular demand for social security measures and government economic planning. More important, the King government came up against the problem of "provincial rights" as it had done in the late 1930's. The leading opponent of any expansion of federal powers or functions was Premier Duplessis of Quebec, who met every federal proposal for social security measures, federal assistance to higher education, or revenue-sharing agreements that would spread the national wealth more evenly among the provinces, with the charge that provincial autonomy was being threatened. Nevertheless, the last three years of Mackenzie King's long term of office contained some notable achievements. It was a tribute to his political genius that when he gave up the leadership, he left his party in such a healthy state that it was able to retain office for another nine years.

The main domestic achievement of the last King government was the successful completion of Confederation. In 1933 the desperate financial situation in Newfoundland had resulted in a Commission government, appointed by the British, and the suspension of responsible government. After the war there was a conference of elected representatives to make recommendations on the future government of the colony. Since 1867 Newfoundland had rejected every Canadian invitation to unite with Canada. But increasing contacts during the war, the decline in British power and the growing prosperity and strength of Canada, together with attractive financial inducements, enabled Joseph Smallwood, leader of the pro-Confederation forces, to persuade the voters to make Newfoundland Canada's tenth province on March 31, 1949.

By the time this union came about and the Newfoundlanders had somewhat reluctantly given up their centuries of independence for the economic advantages of Canadian citizenship, King had left the political scene. The new Prime Minister was the man whom King had brought into the cabinet at the height of the conscription crisis. He was the dignified, wealthy, and bilingual Quebec lawyer Louis St. Laurent, soon to be known as "Uncle Looie" by the Canadian electorate.

Unlike King, Louis St. Laurent had never considered himself a career politician, and had planned to return to private life as soon as the war was over. But he had stayed on, moving from the position of Minister of Justice to that of Minister of External Affairs in 1946. In the shrewd judgement of Mackenzie King, St. Laurent, the French Canadian, was his natural successor as leader of the Liberal party in 1948.

St. Laurent was a worthy successor to Laurier and King as Prime Minister. He lacked Laurier's spellbinding oratorical powers and the deft political acuteness of King, but he was intellectually keen, an efficient administrator, and gave the appearance of a kind, elderly uncle whose integrity was beyond question. Like Laurier, he placed his Canadianism before his French Canadianism, and even quarrelled publicly with Quebec's autonomy-minded Premier, Maurice Duplessis, over such matters as federal taxing powers.

Under St. Laurent's leadership, and with the able assistance of such men as C. D. Howe, Minister of Trade and Commerce, the country's economic development moved ahead rapidly. In the field of international affairs, St. Laurent found an able minister in Lester B. Pearson, who moved from the civil service to active politics in 1948. Despite the emergence of such difficult problems as the growing grain surplus, increasing American control of the Canadian economy, and the dangers of the Cold War, the Canadian people showed their continued confidence in the policies and the administrative competence of the Liberals by re-electing them in 1949 and again in 1953 with overwhelming majorities.

Throughout the years of Liberal ascendancy, three opposition parties continued an apparently fruitless competition for the support of the electorate. Since R. B. Bennett's defeat in 1935 the Conservatives had suffered numerous setbacks. Three successive leaders had tried without success to revive the party's fortunes, and by 1948 the Conservatives had been reduced to little more than an Ontario party. However, at their convention that year they proved their fighting spirit as they chose a new leader, George Drew, and renamed themselves the Progressive Conservatives. The C.C.F., led by M. J. Coldwell after Woodsworth's death in 1942, had its main strength in the prairies, especially in Saskatchewan where T. C. Douglas had won office for the C.C.F. in 1944. The Social Credit party, led by Solon Low, drew its

No, no. It's not TCA — it's the Super-Howe!

W. B. Nesbitt, Conservative M.P. for Oxford, Ontario, accused the Liberal government of putting "the jet-propelled engine of closure on its steam-roller majority to speed the crushing of the Opposition."

chief support from Alberta, which had remained loyal to the party ever since 1935. In 1952, British Columbia joined Alberta and elected a Social Credit administration. On the national level, however, none of the opposition parties was able to find the formula that would bring an end to the long years of Liberal rule.

But by 1956 the Liberal government was beginning to show signs of weakness and old age. Accustomed to wielding power, the Liberals developed a careless attitude towards public opinion, clearly revealed during the bitter parliamentary debate in 1956 over the construction of the trans-Canada pipeline. The Liberal policy was to provide public money to aid in the construction of this pipeline, which would be owned by a private company controlled by American investors. "Canada, through the agency of this government, will put up the money," George Drew charged, "and then an organization owned in the United States to the extent of eighty-three per cent is going to get the benefit of the Canadian investment." This was a charge that won the sympathy of many Canadians who were growing uneasy about the degree of American control over Canada's economy. The Liberals weakened themselves further by attempting to force the pipeline measure through the House of Commons by the introduction of closure, a parliamentary device designed to limit debate. The Conservative and C.C.F. parties fought the measure with a vigour that seemed to restore their vitality. The government measure finally passed, but throughout the nation the pipeline affair was taken as a sign that the Liberals had held office long enough. As a parliamentary reporter wrote: "If the Liberal government is beaten at the next election—a prospect less unlikely now than it has been for twenty-one years—this session of Parliament will appear in retrospect as a 'Gritterdammerung' or 'Twilight of the Grits.' Political historians may well conclude that the Liberals fell, not because of any one policy, and certainly not a pipeline policy of which the average voter knew little and cared less, but because they failed to observe the proper limits of power."

In the same year, the Progressive Conservatives elected a new leader, John G. Diefenbaker, a prairie lawyer who had been a member of parliament since 1940. By the time a new election was called in 1957, this evangelical orator had instilled in his party a new spirit. Campaigning strenuously and playing upon national fears of undue American influence in Canadian affairs, Mr. Diefenbaker succeeded in dislodging the Liberals. But the Diefenbaker victory was so slim that a new election had to be called in 1958, when the Progressive Conservatives, with two hundred and eight seats, were swept into office with the largest parliamentary majority in Canadian history.

In 1958, a new era opened in Canadian politics. After twenty-two years of Liberal government, the country had turned to the Progressive Conservatives and their new leader, John Diefenbaker. After the 1957 defeat, the Liberals too chose a new leader, the internationally known Lester B. Pearson. For the first time since 1921, national minor parties were nearly erased in 1958. The C.C.F., which had won only eight seats, looked towards a future in which its identity would be submerged in the New Democratic Party formed in alliance with the Canadian Labour Congress. The Social

Credit party, though it was far from dead, was left without representation at Ottawa.

4. PROGRESSIVE CONSERVATIVES IN POWER

During the first four years of Progressive Conservative government the pace of economic expansion gradually slowed down. Both Canada and the United States experienced economic recessions during 1959, and by 1962 unemployment figures in Canada reached a level that was higher than any year since the depression. Among the reasons for the country's economic difficulties was the gradual decline of American investment which had been so important in financing the developments of the early 1950's. In addition, Canadian products were harder to sell in overseas markets, since the countries of Europe whose industrial power had been destroyed by the war were now once again operating at full capacity. With declining exports the country experienced financial difficulties which included a balance of payments problem caused, in part, by a failure of export sales to balance the imports of goods and capital.

Though the industrial sector of the economy suffered from stagnation, agricultural prosperity revived. Not only did the Conservative government give generous aid to the farmers, but the large wheat surpluses which had piled up during the late 'fifties gradually disappeared, when poor harvests in 1959 and 1960 reduced grain production. Moreover, the Conservatives succeeded in finding new markets for Canadian grain, especially in eastern Europe and Communist China. The political result of this agricultural prosperity was the transformation of western Canada, once the fortress of protest movements, into a Conservative stronghold.

Elsewhere, too, the Diefenbaker government made some notable innovations. To meet the problems of slack trade and unemployment, the government established a National Productivity Council in 1960, whose function it was to advise the government on methods of increasing Canadian productivity and trade. In social welfare the government increased the pensions of the aged, the disabled and the war veterans. One action for which the Prime Minister made himself personally responsible was the enactment in 1960 of a Bill of Rights. This Act, unlike the American Bill of Rights, was not a constitutional amendment. It was simply a parliamentary statute declaring that Canadians have a right to enjoy such traditional liberties as freedom of speech, association, religion and the press, and also the right to a fair trial, habeas corpus, and legal counsel. Though the Bill of Rights applied only to federal legislation and would have no effect during wartime, it represented an important reminder to Canadians that even the power of government was limited.

In foreign policy the Diefenbaker government faced several serious decisions. The Prime Minister, at a Commonwealth Conference in 1959, joined with the leaders of the African and Asian members in condemning the racial segregation practices of South Africa. The result was South Africa's decision to leave the Commonwealth in 1960. Another Commonwealth problem arose with Great Britain's announcement of her decision to seek entry into the European Common Market. The Diefenbaker government, naturally concerned about the possible loss of British markets for Canadian agricultural products, insisted that a Commonwealth Conference should be held before Britain made any final decision to join the E.C.M. With the breakdown of negotiations between Britain and the European trading partners early in 1963, Canadian worries were temporarily postponed.

No question of foreign affairs received more serious attention from the Diefenbaker government than disarmament. Mr. Howard Green, the Minister of External Affairs, made repeated attempts at both the Geneva Disarmament Conference, and at the United Nations, to break the deadlocked negotiations for controlled arms' reduction and a ban on nuclear testing. In 1963 his efforts remained unsuccessful. The Diefenbaker government's policy on disarmament raised some difficulties in the field of Canadian-American relations.

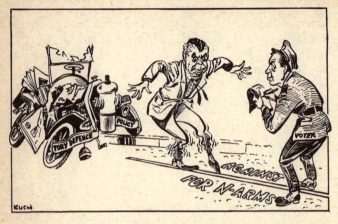

How **Winnipeg Free Press** cartoonist Kuch saw Canadian defence policy early in 1963.

Shortly after coming into office in 1957 the Conservatives signed an agreement with the United States establishing the North American Air Defence Command. This organization, with its headquarters at Colorado Springs, Colorado, provided for an integration of the Canadian and American air forces and air defence weapons under joint command. Despite the agreement, the Conservative government refused to accept nuclear weapons either for missiles or aircraft based in Canada, or for Canadian forces under N.A.T.O. command in Europe. The government, and especially Mr. Green, argued that for Canada to accept nuclear weapons, would be to jeopardize the world disarmament negotiations. By 1963 the indecision on the question of nuclear weapons was one cause of the growing criticism of the Diefenbaker government.

By the end of 1962 there were several other signs that the Diefenbaker party was losing its popularity. Though the party had won a majority of the seats in Quebec in 1958, its strength in that province had almost immediately begun to decline, partly because the Prime Minister was unable to find a French-Canadian lieutenant who could convince his compatriots that the Conservative government was sympathetic to their needs. Moreover, in 1960, the Union Nationale government, cautious ally of the Conservatives, was defeated by a vigorous Liberal party led by Jean Lesage, a former member of the St. Laurent government. The provincial Liberal platform called for reforms that would root out the political corruption that had grown up during Duplessis' long tenure of office, modernize Quebec's educational system, and increase French-Canadian control over the economic life of the province. Some French Canadians were convinced that these reforms could not be carried out unless Quebec seceded from Confederation. These extreme French-Canadian nationalists, or separatists, argued that Quebec was a colony of English-speaking Canada and like other colonies in the world, should be given full independence. While only a minority of Quebec people accepted this view, the existence of the vocal separatist movement was another sign that Canada, and the Diefenbaker government, was entering a difficult period.

Another sign of political discontent was the formation of the New Democratic Party. Negotiations between the C.C.F. and the Canadian Labour Congress had begun shortly after the election of 1958, and as unemployment increased so did the desire of many trade unionists for direct political action. In the summer of 1961 the New Democratic Party was born of the trade union-C.C.F. alliance. The platform of the New Democratic Party was less socialist than that of the C.C.F. had been, but it advocated government planning and control of economic development, and such social security measures as a national medical insurance scheme. As its first leader, the New Democratic Party chose T. C. Douglas, the colourful Premier of Saskatchewan.

The Social Credit party, too, underwent a reorganization during the summer of 1961. While the party continued to hold office in Alberta and British Columbia, it had lost all its federal representatives in 1958. The party's 1961 convention chose a new national leader, an inexperienced politician from Alberta, Robert Thompson. With a view to

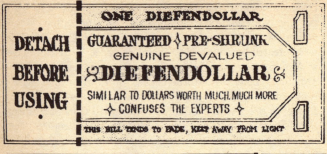

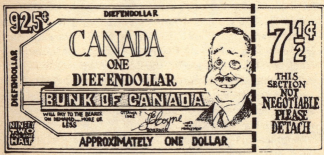

Devaluation in 1962. Election material in 1963.

attracting support in Quebec, where the party was beginning to show signs of growth, the convention chose as deputy leader Réal Caouette, a fiery orator and enthusiastic organizer.

When a new election was called in 1962 the Conservatives asked for a vote of confidence and a renewed mandate to continue their policies of national expansion, including the development of Canada's northland. The Opposition leader, Lester Pearson, and the Liberal party charged that the government had mishandled the country's economic affairs, created increased unemployment and weakened the value of the Canadian dollar. The New Democratic Party agreed that the Conservative record was one of failure, but argued that only a policy of government control and increased social security could guarantee full employment and economic growth. The Social Credit party's chief campaign argument was that the country's economic difficulties were the result of the heavy national debt that had grown up under the Conservative government. In Quebec, Réal Caouette coined the improbable but appealing slogan, "You have nothing to lose, vote Social Credit."

When the ballots were counted on June 18, no party had won a clear majority. The Conservatives retained only one hundred and sixteen of their two hundred and eight seats. But the Diefenbaker government was not turned out of office, for despite a gain of over fifty seats, the Liberals had elected only one hundred of their supporters. The New Democratic Party won nineteen seats, while Social Credit was victorious in thirty, twenty-six of them in Quebec. Clearly, Mr. Caouette had succeeded in capitalizing on the dissatisfaction many people in his province felt with both the Conservatives and the Liberals.

The election held on June 18, 1962, was only the first step in the collapse and defeat of the Diefenbaker administration. Others followed quickly. Six days after the election the Prime Minister admitted that the country faced a serious economic crisis. Steps taken to meet the crisis included the devaluation of the Canadian dollar to 92.5 cents in terms of American currency, but despite this measure the dollar continued to decline in value and the nation began to run short of foreign exchange. On June 24 the Prime Minister announced to the nation the terms of an austerity programme which included the borrowing of a billion dollars from the International Monetary Fund, the United States and the United Kingdom; increases in the tariff on a wide range of goods; and reductions in the value of goods tourists could bring back to Canada. These measures were designed to reduce Canadian imports, expand exports, and maintain an adequate supply of foreign currency.

When parliament assembled in September, Prime Minister Diefenbaker, with the aid of the Social Credit members, was able to defeat motions of non-confidence. But the anticipated legislation to deal with the economic crisis and to fulfil his election promises did not materialize. The House of Commons drifted and reporters coined for it such names as the "Do-nothing Parliament." The government's defeat was inevitable, but before it came the simmering dispute over Canada's defence policy had boiled over.

As part of her NA.T.O and N.O.R.A.D. commitments, Canada had accepted weapons like the Bomarc missiles in Canada and the CF-104 aircraft and the "Honest John" rockets in Europe, all of which were effective only with nuclear warheads. Despite constant prodding by the opposition parties, however, the government refused to state whether it would accept nuclear weapons. In January the Liberal leader, Mr. Pearson, reversing his previous position, called for the acceptance of nuclear weapons to honour Canadian commitments. The Liberal party's endorsement and statements by United States government officials, which reflected impatience with Canada's lack of policy, set off a debate in the Conservative party which led to the resignation of the Honourable Douglas Harkness, the Minister of National Defence, who favoured acquisition of the weapons. On February 5, 1963 the government was defeated on a general non-confidence motion. The debate over nuclear arms became one of the major issues in the ensuing campaign.

After the defeat of the Diefenbaker government a group in the Conservative cabinet attempted a *coup d'état*, whose purpose was to replace Mr. Diefenbaker as leader of the party. The revolt failed, but two more ministers, Mr. Hees, Minister of Trade and Commerce, and Mr. Sévigny, Associate Minister of National Defence, resigned, and several other ministers decided to retire from federal politics. It was a tattered remnant of a great party that Mr. Diefenbaker led into the campaign.

The electoral war was vigorous and bitter. Casting himself in the role of the underdog, the Prime Minister, in the hope that he could imitate Borden's success in 1911, lashed out at the Liberals, at the traitors within his own party, at the press barons in the big cities who had deserted the party, and at the Americans. The Liberals attacked Conservative mismanagement of the nation's economic and financial affairs, indecision on defence policy, the fading image of Canada abroad, and appealed above all for the return of a stable government with a majority. Mr. Douglas and the New Democratic Party hoped that their opposition to nuclear weapons and their extensive programmes of economic planning and social security would attract voters. The Social Credit party was divided between Robert Thompson's English-speaking wing, which advocated nuclear weapons for Canadian troops in Europe, and Réal Caouette's followers in Quebec who rejected any idea of nuclear weapons. All of the opposition parties, in an effort to lay the basis for better relations between French- and English-speaking Canadians, promised the establishment of a Royal Commission on biculturalism to examine the role of French Canadians in the civil service, government-owned businesses like the C.N.R. and other areas of Canadian life.

On April 8 the national jury returned its verdict. No party gained a clear majority. The Liberals won one hundred and twenty-nine seats and forty-one per cent of the popular vote. Conservative representation fell to ninety-five seats and thirty-three per cent of the total vote. Social Credit lost six seats in Quebec and returned twenty-four members, while the N.D.P. retained fourteen per cent of the popular vote but elected only seventeen members. With increased support in the Maritimes, Quebec, Ontario and British Columbia, the Liberals emerged as the party with the best claim to national representation. Its largest measure of support came from the cities, for in the farmlands of Ontario and the West the Conservative defences were impregnable. Only in Calgary and Winnipeg were the Liberals successful.

Two weeks after the election Mr. Diefenbaker resigned and Mr. Lester B. Pearson became Canada's fourteenth Prime Minister. Four years before its centennial, the nation he was called on to govern faced serious economic problems at home and abroad, was sorely divided between city and country, between French and English, and still had not solved the pressing problems of foreign and defence policy.

19 MAJORITY GOVERNMENT RESTORED

1. THE TRIALS OF LESTER PEARSON

Lester B. Pearson's new government, though a minority government once more, promised a return to expert administration and cautious reform. During the years of opposition the Liberals had attempted to reorganize their decimated party and develop a new platform. A group of new candidates were recruited to give the party vitality and direction. From Quebec came Maurice Lamontagne, a political economist of established reputation, Guy Favreau, a constitutional lawyer, and a handful of others. Ontario provided the Pearson party with Walter Gordon, a prominent consultant of both business and government in the management and accounting fields, and Mitchell Sharp, once Deputy Minister of Finance, now turned politician.

During the election campaign the Liberals had promised "sixty days of decision" designed to clean up what they claimed was the mess left by the disintegrating Diefenbaker administration. Those sixty days turned quickly into misadventure, misjudgement and the near collapse of a government that had advertised itself as a paragon of competence and organizational skill. At the centre of the Liberal government's problems were two individuals: Walter Gordon, Minister of Finance, and Jean Lesage, Premier of Quebec. In addition, of course, there was the fundamental problem that the Pearson government lacked a majority in the House of Commons and was therefore constantly conscious of potential defeat should the opposition parties ever unite in vote of non-confidence.

The trouble began with Gordon's budget shortly after the new parliament met for the first session. Over a long period Gordon had grown increasingly concerned about the domi-

"I'm Afraid You New Lads—and Lady—Will Have To Take Your Basic Training Under Fire"

Many of them panicked under fire, and the veterans seemed of very little help.

nating role played by the United States' direct investment in the Canadian economy. While professional economists tended to dismiss the problem, Gordon and many others believed that economic domination would eventually lead to loss of political independence. In his first budget the new Minister of Finance proposed a series of complicated measures designed to place some controls on foreign direct investment in Canada and to encourage increased Canadian ownership. The measures were sharply attacked by the opposition parties as clumsy and ill-advised. But more serious, perhaps, was the discovery by the Opposition that Gordon, in preparing his budget, had obtained the advice of three private consultants from Toronto financial houses. That the contents of the budget should be known to individuals outside of the Minister's official circle was clearly contrary to parliamentary practice. Although no one questioned Gordon's integrity, his actions made it plain that an inexperienced minister could be a serious liability to a government, especially a minority government. Most of that first budget, which had promised so much, was ultimately withdrawn and the government thus saved from defeat.

Several other measures produced similarly unfortunate results, and it soon became clear that the Pearson administration was to be repeatedly plagued by the results of its own bad management and political ineptitude. Relations with Quebec placed the government in an especially difficult position, not least of all because Pearson's Quebec supporters seemed even more accident prone than the government as a whole. Nevertheless, it was in dealing with Quebec that the Liberal government experienced some of its most notable successes. Most important was the decision in 1963 to appoint the Royal Commission on Bilingualism and Biculturalism with André Laurendeau, Editor of *Le Devoir*, and H. Davidson Dunton, President of Carleton University, as Co-Chairmen. The purpose of the ten-member Commission (four French-speaking, four English-speaking, and two representatives of the other ethnic groups) was to "inquire into and report upon the existing state of bilingualism and biculturalism in Canada and to recommend what steps should be taken to develop the Canadian Confederation on the basis of an equal partnership between the two founding races, taking into account the contribution made by the other ethnic groups to the cultural enrichment of Canada and the measures that should be taken to safeguard that contribution." The Commission set out at once on what was to prove a seven-year task. After a series of public hearings, which were often characterized by vigorous debate, the Commission issued a Preliminary Report. The Report's most striking comment was that "Canada, without being fully conscious of the fact, is passing through the greatest crisis in its history." The nature of that crisis was the growing tendency of French Canadians to identify their future with Quebec alone, and, at the same time, the apparent unwillingness of many English Canadians to accept French Canadians as equal partners throughout the Canadian federal system. As yet the Commissioners made no effort to define the term "equal partnership."

The frankness of the Preliminary Report shocked many

English Canadians in 1965, but the next few years confirmed the validity of the Commissioners' concern. During the following five years the Commission issued a series of Reports suggesting the acceptance of official bilingualism in the operations of the federal government and also in New Brunswick and Ontario where most of the French Canadians who resided outside Quebec lived. Obviously Quebec would also be a bilingual province. Moreover, the Commission called upon the provinces to provide French-language instruction, or English-language instruction, in all areas where the minority represented ten per cent of the population. In addition to upgrading bilingualism in the federal civil service, the Commission recommended the creation of an effectively bilingual federal capital at Ottawa. Finally, the Commissioners conducted important investigations into the economic status of French Canadians and demonstrated the dominance of the English language in the economy, showing that even in Quebec the French Canadians occupied an inferior economic status. The Commissioners remarked:

> Our examination of the social and economic aspects of Canadian life (based on 1961 census figures) shows that there is inequality in the partnership between Canadians of French origin and those of British origin. By every statistical measurement which we used, Canadians of French origin are considerably lower on the socio-economic scale. They are not as well represented in the decision-making positions and in the ownership of industrial enterprises; they do not have the same access to the fruits of modern technology. The positions they occupy are less prestigious and do not command as high incomes; across Canada their average annual earnings are nine hundred and eighty dollars less than those of the British. Furthermore, they have two years less formal education. Quebec manufacturing firms owned by francophones produce only fifteen per cent of the provincial output.

In an effort to alter this situation the Commission recommended the increased use of French as a language of work

"There! That's The B and B Commission's Order For Today."

Whatever the long-term value of the B. and B. Commission, there was considerable contemporary criticism of the millions of dollars spent by the Commission and its research staff.

throughout all levels of economic activity in Quebec in both the public and private sectors. By 1970 many of the Commission's major recommendations had been implemented at least in part. The problem of the use of French in the economic life of Quebec was obviously the most difficult to solve, but its importance was indicated by the small but vocal group of French Canadians who began demanding that Quebec should become an unilingually French province.

While the Pearson government experienced some marked successes in its desire to improve the status of the French language in Canada, it was less successful in finding a formula to satisfy Quebec's growing demand for autonomy within the federal system. Despite Pearson's strong support in Quebec, his government was faced with several critical problems in dealing with Jean Lesage's provincial Liberal administration.

After the 1962 Quebec election, which the Lesage government won on the issue of bringing the remaining privately owned power companies into the publicly owned Hydro-Québec, the Quebec government grew increasingly nationalistic. Its slogan during that election indicated the new trend: *maître chez nous*. To some degree this cry reflected the mood of the province in the process of modernization. Some Quebeckers had begun to advocate a complete reform of the Canadian federal system in the direction of greater autonomy for Quebec. Some called for a special status which would recognize that Quebec was not a province like the others. Some suggested that a "two nations" theory be built into a structure of two equal associate states, Quebec and English Canada. And some advocated complete independence.

The Lesage government accepted none of these formulas though some of its members, notably René Lévesque, the popular Minister of Natural Resources, often seemed sympathetic to even the most extreme suggestions about constitutional change. Lesage, however, was determined to defend and extend the autonomy of his province, particularly in the division of tax revenues. His government had embarked upon a series of social reforms whose cost made it necessary to attempt to press Ottawa out of some part of the important fields of income—especially corporation and death taxes. Both money and jurisdiction were involved in the most critical of several disputes between Quebec and Ottawa: the Canada Pension Plan controversy in 1964. This plan, a major social enactment, was designed to establish a government-sponsored portable contributory retirement scheme for every Canadian. The Quebec government, concerned to prevent federal infringement on the provincial field of social welfare and equally anxious to have access to the large sums of money that would be paid into the fund, refused to accept the federal proposal. After a series of difficult negotiations in which Pearson's aggressive young Minister of Forestry, Maurice Sauvé, played a major role, a compromise was reached. The seriousness of the dispute was later revealed by Mr. Pearson who told a reporter: "That issue could have broken up the country. If

Quebec had gone ahead with a pension plan of its own that bore no relation to the national plan, it would have been disaster."

The compromise plan provided that both Canada and Quebec would establish pension funds, but that certain changes would be made in the federal plan to allow for the integration of the Quebec plan into it. Thus, the important element of portability was maintained. The settlement of this dispute was seen by many as setting a pattern for future relations between Ottawa and Quebec, for it accepted the idea, at least in a limited fashion, that Quebec had a special status in Confederation. Subsequently, the federal government passed legislation providing for the right of a province to "opt out" of federal shared-cost programmes, a policy clearly designed to meet the demands of Quebec. At this point, very few people asked how special Quebec's status could be without the province gradually acquiring independence.

As these delicate federal-provincial questions were being debated, the Pearson government was rocked by a series of minor scandals that reached right into the Cabinet and destroyed the careers of three of the most promising Quebec ministers. Then came a further blow: the rejection by Quebec of a constitutional amending formula that had taken years to devise. Though the so-called Fulton-Favreau formula, which provided that most parts of the B.N.A. Act could be amended with the approval of Ottawa and two-thirds of the provinces with at least fifty per cent of the population, was tailored to meet Quebec's demands in particular, a strong nationalist campaign in Quebec forced Lesage to withdraw his support from the proposal after it had been accepted in every other province.

These events strongly suggested that divisions within the country were deepening. Those divisions, and the emotions surrounding them, were loudly expressed in 1964 during the lengthy debate over the adoption of a new national flag. After a number of proposals had been rejected, the government settled on a design that placed a red maple leaf on a white and red background. Many Canadians, especially in English

Canada, were most reluctant to see the last sign of the country's British heritage disappear from the flag, while others felt that the new design lacked distinction. In the end, after months of debate, the government's proposal was adopted and soon won wide acceptance.

Despite its difficulties the Pearson government gradually succeeded in implementing a series of useful proposals. Improved manpower retraining programmes helped to meet the challenge of automation, wheat sales increased, and the government moved towards the integration of the army, navy and air force. The country's foreign policy remained unchanged, though as well as continuing to serve on the United Nations' Peacekeeping Force in the Middle East, Canada made a significant contribution to the United Nations' Peacekeeping Force in Cyprus in early 1964. An increasingly buoyant economy and the evidence of serious divisions in the Conservative party convinced the Liberals in the spring of 1965 that the time had arrived for another attempt to obtain a majority government.

The Liberals' campaign was founded on an appeal for a stable majority and its major promise was a national medicare plan. The Conservative opposition concentrated on the government's fumblings and scandals, and strongly implied that the Liberals were unduly soft on Quebec. Once again John Diefenbaker, increasingly under attack even in his own party, confounded his critics by stumping the country with vigour and effect. The electorate again denied the Liberals their majority, returning one hundred and thirty-one Liberals, ninety-seven Conservatives, twenty-one New Democrats, five English-language Socreds and nine who followed Réal Caouette's Quebec party.

The Liberal's major gain in 1965 was a powerful new leadership team from Quebec: Jean Marchand, former President of the Confederation of National Trade Unions; Gérard Pelletier, former editor of *La Presse*; and Pierre Elliott Trudeau, trade union lawyer, professor of constitutional law, journalist and general non-conformist. The "three wise men," as they were called, who together had fought many battles against the Duplessis regime in the 1950's, had never been Liberal partisans. However, by the mid-sixties they had become convinced that the growing intensity of nationalism in Quebec threatened the future of both Quebec and Canada. They chose, therefore, to join the Liberal party, the only party with enough support in Quebec to make it an effective tool through which to defend federalism in French Canada.

The appearance of the three strong French Canadians in federal politics brought an almost immediate change in the Pearson government's approach to federal-provincial relations. A new tough line became the order of the day. While the legitimate jurisdiction of all the provinces was to be fully respected, and taxing powers shared accordingly, all provinces were to be treated equally. Otherwise, Pearson's New Quebec advisers argued, Quebec might gradually assume such a "special status" within Confederation as to be effectively separate. The chief theorist of the new federalism was Pierre Trudeau, who for years had been advocating just such an approach to federalism in his articles and speeches, later published in his book *Federalism and the French Canadians*. He summed up his views when he wrote: "Better than the American melting pot, Canada could offer an example to all those new Asian and African states . . . who must discover how to govern their polyethnic populations with proper regard for justice and liberty. What better reason for cold-shouldering the lure of annexation to the United States? Canadian federalism is an experiment of major proportions; it could become a brilliant prototype for the moulding of tomorrow's civilization." Trudeau and his friend Marc Lalonde, who became Pearson's special assistant after 1965, were soon hard at work preparing the federal government's case for a full-scale re-examination of the constitution.

2. GENERAL DE GAULLE INTERVENES

The surprising defeat of the Lesage government in the provincial election of June 1966 did nothing to reduce friction between Ottawa and Quebec. The eight point eight per cent of the vote that the two separatist parties received in that election indicated the nationalist impulse was still strong. Moreover, Daniel Johnson, the new Premier, had committed his Union Nationale party to a programme of "equality or independence." He called for a complete revision of the Canadian constitution that would recognize Quebec as a "nation" within a Canadian union.

One area in which the Johnson government attempted to press for a larger Quebec role was in the international field. The Lesage administration had already moved in this direction by establishing, under an umbrella agreement with Ottawa, direct relations with France. Premier Johnson pressed further, insisting that in areas under provincial jurisdiction a province could deal directly with foreign governments and attend international conferences—particularly in the field of education.

FATHERS OF DECONFEDERATION

In 1963 the radical separatist Front de Libération du Québec began its campaign of terror and violence. In October 1970 the F.L.Q. moved from bombs to kidnapping and murder, when two cells kidnapped James Cross, the British Trade Commissioner in Montreal, and kidnapped and executed Pierre Laporte, a cabinet minister in the Quebec government.

This view was rejected by the federal authorities, who claimed complete jurisdiction in international affairs, though they agreed that the provinces must be involved where their areas of jurisdiction were under discussion.

The conflict between Quebec and Ottawa was dramatized in August 1967 by a visit of the President of France, General Charles de Gaulle, to Quebec. De Gaulle came to Canada on the suggestion of the Quebec government, which had invited him to inspect the magnificent site of Expo '67, Montreal Mayor Jean Drapeau's brilliant edition of the World's Fair. From the outset Quebec and Ottawa were locked in petty quarrels over the details of the visit. The climax came with the appearance of the General in Montreal, after several days of meeting enthusiastic welcoming crowds as he moved as though in royal procession along "le chemin du roi" from Quebec City to Montreal. Standing on the balcony of Montreal city hall, he concluded his words of appreciation with an appeal that startled even those most familiar with his great sense of occasion." *Vive la France!"* his resonant voice proclaimed, *"Vive le Québec! Vive le Québec libre!"* The effect was electrifying. While the intention of the message was never made clear, many, both in French and English Canada, believed that de Gaulle had thrown his support behind the movement for an independent Quebec. The federal government at once pronounced the remarks an "unacceptable" interference in the domestic affairs of Canada. The General cancelled his planned trip to Ottawa, and ordered his aircraft to return directly to Paris.

General de Gaulle did not create the crisis between the French and English in Canada, but he certainly helped to bring it to a head. French-Canadian demands for a fundamental constitutional revision were now taken more seriously. And when, in the autumn of 1967, René Lévesque, one of the most popular politicians in Quebec, left the Liberal party to begin the work that led the following year to the establishment of the separatist Parti Québécois, few doubts remained about the seriousness of the situation. The federal government, quietly preparing itself for constitutional talks, responded slowly to demands for a full-scale conference on constitutional matters. Premier John Robarts of Ontario stepped in to bridge the gap by announcing a Confederation for Tomorrow Conference to be held in Toronto at the end of 1967. Though the federal government refused to attend this conference on the grounds that a meeting of this type should be called by Ottawa only, Premier Robarts' gathering did contribute significantly to opening up a constitutional discussion. In the meantime the federal government announced that a full federal-provincial conference would be convened in February 1968, to consider proposals for constitutional revisions, including the entrenchment in the constitution of a Charter of Human Rights defining and protecting individual liberties and language rights.

3. THE RISE OF PIERRE ELLIOTT TRUDEAU

Even while the Centennial of Confederation was being celebrated across the country in 1967, many people were asking themselves if the country could survive another century, or even a decade. Internal strains, which included not only Quebec nationalism but also a general drive for more autonomy on the part of several provinces and a sense of neglect in western Canada, endangered the country from within. In addition, there was the ever-present concern about the growing influence of the United States upon Canada. Indeed, in 1965, one well-known Canadian intellectual, Professor George Grant, published a book entitled *Lament for a Nation* in which he pronounced Canada's funeral oration. Canada, Grant asserted, had been inevitably destroyed by modern technology, which undermined all differences between nations, and "continentalism," which made the Canadian economy dependent upon the United States.

Within the Pearson government the issue of the United States direct investment in Canada was a cause of concern and division. Walter Gordon, no longer Minister of Finance, continued to fight for action on this front. In 1967 he won approval for the appointment of a Task Force of economists to investigate the implications of the foreign ownership issue. Its report, which appeared early in 1968, called for the development of a new national policy designed to regulate more closely foreign-owned firms in Canada and to promote Canadian investment in future economic development. It gave its approval to Mr. Gordon's proposed Canada Development Corporation, which was to channel Canadian funds into local developments. The Task Force report concluded: "The old National Policy served Canada, in its day, as an instrument of nation-building and a means of facilitating economic growth.

Conditions have changed and a new National Policy is required. The nation has been built but its sovereignty must be protected and its independence maintained. A diversified economy has been created, but its efficiency must be improved and its capacity for autonomous growth increased."

Thus, as Centennial Year drew to a close, the two questions that had dominated so much in Canadian history, the relations between French and English Canadians and the United States presence, once more moved to the front of the political stage. And on that stage, the principal actors were beginning to change. Even though his party had come through the 1965 general election more successfully than anyone would have predicted, John Diefenbaker was unable to unite his warring factions. A growing number of party supporters, especially in urban areas and in Quebec, were convinced that their greatest need was a new leader. Dalton Camp, national president of the party, made himself the most influential proponent of a convention to reassess the leadership. His campaign proved successful and the party called a leadership convention for Toronto in 1967.

Competition for the Conservative leadership was spirited and colourful. The two leading contenders were both provincial premiers, Duff Roblin of Manitoba and Robert Stanfield of Nova Scotia. Stanfield, the winner, was a thoughtful, modest man with a sound record of achievement as a provincial Premier behind him. He was looked upon as a man who could heal the party's wounds and rebuild its organization. The declining popularity of the Liberals seemed to leave opportunity beckoning to Robert Stanfield.

Once the Conservative choice was made, the Liberals moved to follow suit. It took no campaign to obtain Pearson's resignation as party leader: he left voluntarily. At once a succession of candidates, all but one members of the federal cabinet, began to announce their intentions to run for the leadership. At first it appeared that the Liberals, like the Conservatives, would be unable to produce a single French-speaking contender. This was a matter of special concern at a time when French-English relations were in such a critical state. Suddenly a candidate emerged almost in spite of himself.

This was the Minister of Justice, Pierre Elliott Trudeau, who in the late months of 1967 and the early months of 1968 had begun to make his mark on Canadian political life, first by sponsoring of a series of advanced reforms to the criminal code. This was followed in February 1968 by his strong defence of the federal government against the attacks of Quebec's Premier Johnson. Finally, there was Trudeau's intriguing and unusual personality combined with a great capacity to communicate, especially on television. At the Liberal Convention in April 1968, Trudeau, who fewer than three years before had not even been a member of the Liberal party, was elected the party's leader.

In virtually his first action as Prime Minister, Trudeau called a general election in order to capitalize on the popularity and interest that his campaign for the party leadership had stimulated. He made national unity his central campaign issue, promising to continue the process of constitutional revision and asserting his determination to establish bilingualism as a central foundation in the Canadian federal system and to treat all provinces as equals. He promised further to renew the federal government's attack on regional economic disparity, take action to encourage Canadian control of the Canadian economy, and conduct a full-scale reassessment of the country's foreign policy, including an attempt to reach an agreement with Mainland China on the question of diplomatic recognition. In the election campaign Trudeau's personality often seemed more important than issues. Everywhere he went, criss-crossing the country by jet, the crowds flowed around him exhibiting a phenomenon which the newspapers quickly dubbed "Trudeaumania." In their growing frustration, the opposition parties charged that he refused to debate issues. Stanfield, in his first federal election, fought hard but was plagued by ambiguities in his party's stand on Quebec and by his difficulty in finding a unifying theme for his campaign. Tommy Douglas and the N.D.P. worked hard to hold back the strong urban swing toward Trudeau, and in Quebec, Réal Caouette struggled to maintain his party's rural stronghold. The final returns gave the Liberals the first majority government since 1962: they won 155 seats, to the Conserva-

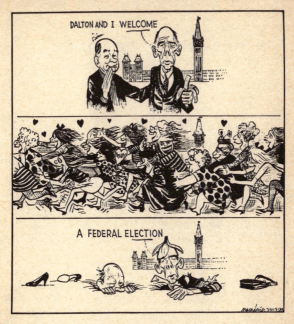

DALTON AND I WELCOME

A FEDERAL ELECTION

Duncan Macpherson's wry comment on the 1968 general election, when Trudeaumania upset the wise calculations of Robert Stanfield and his chief strategist, Dalton Camp.

tives' 72, the N.D.P.'s 22 and the Créditistes' 14.

With this solid majority behind him and support drawn from every section of the country, Trudeau now had an opportunity to turn his government's attention to the many difficult problems that had plagued the country during the 1960's and demanded solutions if the nation was to survive the 'seventies. He had spoken of his desire to work towards the building of a "Just Society." Awaiting him in a generally affluent Canada were problems of poverty, especially among the native peoples; inflation; economic under-development, especially in the East; pollution and urban decay; wheat surpluses and many other pressing economic, social and cultural questions. Behind all of these issues were Canada's perennial problems: national unity and relations with the United States.

20 NATIONALISM, REGIONALISM, SEPARATISM

THE OPTIMISM and enthusiasm of Centennial Year, which carried over into the election of Pierre Elliott Trudeau's majority government in June 1968, quickly dissipated. As the new government attempted to find solutions for some of the problems which the celebrations of 1967 had temporarily pushed aside it soon discovered that Canada remained a difficult country to govern. That difficulty arose out of three characteristics of the country which, at various times, have dominated public debate: the sensitive relations between French and English, the persistence of regionalism and the unequal partnership between Canada and the United States. By the 1970's all of these difficult challenges to the country's unity had re-emerged simultaneously and sharply. The country's ability to survive had never before been so seriously in jeopardy.

1. CANADA, THE WORLD AND THE UNITED STATES

One of the main priorities of the Trudeau government was a reexamination of Canada's foreign policy. That re-assessment was made necessary by external changes as well as by changing Canadian attitudes toward the outside world. By the late 1960's the nearly complete revival of the economies of the European nations and the movement toward European unity had two direct effects upon Canada. In the first place, the restoration of European power reduced the influence that a relatively small country like Canada could exercise in world affairs. While the Western European nations wanted Canada to play a continuing role in NATO, for example, it was plain that Canada's importance in the defence of Europe was far less crucial than it had been in the two decades immediately following the Second World War.

Equally important was the fact that Europe's growing unity, especially in economic matters, had important implications for Canada. As Great Britain moved toward membership in the common market (obtained in 1973), Canada recognized the danger of becoming totally dependent upon her powerful United States neighbour in trade and defence matters. And that at a time when a growing number of Canadians felt uneasy about the powerful impact that the United States had already had upon nearly every aspect of Canadian life.

To these particularly Canadian reasons for a new look at our foreign policy were added two more general ones. During the 1960's the involvement of the United States in the war in Vietnam convinced many Canadians that they should take a more critical view of American foreign policy goals. That war seemed to have very little to do with the defence of the "free world"; indeed it had all of the earmarks of a rather brutal military imperialism. Moreover, Canadians joined in a general movement towards détente, or more peaceful relations with the Soviet Union and its allies. A thaw was beginning in the Cold War and many Canadians thought that this offered Canada an opportunity to formulate some new lines of foreign policy.

For these reasons, then, the Trudeau government moved to define what came to be called a "third option," which meant a diversification of Canada's economic and diplomatic contacts in order to reduce our dependence upon the United States. The Prime Minister summarized his government's intentions in a statement which he made during a visit to the Soviet Union in May 1971. "Canada has increasingly found it important," he observed, "to diversify its channels of communication because of the overpowering presence of the United States of America, and that is reflected in a growing consciousness among Canadians of the danger to our national identity from a cultural, economic and perhaps even military point of view. It has been the desire of the Canadian people, and certainly reflected by the government to, I repeat, diversify our points of contact with the significant powers of the world."

The first new contact established by the Trudeau government was with the People's Republic of China. For two decades the question of extending diplomatic recognition to "Red China" had been debated in Canada, often with an eye to the anticipated reactions of the United States. By 1970 negotiations were completed, and ambassadors exchanged, between Canada and mainland China. Canada's "one China" policy, which involved dropping recognition of the Formosa regime of Chiang Kai-shek, provided a precedent to be followed by some other nations. Canada hoped that diplomatic recognition would gradually lead to an opening up of the enormous Chinese market to an increased volume of Canadian trade. This policy has met with considerable success. Trade between the two countries has increased and so have cultural and athletic exchanges.

The Prime Minister's frequent trips abroad, to China, the Soviet Union and Cuba, as well as to the United States, Great Britain and Europe, often evoked criticism at home. Yet they were part of an effort to develop the "Third Option," and to promote the sale of Canadian technology, especially nuclear power plants, abroad. An important step in this direction was the establishment of a "contractual relationship" with the European Common Market in the spring of 1975, under which Canada hoped to obtain trading advantages in Europe.

Despite this effort to find new international contacts, Canada's relations with the United States remained the principal axis on which Canadian external policy turned. In foreign and military policy Canada remained a firm ally of the United States both in NATO and NORAD. Defence production sharing agreements and the heavy dependence of Canada on United States military technology and intelligence were all policies inherited by the Trudeau government and which remained unaltered. These close connections were further confirmed by the high level of U.S. direct investment in Canada and the critical importance of the U.S. market for Canadian exports. No two countries in the world enjoy a greater volume of trade than Canada and the United States. By the late 1960's many Canadians wondered if this relationship should not be altered before Canada totally surrendered control over its economy to foreigners. By 1968 United States investors controlled 97% of the capital invested in the automobile industry, 90% in rubber, 54% in electrical equipment, 62% in mining, and 74% in the oil and natural gas industries. In total, about 27% of all Canadian business assets were foreign controlled.

This heavy American penetration of the Canadian economy appeared to be paralleled in the less easily measurable area of culture. The extent to which Canadians watched American TV and movies, read American books and magazines, and were taught by American-trained professors in Canadian universities became a subject of widespread controversy. "The tremendous expansion of communications in the United States," a Royal Commission observed in 1961, "has given that nation the world's most penetrating and effective apparatus for the transmission of ideas. Canada, more than any other country, is naked to that force, exposed unceasingly to a vast network of communications which reaches to every corner of our land: American words, images and print — the good, the bad, the indifferent — batter unrelentingly at our eyes and ears."

In response to what was sometimes called the "Americanization" of Canada, governments and voluntary organizations offered a variety of proposals. Following several studies of the U.S. economic impact on Canada, and a great deal of debate, the Trudeau government implemented several new policies. In 1971 the Canada Development Corporation was set up as a government-sponsored corporation that would invest Canadian money in the development of Canadian enterprises. Two years later the government adopted the Foreign Investment Review Act whose purpose was to oversee new investment in Canada in an effort to ensure that Canadians would gain as many benefits as possible out of foreign investment. Where disadvantages outweighed advantages such investments were to be prohibited. One particularly critical area in which the government took an interest was petroleum production. During the world oil crisis in the winter of 1974 the Canadian government established Petro-Can whose purpose was to explore and exploit Canadian oil resources in competition with the existing, foreign-owned companies.

The cultural field was more complicated, particularly because education and some other aspects of culture rested within provincial jurisdictions. Nevertheless the federal government took several steps to aid publishers of Canadian books, encourage the development of a Canadian film industry, set limits on United States programming on Canadian television, promote Canadian recorded music and remove tax privileges enjoyed by some American magazines in Canada. Moreover, some provincial departments of education, and some schools and universities, introduced programmes in "Canadian studies" designed to ensure that Canadian students acquired greater familiarity with the culture of their country.

Despite these measures, and many declarations by Canadian and United States politicians affirming the independence of Canada, the impact of the two hundred million Americans on twenty-two million Canadians remained pervasive. The relationship resembled that of "an elephant and a mouse," Canada's Prime Minister told an American audience. "Cultural survival is perhaps the most critical problem our generation of Canadians will have to face," a Canadian Senate committee concluded in 1970, "and it may be it can only be achieved by using all the means at our command."

2. THE POLITICS OF REGIONALISM

Critics of the Trudeau government's efforts to defend Canadian sovereignty and encourage Canadian cultural growth advanced three arguments. Some members of the Progressive Conservative party, and even some Liberals, contended that the government's policies threatened the cultural and economic freedom of Canadians. By contrast the NDP, and some voluntary groups like the Committee for an Independent Canada, complained that the government was too slow to act and, even when it did act, rarely went far enough. A third criticism, and perhaps the most serious one, was expressed by people in the West and the Atlantic provinces who argued that national cultural and economic policies were often better suited to a rich province like Ontario than to a less prosperous one like New Brunswick. This point was made by the federal PC leader, Robert Stanfield, himself a former premier of Nova Scotia, when he observed in 1971, "I have nothing against this new nationalism, but I must say that in the circumstances it expresses more a preoccupation of the central Canadian financial community, and especially of Ontario, than a sentiment of national independence from coast to coast."

Mr. Stanfield, in that remark, placed his finger on the central paradox of Canada in the late sixties and early seventies, for the country appeared to be experiencing contradictory emotions. One was an outburst of nationalism. The second was a rebirth of intense provincial, regional and ethnic loyalties. Could there be a single Canadian culture and nationalism in a country divided into distinct regions, recognizing two official languages, and inhabited by people from numerous cultural backgrounds? Every attempt by the federal government to devise national cultural and economic policies seemed to encourage a regional reaction.

In the western provinces and the Atlantic region policies designed to encourage Canadian publishing, for example, often appeared to benefit Toronto publishers in particular. And those publishers were suspected of ignoring authors who lived outside of central Canada. Similarly Canadian content rules for radio and TV seemed to fall most heavily on regions with few TV outlets, and to have the least impact on areas where U.S. channels were easily accessible. As a result there developed a demand for the decentralization of constitutional power in the field of communications so that provinces could establish TV outlets, such as Ontario Educational Television, which would concentrate on local subjects. Similarly a number of new publishing companies were organized to specialize in the publication of local and regional writing.

Efforts to establish national economic policies met with many of the same criticisms. The provinces which were less highly developed economically, particularly the Atlantic provinces and Quebec, expressed strong reservations about policies designed to slow down the flow of foreign capital investment into Canada. Ontario might have enough development capital, they argued, but they had too much unemployment and too little industrial development to be able to refuse capital investment, whatever its source. These criticisms made the Trudeau government very cautious in its application of the Foreign Investment Review Act.

Few issues displayed the continued existence of regional conflict in Canada more vividly than the energy crisis of 1973-74. Since the provinces have jurisdiction over natural resources, Alberta's near monopoly on Canadian petroleum supplies gave that province a powerful bargaining position as world oil prices rapidly increased. Yet the federal government's jurisdiction over inter-provincial and international trade provided it with the power to establish domestic oil prices. For the industrial provinces, especially Ontario, controlled oil prices were especially important if the cost of manufactured goods was to remain internationally competitive. Alberta, on the other hand, felt a natural desire to reap a fair profit from its non-renewable resources in order to finance its own industrial development. Ottawa had to mediate these conflicting demands. Since Ottawa, in concert with the provinces, established a domestic oil price lower than the international market price, many Albertans, and other Westerners, concluded that the Trudeau government was too much dominated by central Canada, too little aware of Western needs and aspirations.

The political complexion of the country after 1968 fairly

accurately reflected regional differences. While the Liberal party, with its strong central Canadian base, remained in power in Ottawa, the West and the Atlantic provinces turned to the opposition parties — Social Credit, Progressive Conservative and NDP — to form provincial governments. A similar trend was apparent in federal politics. In 1972, after four years in power, the Trudeau government confidently faced the electorate. In what turned out to be the closest election in Canadian history, the Liberals were barely returned as a minority government: 109 Liberals, 107 Progressive Conservatives, 31 New Democrats, 15 Créditistes and 2 independents.

There were many reasons for this result: high unemployment and rising inflation, a mismanaged electoral campaign by the Liberals and strong campaigns by Robert Stanfield, David Lewis and Réal Caouette of the opposition parties. But in the West, where the Liberals had not been strong since the election of John Diefenbaker, the Government received an especially severe thrashing. It won only seven seats, not one of which was in Alberta. For the first time teenagers were voting in a federal election, since the federal government had passed an act in 1970 reducing the voting age to eighteen.

Trudeau's minority government, supported on a day-to-day basis by the NDP, attempted to rebuild its support in the western and Atlantic provinces by two types of policies. The first was a new emphasis on policies to reduce regional economic disparities. The Department of Regional Economic Expansion attempted to encourage investment in industrial developments, in areas of Quebec and the Atlantic region, in particular, where unemployment was above the national average and economic growth slow or non-existent. While these policies were controversial, both because they provided large public subsidies to private companies and because their results were difficult to measure, the essential goals were supported by all political parties.

The effort to respond to Western grievances was no less controversial and much less productive of immediate results.

During the early 1970's British Columbia, Alberta and Saskatchewan, because of such natural resources as natural gas, oil, uranium and potash, experienced industrial development and prosperity. Yet each of these provinces believed that national economic policies, especially freight rates, tariffs and oil-pricing policies, prevented them from attaining levels of growth, diversification and affluence that they deserved. In an effort to meet these claims the federal government convened the Western Opportunities Conference in July 1973. At that meeting the well-briefed premiers of the western provinces set out in detail the causes of Western alienation and offered some suggestions to improve the situation. In essence what the western provinces wanted was a shift from national economic policies which favoured Eastern industry through tariff and freight rate structures to ones which would stimulate industrial development in the West. The federal ministers expressed great sympathy for Western aspirations, but indicated that solutions would have to be implemented over a long term and after detailed studies. Many Westerners suspected that this response meant that little, if anything, would be done to meet their complaints.

Trudeau's minority government survived until the spring of 1974. During those years economic issues increasingly dominated public discussion. Energy was one matter of critical concern. Unemployment, particularly among women and in the under-twenty-five age group, was another. The Conservative Opposition concentrated in particular on the Government's inability to control the rising rate of inflation which by the spring of 1974 was threatening to exceed 10 per cent annually. Robert Stanfield urged the Government to adopt some scheme of wage and price controls, but both the Liberals and the NDP rejected this proposal. Inflation, the Government argued, was an international problem that could not be effectively dealt with by domestic controls.

The debate over inflation became one of the issues in the federal election of June 1974, which followed the withdrawal of NDP support from the minority Liberal government. During the campaign the Liberals emphasized the need for a majority government, insisting that the country faced serious economic, international and constitutional problems that only a strong government could resolve. Robert Stanfield argued that the Liberals, supported by the NDP, had mismanaged the economy and he advocated short-term controls. The Liberals replied that the situation was not yet so serious as to demand such a radical, and probably unworkable, solution as wage and price controls. The NDP agreed. When the votes were counted Prime Minister Trudeau found that his majority had been restored: Liberals, 141; Progressive Conservatives, 95; New Democrats, 16; Créditistes, 11; and 1 independent. The Government remained extremely weak in the prairie provinces, once again without a seat in Alberta.

Nevertheless Trudeau's comeback was quite remarkable. As the leader of a minority government he had displayed more flexibility and political agility than his critics had expected. His 1974 campaign, in contrast to 1972, again revealed his ability to communicate with the electorate, almost reawakening the "Trudeaumania" of 1968. Robert Stanfield and David Lewis campaigned vigorously, too. The NDP leader bore the burden of having supported the Liberal minority government at first, and then having brought it down. He suffered from the electorate's apparent desire for a majority government.

Shortly after the election, in which he was personally defeated, David Lewis resigned as NDP leader. Edward Broadbent, the Member of Parliament for Oshawa, Ontario, was elected to succeed him. Robert Stanfield, who had reunited the Progressive Conservative Party and nearly won office in 1972, also announced his decision to give up the leadership of his party before another election. At its leadership convention in February 1976, the party chose the youthful Alberta M.P. Charles Joseph "Joe" Clark as its new leader. He rapidly proved his determination to challenge the Liberal government. The failing health of Réal Caouette in the fall of 1976 made the choice of a new party leader necessary for the Créditistes. A convention elected André Fortin for the position only one month before the death of Mr. Caouette on December 16, 1976.

The Government, Trudeau's third, quickly found itself faced with a number of complex difficulties. Though there was growing evidence of dissatisfaction with the Government's policy of expanding bilingualism in the government service, the most immediate issues were economic. Economic growth was slow, unemployment high and inflation rising. Canada, like several other industrial nations, was suffering from a disease which economists called "stagflation." The country's stagnating economy obviously required some new medicine, but the government lacked a prescription. Amid growing criticism for lack of leadership, and an increasing number of demands for controls to combat inflation, John Turner, the Minister of Finance, resigned in the summer of 1975. In October, the government reversed its previously stated position on wage and price controls. The Prime Minister announced his government's decision to impose wage and price limits for a three-year period.

Legislation was soon passed establishing an Anti-Inflation Board to rule on wage and price increases. A series of complicated regulations were issued to inform the public of guidelines for wage, price and profit increases. In addition, federal and provincial governments, all of which accepted the anti-inflation programme, moved to reduce government spending, which was considered one of the factors contributing to the inflationary pressure on the economy.

The new policy, while welcomed by those who believed that inflation was out of control, was sharply criticized. The opposition parties charged that the Government had broken its election promise to fight inflation without controls. Organized labour, led by President Joe Morris of the Canadian Labour Congress, launched a campaign against the controls, which, labour argued, would hold down wages while prices and profits grew. Businessmen complained that the regulations were difficult to understand and apply, and that limits on profits would reduce investment and cause further economic stagnation. After the first year of operation the controls appeared to have contributed, along with other factors, to a gradual slowdown in the inflation rate.

The implementation of wage and price controls, a drastic measure in peacetime, indicated how serious some of Canada's economic problems had become. Another problem of critical importance which remained unresolved was that of energy. Of particular concern was the question of a new pipeline to bring Arctic gas and oil down the Mackenzie Valley to the south. This prospective project involved energy, foreign investment, ecological danger and, above all, the rights of Canada's native peoples in the North. The resolution of this difficult question waited the finding of a Royal Commission appointed to examine the native peoples' claims and the ecological problems, and a decision of the National Energy Board on future oil and gas needs.

3. FEDERALISM VERSUS SEPARATISM

The first priority of the Trudeau government after 1968 was the improvement of the position of French Canadians within Confederation. As the Royal Commission on Bilingualism and Biculturalism had pointed out, the French language did not enjoy a position of equality with English in federal institutions, nor did French-language minorities outside Quebec generally have access to education in their own language. Nor did French Canadians, as a group, appear to have equal opportunity with English-speaking Canadians in the country's economic life. If Quebec was to remain part of Confederation, steps to modify these conditions were obviously necessary.

The Liberal government's approach to French-Canadian grievances was three-pronged. The first was the passage of the Official Languages Act in 1969. It declared: "The English and French languages are the official languages of Canada for all purposes of the Parliament and Government of Canada and possess and enjoy equality of status and equal rights and privileges as to their use in all the institutions of the Parliament and Government of Canada." The purpose of this act was to guarantee that both French and English Canadians could deal with their federal government in their own language. Moreover the act ensured that French Canadians who wished to work in federal institutions would have equal opportunity in appointments and promotions. Since French Canadians held only about 14 per cent of the higher civil service positions (although they represented over a quarter of the population), it was necessary to increase that proportion by making the public service attractive to French-speaking candidates.

The second aspect of government policy, though not designed for Quebec alone, was regional economic development. Through the encouragement of industrial growth in the poorer parts of Quebec, it was hoped that the economic status of French Canadians would be improved.

Finally, the Trudeau government believed that the process of constitutional revision, begun under Prime Minister Pearson, should be continued. The purpose of this revision was to remodel the constitution to meet the criticisms of several of the provinces, while at the same time encouraging all of the provinces, wherever practical, to guarantee equality in education for French and English Canadians. These policies, the Trudeau government hoped, would prevent the growth of support for demands that Quebec be given a "special status" within Confederation or that it secede from Canada.

The importance of these policies was underlined by the growing strength of René Lévesque's Parti Québécois, a party devoted to establishing an independent Quebec. Though public opinion polls revealed only a very small increase in the number of convinced separatists (the separatists totalled between 15 and 20 per cent), Lévesque's personal popularity and the social reform aspects of his party's programmes were attractive to non-separatist voters. In the Quebec election of April 1970, in which the new Liberal leader Robert Bourassa won power, the PQ won seven seats, though Lévesque himself suffered defeat.

Separatist fervour reached a high pitch during that election and a mood of bitterness followed the party's defeat. Social tensions in the province were also quite severe both because of high unemployment and because of several particularly difficult labour disputes. Montreal was the centre of this tense atmosphere. It was also the centre of a small terrorist organization known as the Front de Libération du Québec, or the FLQ. Since 1963 the FLQ had been responsible for sporadic bombings of mail boxes, federal buildings and factories involved in labour strife, causing at least six deaths, many injuries and much property damage. On October 5, 1970, one FLQ cell carried out a spectacular new action — the kidnapping of the British diplomat James Cross. That night the FLQ released a manifesto, filled with revolutionary rhetoric, and listing a series of demands, the main one being the release of all imprisoned FLQ members. The government authorities agreed only to the demand that the manifesto be read over nation-wide television. After five days of demands and counter demands, a second FLQ cell struck, this time kidnapping Pierre Laporte, the Quebec Minister of Labour. With the police hunt for the kidnappers producing no result, and tension rising in Montreal, the federal government called out the army. Then, on October 16, in response to a request from the Mayor of Montreal and the Premier of Quebec, the Trudeau government invoked the War Measures Act. This legislation, used previously only in wartime, provided the police with wide, arbitrary powers of search and arrest. Under these powers more than four hundred were rounded up, questioned and detained. But the kidnappers continued to elude the police.

The implementation of the War Measures Act shocked the country into a state of calm. It did not save the life of Pierre Laporte who, on October 17, was strangled to death by his kidnappers. James Cross was held unharmed until December 3 when the FLQ hide-out was finally discovered by police. His freedom was exchanged in return for safe passage to Cuba for his kidnappers. Some months later Laporte's murderers were arrested. The FLQ had been destroyed; some of its members had been jailed or exiled, while most of its sympathizers had turned their backs on violence. Many questions about the October crisis remained unanswered but one fact seemed plain: that tragic crisis neither created nor resolved the essential constitutional conflict that had been developing in Quebec for a decade.

The Bourassa government in Quebec strongly opposed the separatist movement but at the same time urged a general decentralization of constitutional power, especially in areas of social security, communications, culture and immigration. The federal government, while not opposed to some decentralization, believed that Quebec's full demands could not be met without seriously weakening the national government's capacity to maintain the country's unity. In June 1971 Prime Minister Trudeau and the provincial premiers met in Victoria to discuss constitutional changes and an amending formula that would allow the constitution to be altered without the assistance of the British parliament. The so-called Victoria Charter was a compromise which, without radically altering the division of powers in the constitution, appeared to satisfy all of the provinces and the federal authorities. Nevertheless, at the last moment, Quebec decided to reject the new constitution since it did not, in the Bourassa government's view, give the provinces sufficient authority in the area of social security.

With the rejection of the Victoria Charter, the attempt to revise completely the British North America Act was set aside. Instead governments continued to negotiate about specific powers and policies and about new fiscal arrangements covering transfers of money from the federal government to the provinces. Quebec was especially anxious to obtain increased provincial control over communications and immigration, both of which powers appeared important in defending the French-Canadian culture.

The declining birth rate among French Canadians made many Quebeckers uneasy about their future unless some measures could be taken to control immigration and also to ensure that French was guaranteed a priority position in the province. This was the objective of Bill 22, which proclaimed

French as the official language of Quebec and set down regulations intended to ensure that the children of immigrants attended schools in French rather than English. This legislation met widespread criticism from non-French Quebeckers and also from Quebec nationalists who did not think it went far enough.

The Bourassa government was reelected with an overwhelming majority in the autumn of 1973. The Liberals gained 102 seats, while the PQ won only 6. Yet this vast majority disguised the fact that the PQ percentage of the popular vote had increased and that, among French-speaking voters, it was nearly as large as the percentage won by the Liberals. With such a majority behind him Bourassa's government seemed secure. But it rapidly became careless and complacent, and tainted by charges of corruption. Though Bourassa had presented his party as one which could best deal with the province's economic problems, he seemed unable to reduce unemployment or fight inflation. Moreover his government's relations with the trade unions, especially those in the public service, were very poor. Hydro workers, teachers, hospital workers and others were unable to reach satisfactory agreements. The Premier's personal popularity gradually declined as he acquired a reputation for both arrogance and indecision.

Nevertheless, the Liberal majority was so large that its hold on power seemed unchallengeable. That certainly seemed to be the Premier's view when he called another election, a year earlier than was necessary, for November 15, 1976. He hoped that he could force the electorate to choose between his support for federalism and René Lévesque's separatism in the same way as he had done so successfully in the previous election. But the strategy failed. The electorate was more interested in immediate questions of jobs, strikes and good government than in constitutional questions. Non-Francophone voters, who usually supported the Liberals faithfully, were very unhappy about Bill 22, the language legislation. And most important, René Lévesque refused to debate the question of federalism versus separation. Instead his party insisted that that question should be settled in a future referendum. In the meantime Lévesque offered clean government, tax cuts, economic growth and social reform.

November 15 produced a surprise for most Quebeckers, and a shock for the rest of Canada. René Lévesque's Parti Québécois had driven the Liberals from office, winning 68 of the 106 seats and humiliating the Liberals by defeating the Premier himself. By voting so strongly against the Bourassa government, Quebeckers had elected, for the first time in their history, a government dedicated to the establishment of an independent Quebec nation. "Now we have to build this country of Quebec," Lévesque told his jubilant supporters on election night.

To achieve the party's goal Lévesque knew that he had still to convince a majority of Quebeckers that independence was a desirable aim. But the PQ had won the power that could be used to convince the doubters to join the independence cause. Pierre Trudeau, the Canadian Prime Minister, faced his most critical challenge, for the survival of Canada was now in question. The Prime Minister described the situation clearly shortly after the Quebec election: "Quebeckers, like the citizens of other provinces, are proud," he told the Canadian people. "They seek personal fulfillment in a free and independent way. The central question is whether this growth of freedom and independence is best assured by Canada, or by Quebec alone. Canadians must think about this brutal question now. Not only think of solving it in words, but by deeds and through their attitudes. In the area of the language problem, of course, but also in the very important areas of regional disparity and social justice. . . . I believe that Canada cannot, indeed that Canada must not, survive by force. The country will only remain united — it should only remain united — if its citizens want to live together in one civil society."

INDEX

327